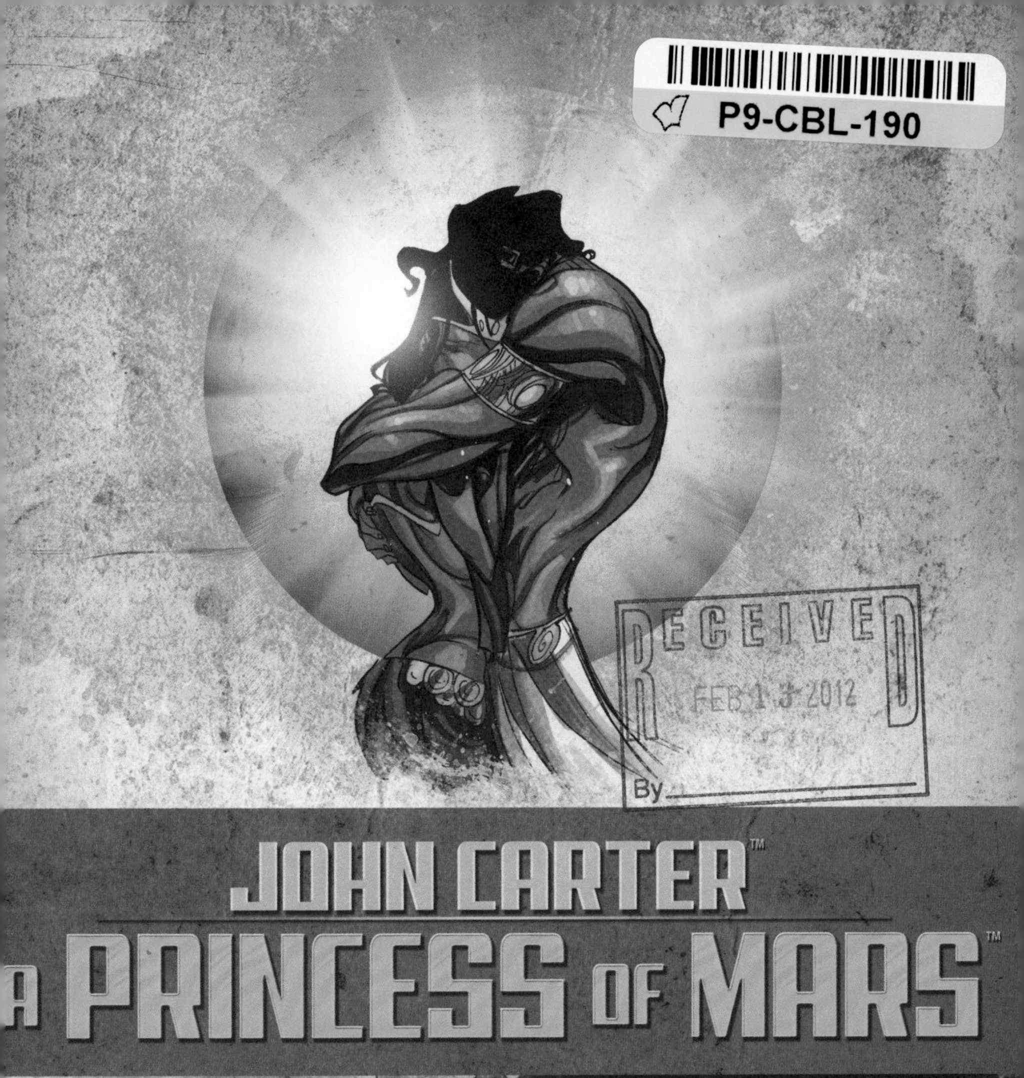

JOHN CARTER™
A PRINCESS OF MARS™

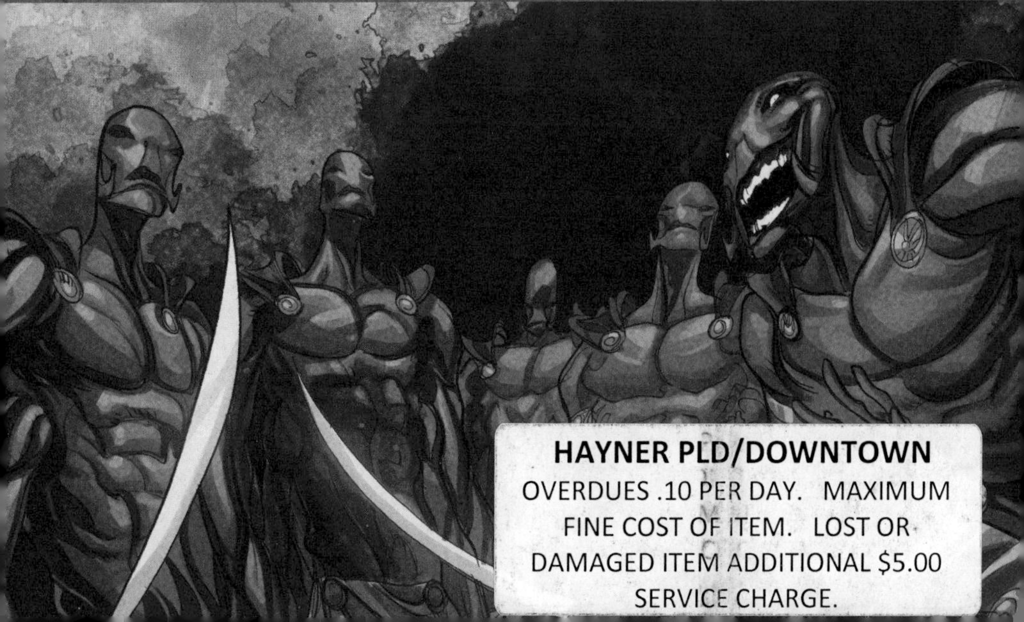

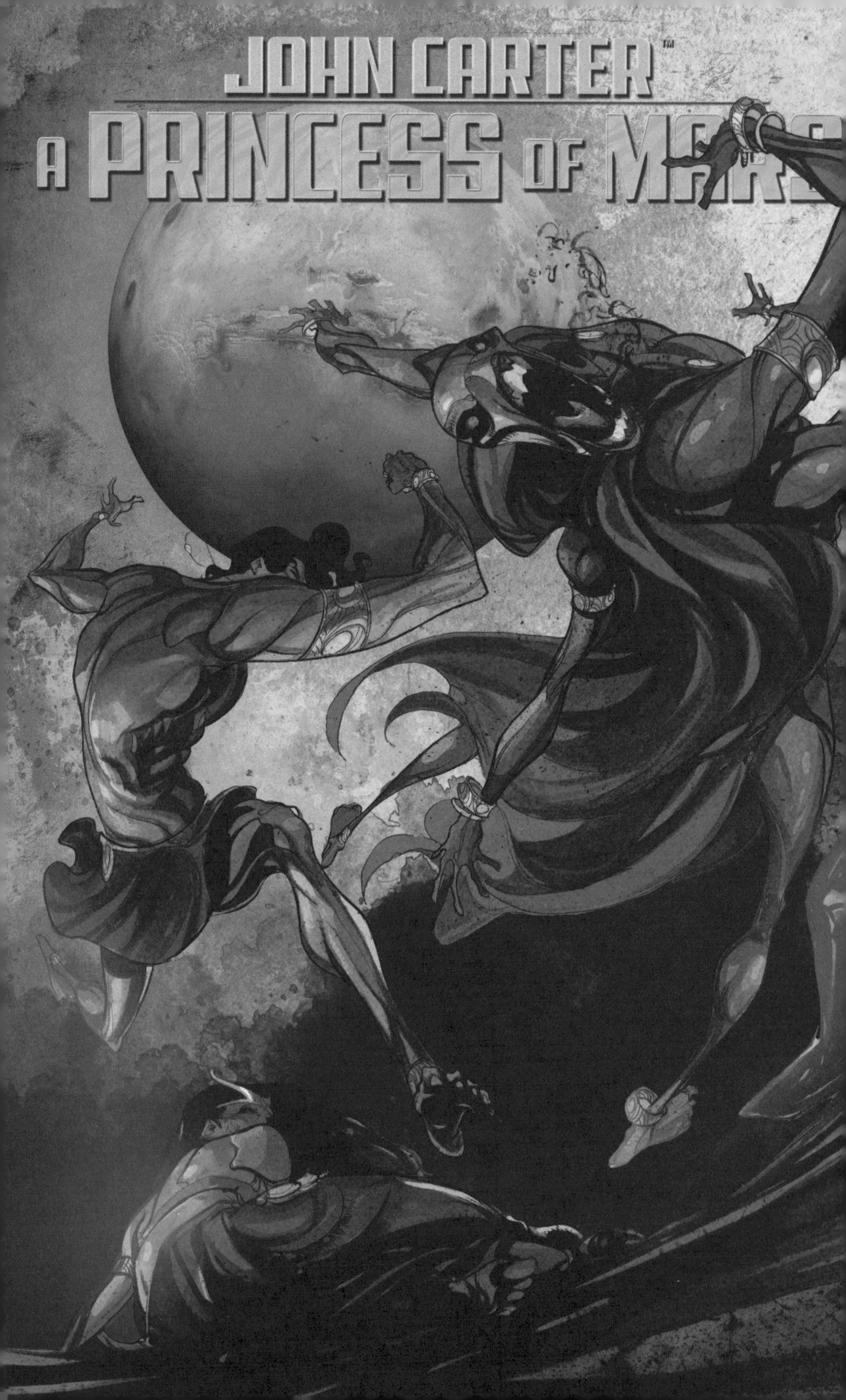
JOHN CARTER™
A PRINCESS OF

BASED ON
THE WORKS OF
EDGAR RICE BURROUGHS

WRITER: ROGER LANGRIDGE   ARTIST: FILIPE ANDRADE
COLOR ARTIST: SUNNY GHO WITH IFC'S ARIF PRIANTO
& BENNY MAULANA AND SOTOCOLOR
LETTERER: VC'S CORY PETIT
ASSISTANT EDITORS: RACHEL PINNELAS & JON MOISAN
EDITOR: SANA AMANAT

FRONT COVER ARTIST: FILIPE ANDRADE
BACK COVER ARTIST: SKOTTIE YOUNG

COLLECTION EDITOR: MARK D. BEAZLEY
ASSISTANT EDITORS: ALEX STARBUCK & NELSON RIBEIRO
EDITOR, SPECIAL PROJECTS: JENNIFER GRÜNWALD
SENIOR EDITOR, SPECIAL PROJECTS: JEFF YOUNGQUIST
BOOK DESIGNER: RODOLFO MURAGUCHI
SENIOR VICE PRESIDENT OF SALES: DAVID GABRIEL
SVP OF BRAND PLANNING & COMMUNICATIONS: MICHAEL PASCIULLO

EDITOR IN CHIEF: AXEL ALONSO
CHIEF CREATIVE OFFICER: JOE QUESADA
PUBLISHER: DAN BUCKLEY

– ONE –

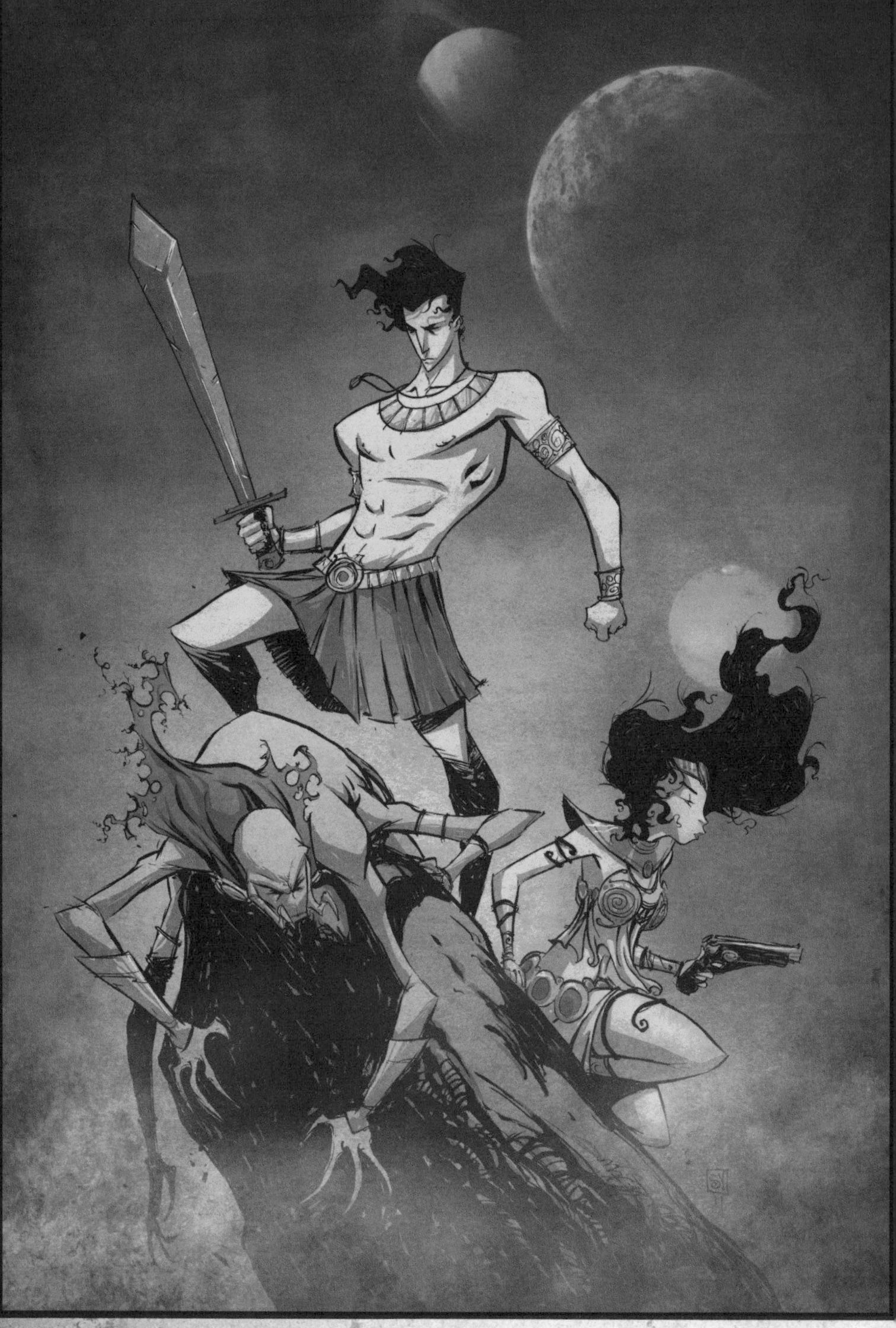

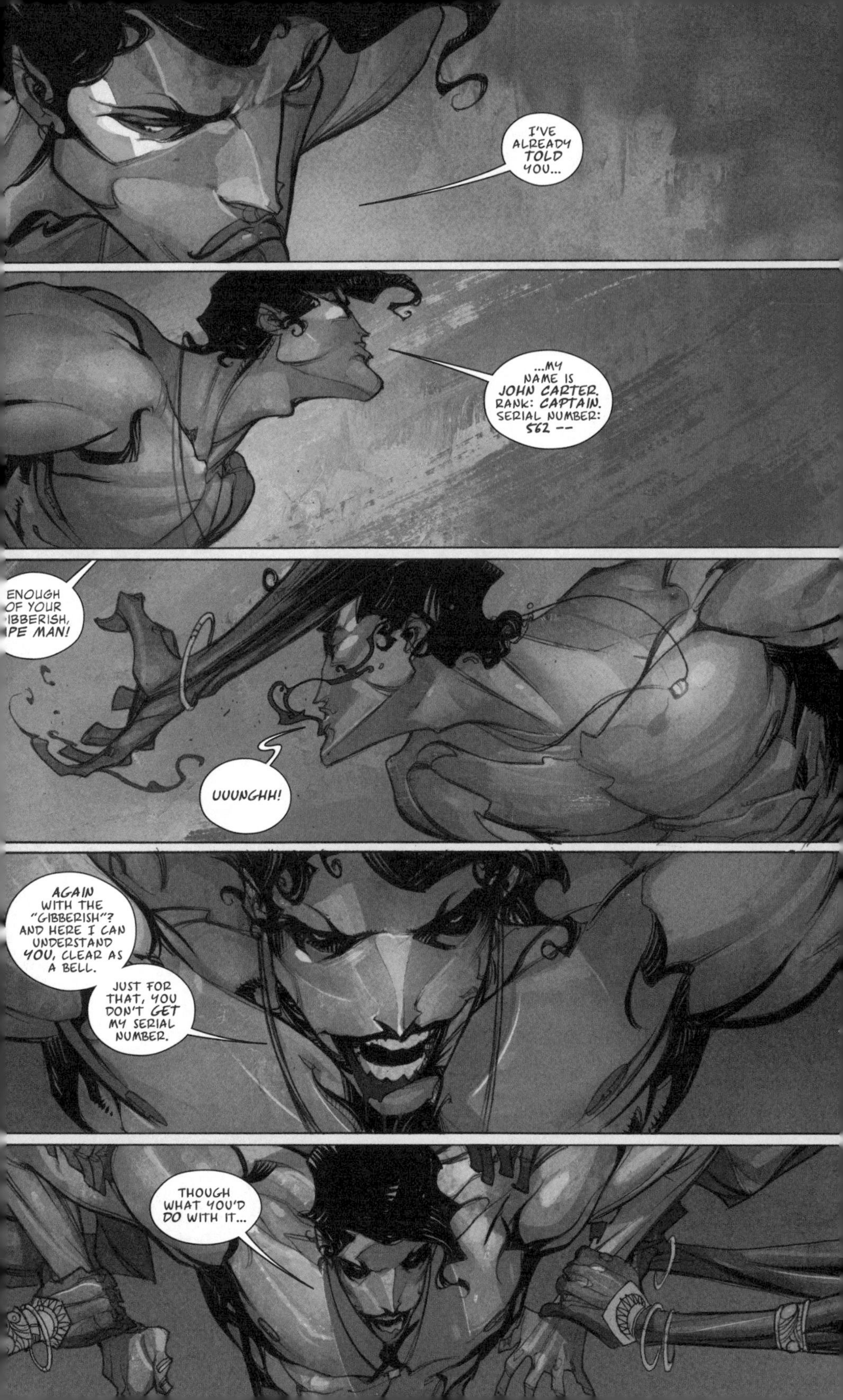

I'VE ALREADY TOLD YOU...
...MY NAME IS JOHN CARTER. RANK: CAPTAIN. SERIAL NUMBER: 562 --
ENOUGH OF YOUR IBBERISH, PE MAN!
UUUNGHH!
AGAIN WITH THE "GIBBERISH"? AND HERE I CAN UNDERSTAND YOU, CLEAR AS A BELL.
JUST FOR THAT, YOU DON'T GET MY SERIAL NUMBER.
THOUGH WHAT YOU'D DO WITH IT...

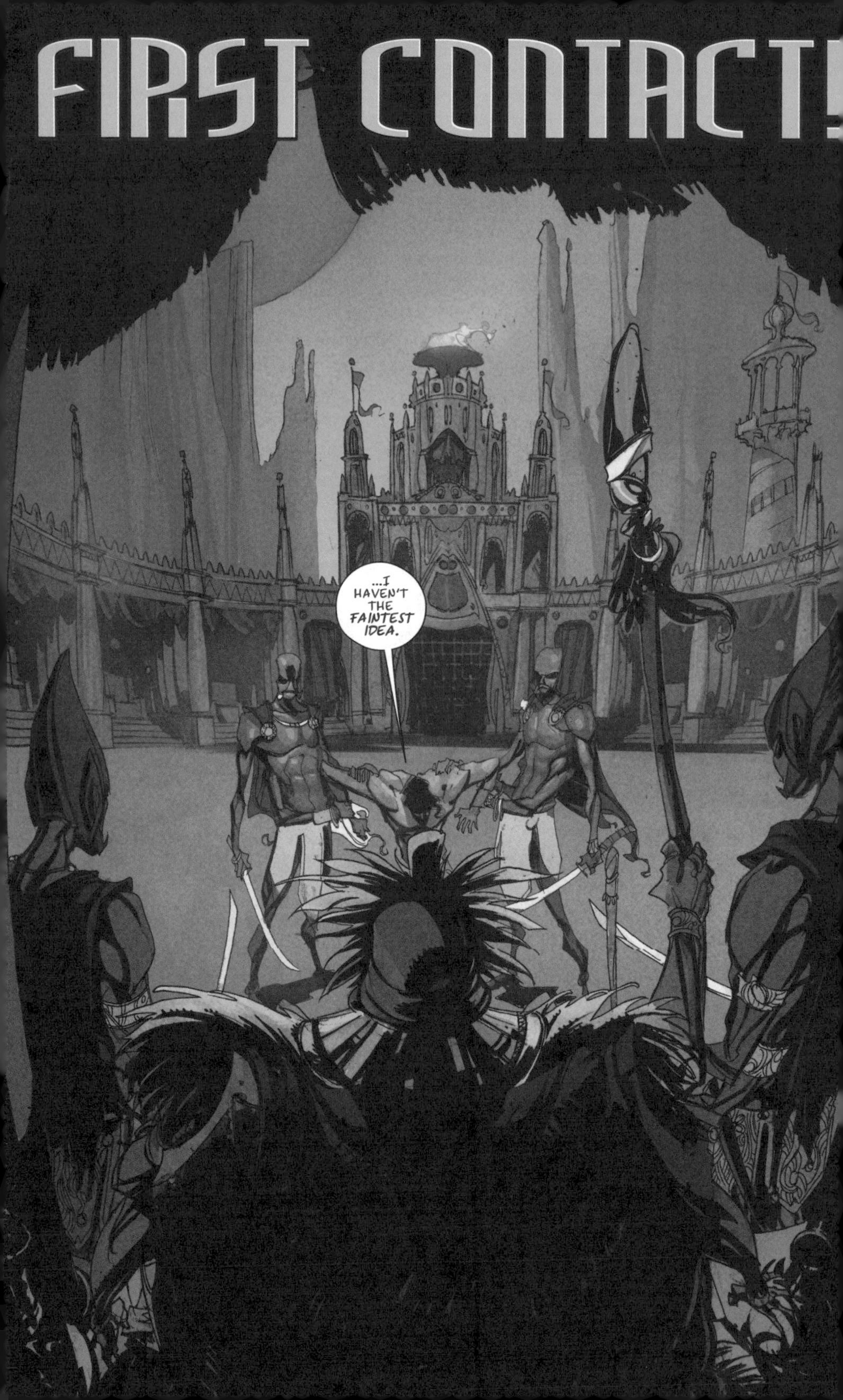
FIRST CONTACT!
...I HAVEN'T THE FAINTEST IDEA.

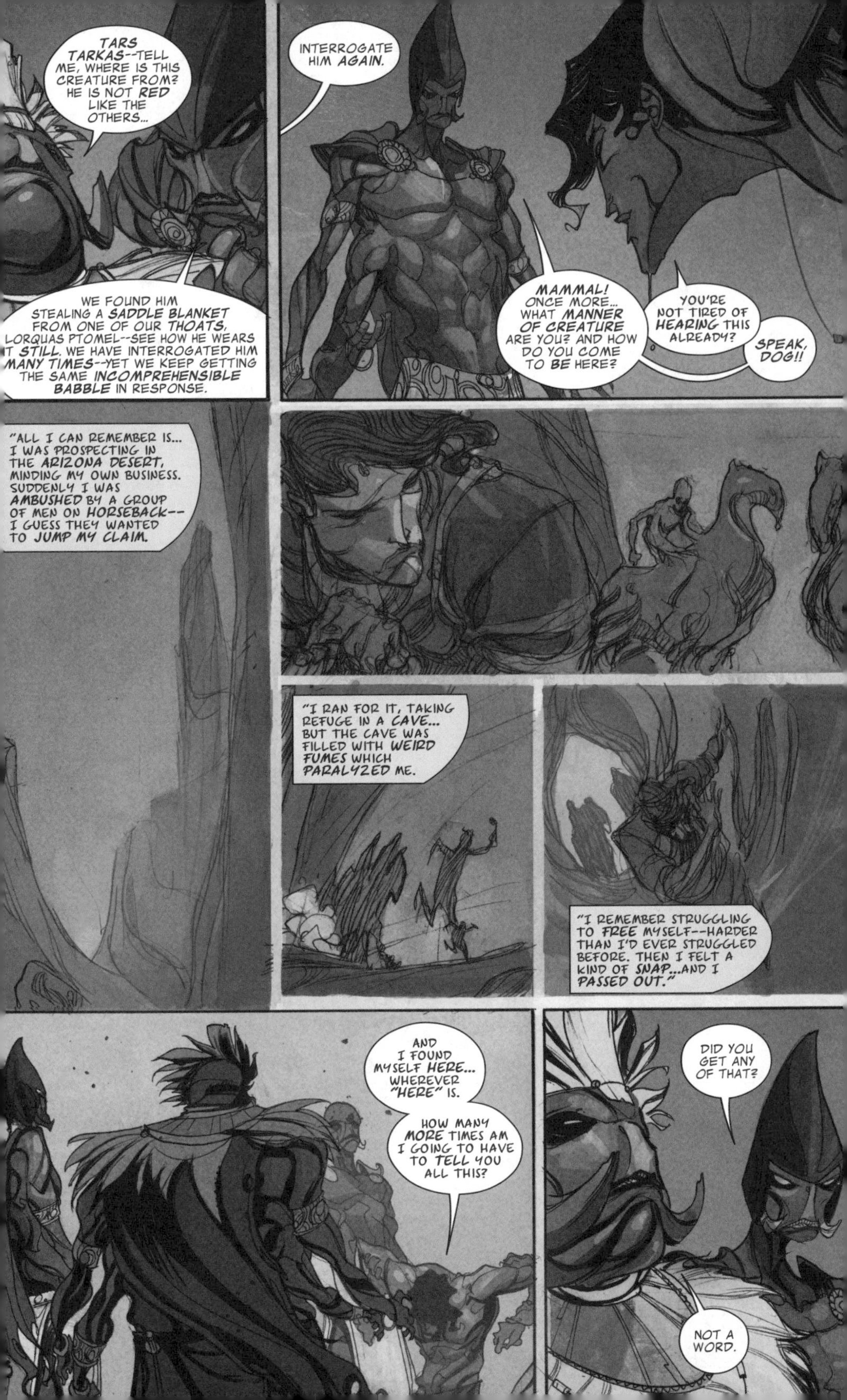
TARS TARKAS--TELL ME, WHERE IS THIS CREATURE FROM? HE IS NOT RED LIKE THE OTHERS...
WE FOUND HIM STEALING A SADDLE BLANKET FROM ONE OF OUR THOATS, LORQUAS PTOMEL--SEE HOW HE WEARS IT STILL. WE HAVE INTERROGATED HIM MANY TIMES--YET WE KEEP GETTING THE SAME INCOMPREHENSIBLE BABBLE IN RESPONSE.
INTERROGATE HIM AGAIN.
MAMMAL! ONCE MORE... WHAT MANNER OF CREATURE ARE YOU? AND HOW DO YOU COME TO BE HERE?
YOU'RE NOT TIRED OF HEARING THIS ALREADY?
SPEAK, DOG!!
"ALL I CAN REMEMBER IS... I WAS PROSPECTING IN THE ARIZONA DESERT, MINDING MY OWN BUSINESS. SUDDENLY I WAS AMBUSHED BY A GROUP OF MEN ON HORSEBACK-- I GUESS THEY WANTED TO JUMP MY CLAIM.
"I RAN FOR IT, TAKING REFUGE IN A CAVE... BUT THE CAVE WAS FILLED WITH WEIRD FUMES WHICH PARALYZED ME.
"I REMEMBER STRUGGLING TO FREE MYSELF--HARDER THAN I'D EVER STRUGGLED BEFORE. THEN I FELT A KIND OF SNAP...AND I PASSED OUT."
AND I FOUND MYSELF HERE... WHEREVER "HERE" IS.
HOW MANY MORE TIMES AM I GOING TO HAVE TO TELL YOU ALL THIS?
DID YOU GET ANY OF THAT?
NOT A WORD.

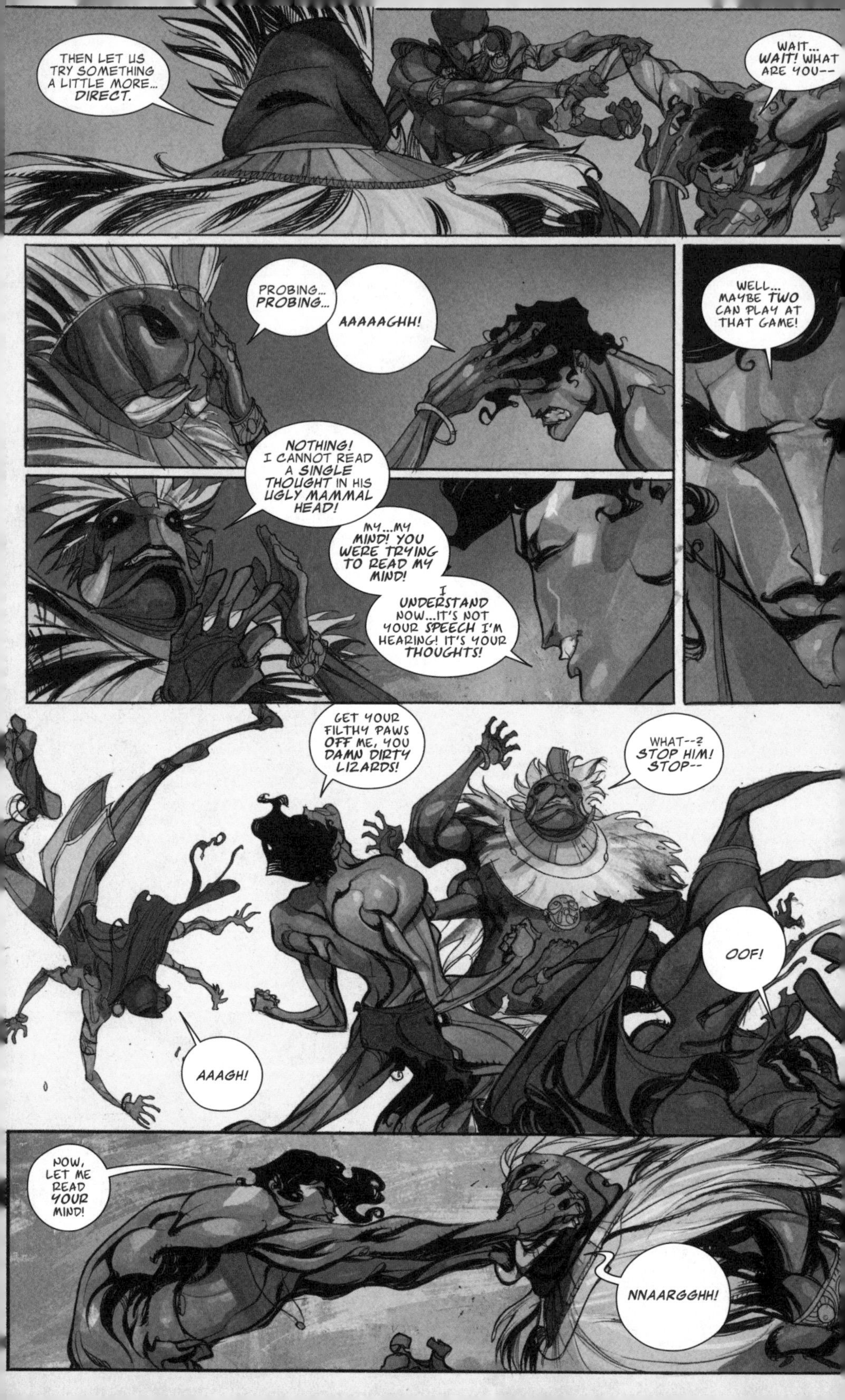
THEN LET US TRY SOMETHING A LITTLE MORE... DIRECT.
WAIT... WAIT! WHAT ARE YOU--
PROBING... PROBING...
AAAAAGHH!
WELL... MAYBE TWO CAN PLAY AT THAT GAME!
NOTHING! I CANNOT READ A SINGLE THOUGHT IN HIS UGLY MAMMAL HEAD!
MY...MY MIND! YOU WERE TRYING TO READ MY MIND!
I UNDERSTAND NOW...IT'S NOT YOUR SPEECH I'M HEARING! IT'S YOUR THOUGHTS!
GET YOUR FILTHY PAWS OFF ME, YOU DAMN DIRTY LIZARDS!
WHAT--? STOP HIM! STOP--
OOF!
AAAGH!
NOW, LET ME READ YOUR MIND!
NNAARGGHH!

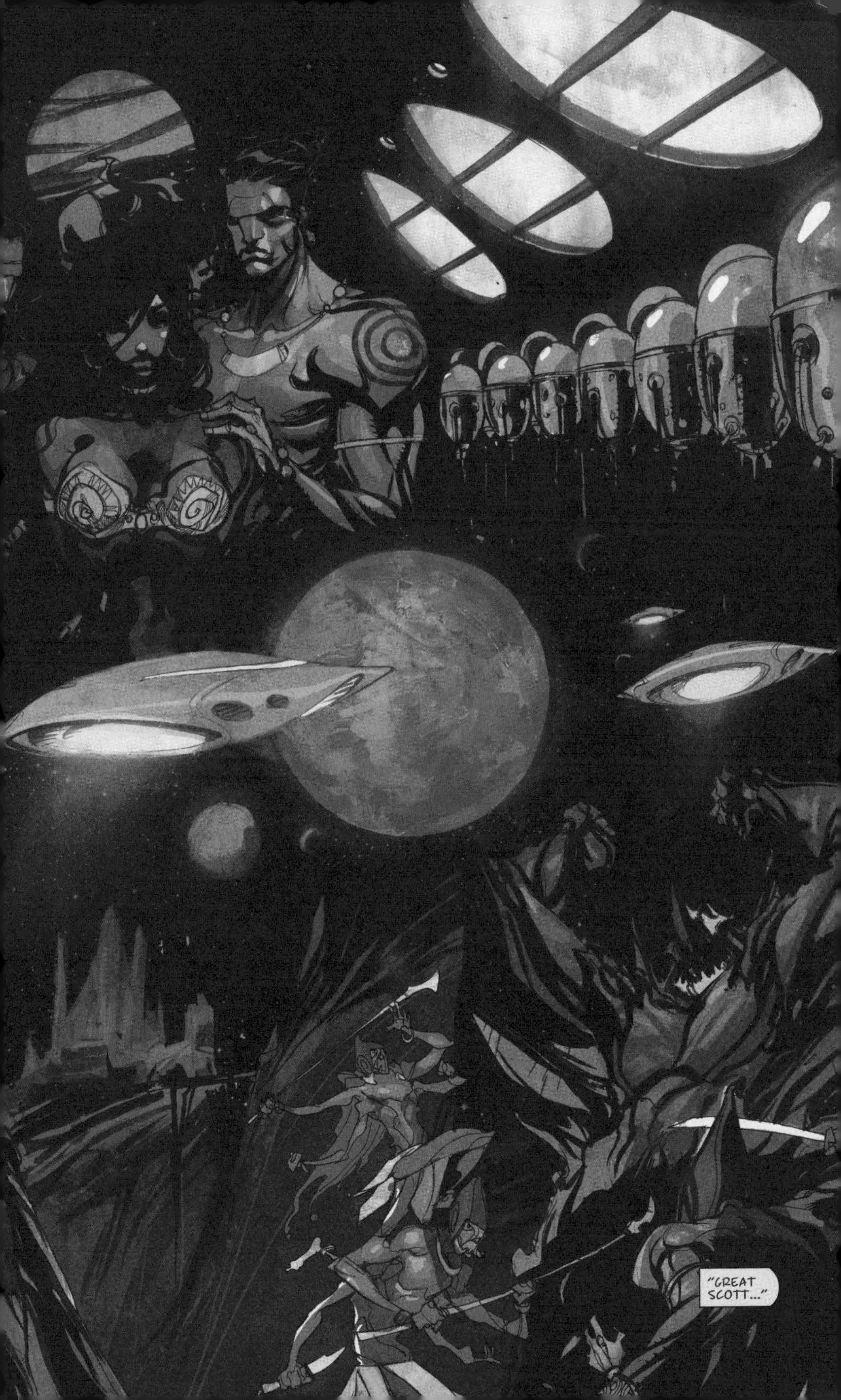
"GREAT SCOTT..."

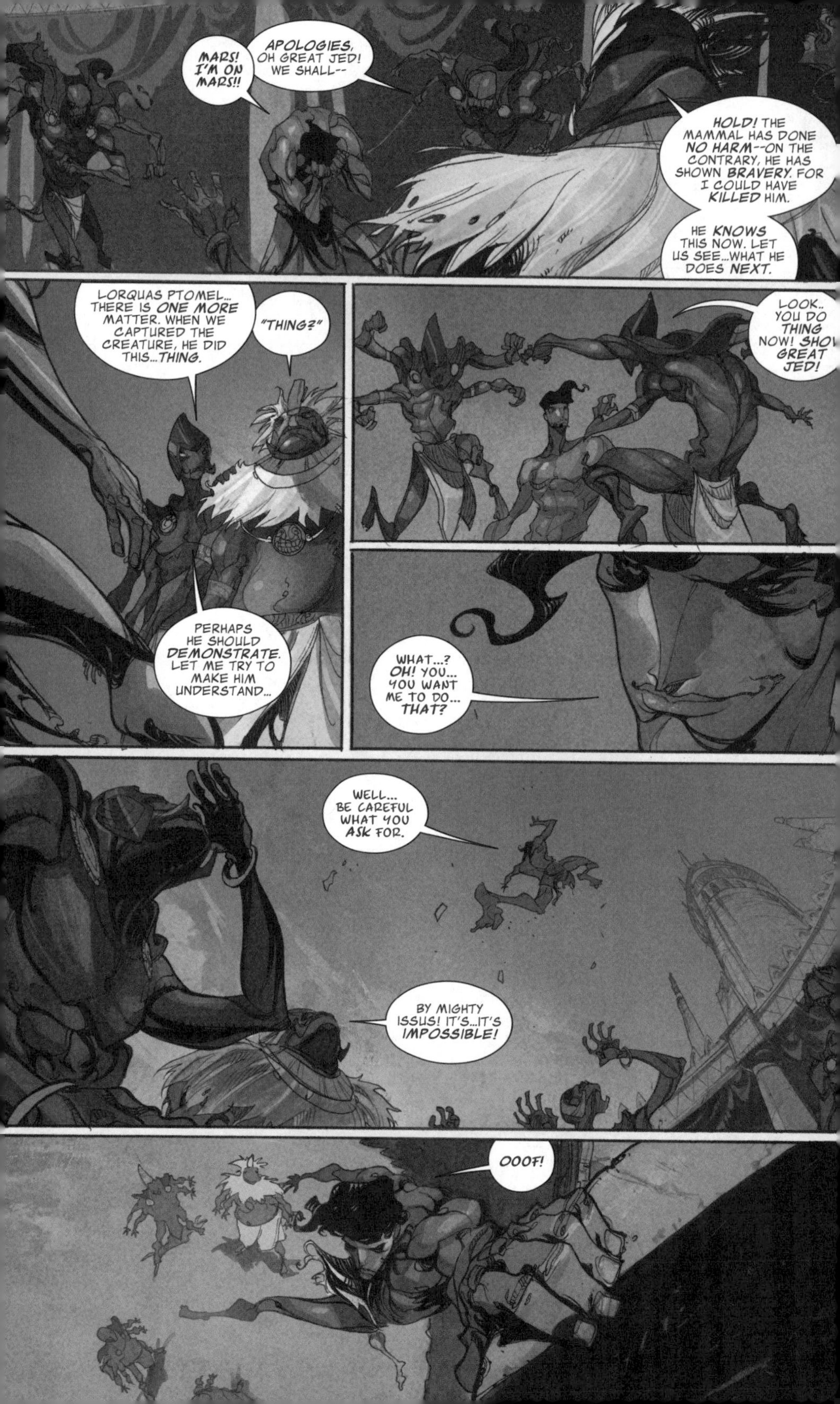
MARS! I'M ON MARS!!
APOLOGIES, OH GREAT JED! WE SHALL--
HOLD! THE MAMMAL HAS DONE NO HARM--ON THE CONTRARY, HE HAS SHOWN BRAVERY. FOR I COULD HAVE KILLED HIM.
HE KNOWS THIS NOW. LET US SEE...WHAT HE DOES NEXT.
LORQUAS PTOMEL... THERE IS ONE MORE MATTER. WHEN WE CAPTURED THE CREATURE, HE DID THIS...THING.
"THING?"
PERHAPS HE SHOULD DEMONSTRATE. LET ME TRY TO MAKE HIM UNDERSTAND...
LOOK.. YOU DO THING NOW! SHO GREAT JED!
WHAT...? OH! YOU... YOU WANT ME TO DO... THAT?
WELL... BE CAREFUL WHAT YOU ASK FOR.
BY MIGHTY ISSUS! IT'S...IT'S IMPOSSIBLE!
OOOF!

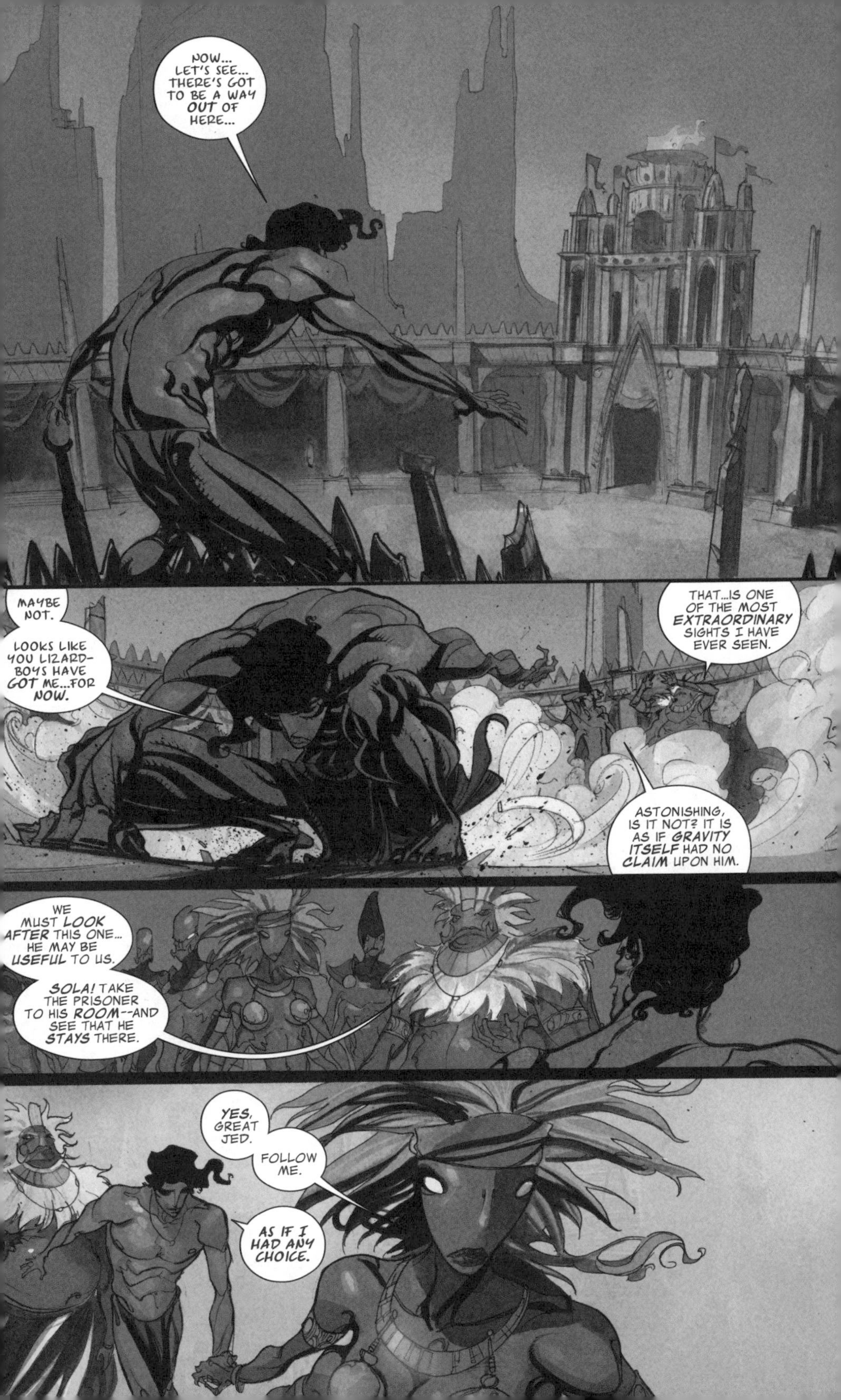
NOW... LET'S SEE... THERE'S GOT TO BE A WAY OUT OF HERE...
MAYBE NOT.
LOOKS LIKE YOU LIZARD-BOYS HAVE GOT ME...FOR NOW.
THAT...IS ONE OF THE MOST EXTRAORDINARY SIGHTS I HAVE EVER SEEN.
ASTONISHING, IS IT NOT? IT IS AS IF GRAVITY ITSELF HAD NO CLAIM UPON HIM.
WE MUST LOOK AFTER THIS ONE... HE MAY BE USEFUL TO US.
SOLA! TAKE THE PRISONER TO HIS ROOM--AND SEE THAT HE STAYS THERE.
YES, GREAT JED.
FOLLOW ME.
AS IF I HAD ANY CHOICE.

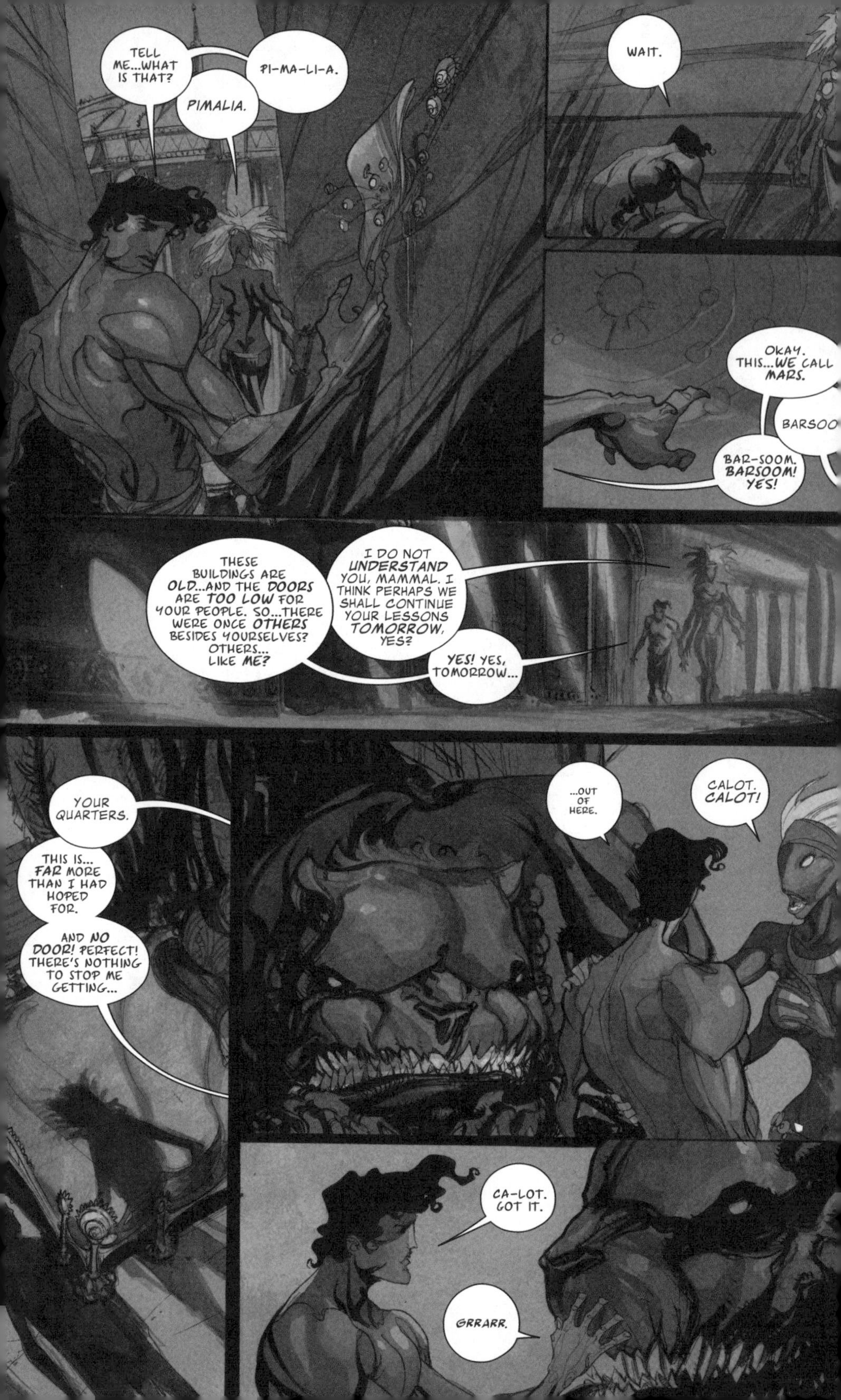
TELL ME...WHAT IS THAT?
PI-MA-LI-A.
PIMALIA.
WAIT.
OKAY. THIS...WE CALL MARS.
BARSOO
BAR-SOOM. BARSOOM! YES!
THESE BUILDINGS ARE OLD...AND THE DOORS ARE TOO LOW FOR YOUR PEOPLE. SO...THERE WERE ONCE OTHERS BESIDES YOURSELVES? OTHERS... LIKE ME?
I DO NOT UNDERSTAND YOU, MAMMAL. I THINK PERHAPS WE SHALL CONTINUE YOUR LESSONS TOMORROW, YES?
YES! YES, TOMORROW...
YOUR QUARTERS.
THIS IS... FAR MORE THAN I HAD HOPED FOR.
AND NO DOOR! PERFECT! THERE'S NOTHING TO STOP ME GETTING...
...OUT OF HERE.
CALOT. CALOT!
CA-LOT. GOT IT.
GRRARR.

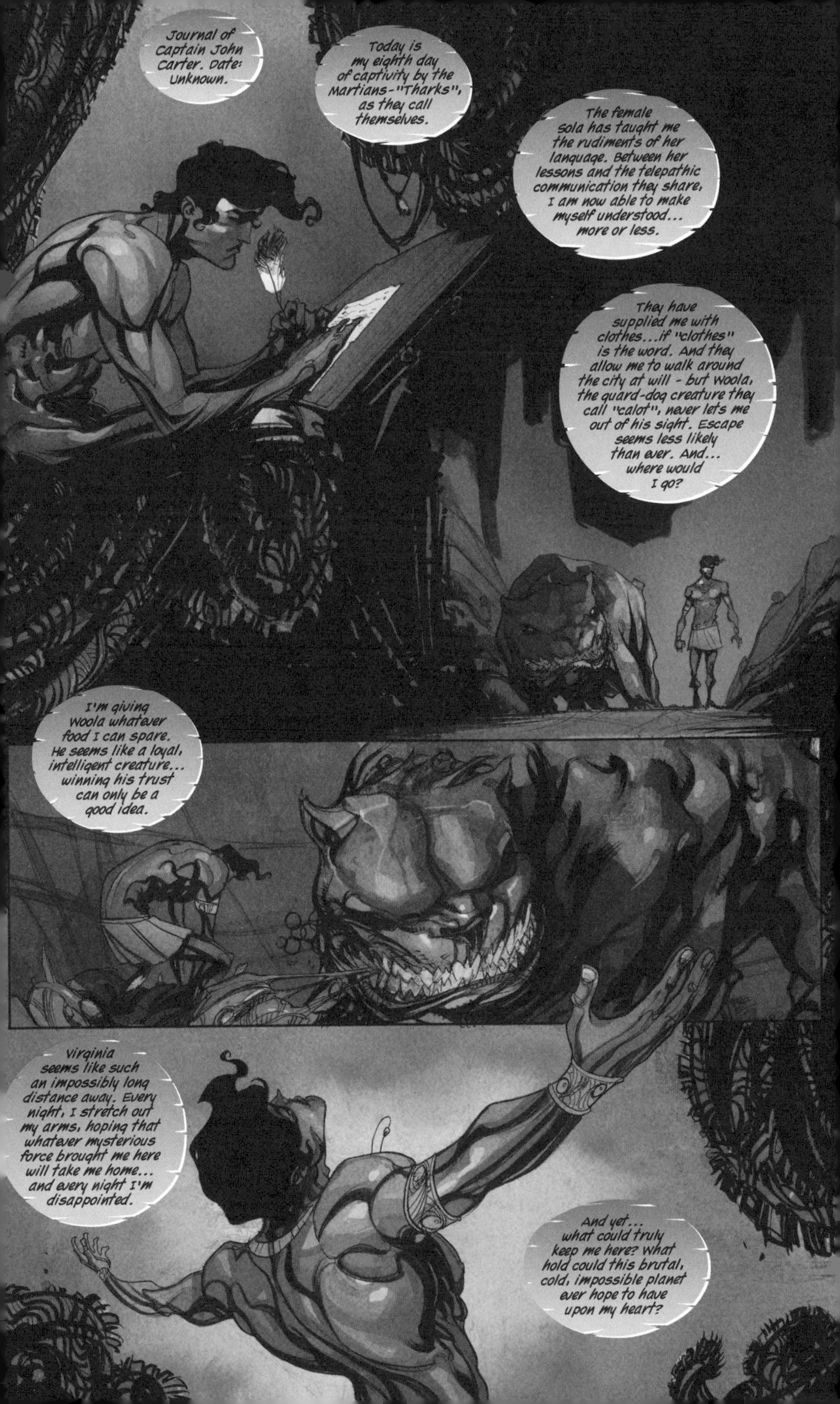
Journal of Captain John Carter. Date: Unknown.
Today is my eighth day of captivity by the Martians-"Tharks", as they call themselves.
The female Sola has taught me the rudiments of her language. Between her lessons and the telepathic communication they share, I am now able to make myself understood... more or less.
They have supplied me with clothes...if "clothes" is the word. And they allow me to walk around the city at will - but Woola, the guard-dog creature they call "calot", never lets me out of his sight. Escape seems less likely than ever. And... where would I go?
I'm giving Woola whatever food I can spare. He seems like a loyal, intelligent creature... winning his trust can only be a good idea.
Virginia seems like such an impossibly long distance away. Every night, I stretch out my arms, hoping that whatever mysterious force brought me here will take me home... and every night I'm disappointed.
And yet... what could truly keep me here? What hold could this brutal, cold, impossible planet ever hope to have upon my heart?

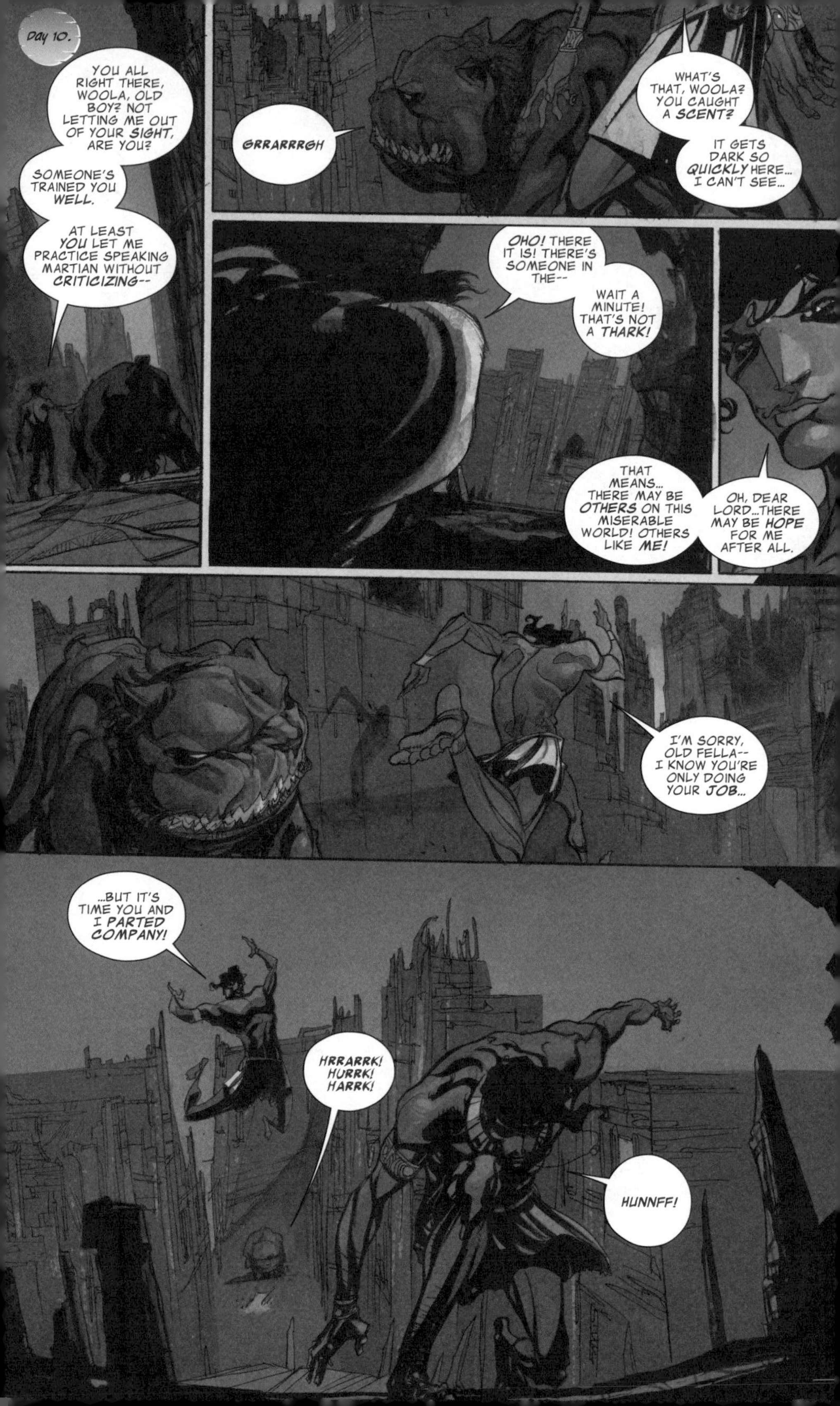
Day 10.
YOU ALL RIGHT THERE, WOOLA, OLD BOY? NOT LETTING ME OUT OF YOUR SIGHT, ARE YOU?
SOMEONE'S TRAINED YOU WELL.
AT LEAST YOU LET ME PRACTICE SPEAKING MARTIAN WITHOUT CRITICIZING--
GRRARRRGH
WHAT'S THAT, WOOLA? YOU CAUGHT A SCENT?
IT GETS DARK SO QUICKLY HERE... I CAN'T SEE...
OHO! THERE IT IS! THERE'S SOMEONE IN THE--
WAIT A MINUTE! THAT'S NOT A THARK!
THAT MEANS... THERE MAY BE OTHERS ON THIS MISERABLE WORLD! OTHERS LIKE ME!
OH, DEAR LORD...THERE MAY BE HOPE FOR ME AFTER ALL.
I'M SORRY, OLD FELLA-- I KNOW YOU'RE ONLY DOING YOUR JOB...
...BUT IT'S TIME YOU AND I PARTED COMPANY!
HRRARRK! HURRK! HARRK!
HUNNFF!

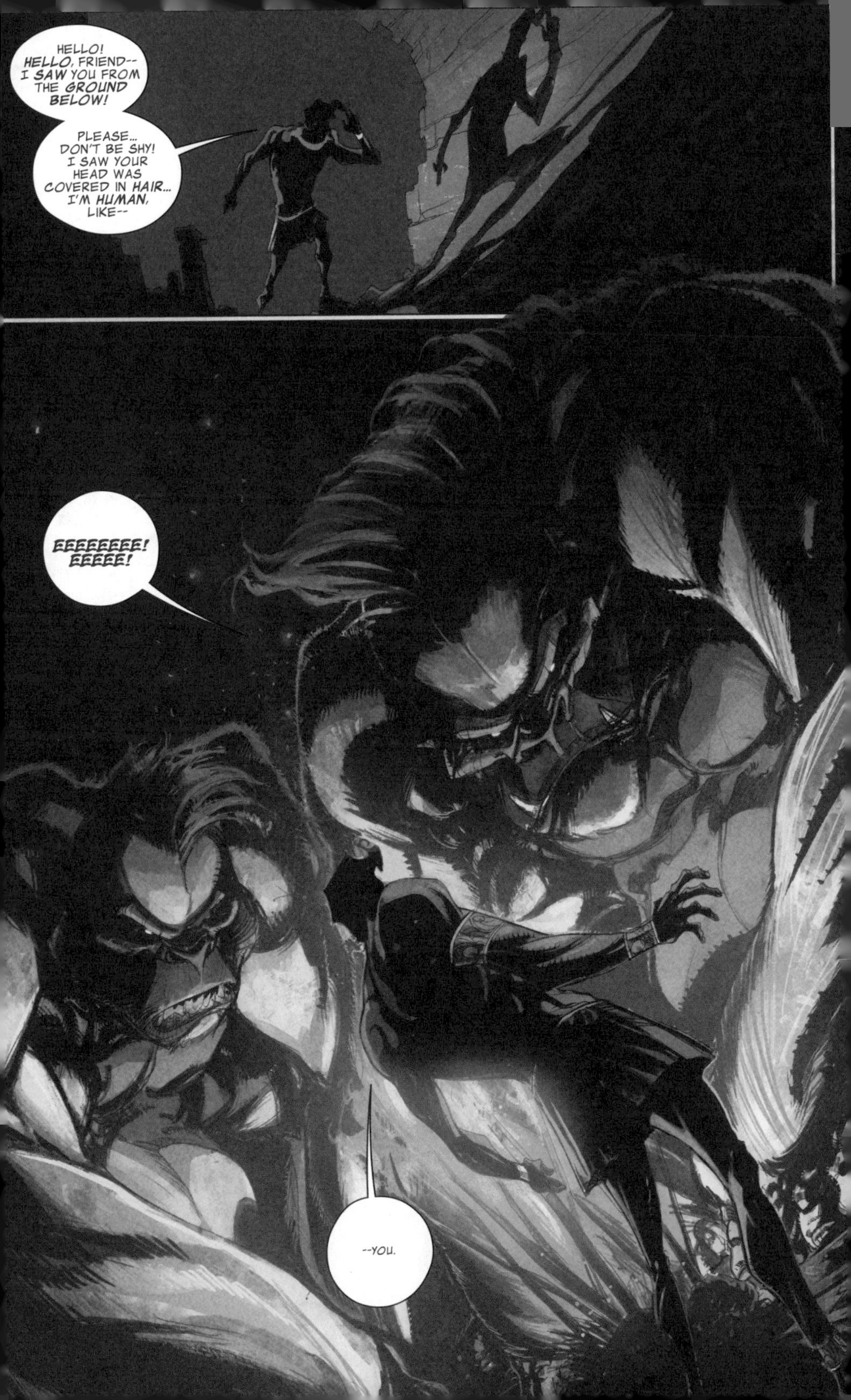
HELLO! HELLO, FRIEND-- I SAW YOU FROM THE GROUND BELOW!
PLEASE... DON'T BE SHY! I SAW YOUR HEAD WAS COVERED IN HAIR... I'M HUMAN, LIKE--
EEEEEEEE! EEEEE!
--YOU.

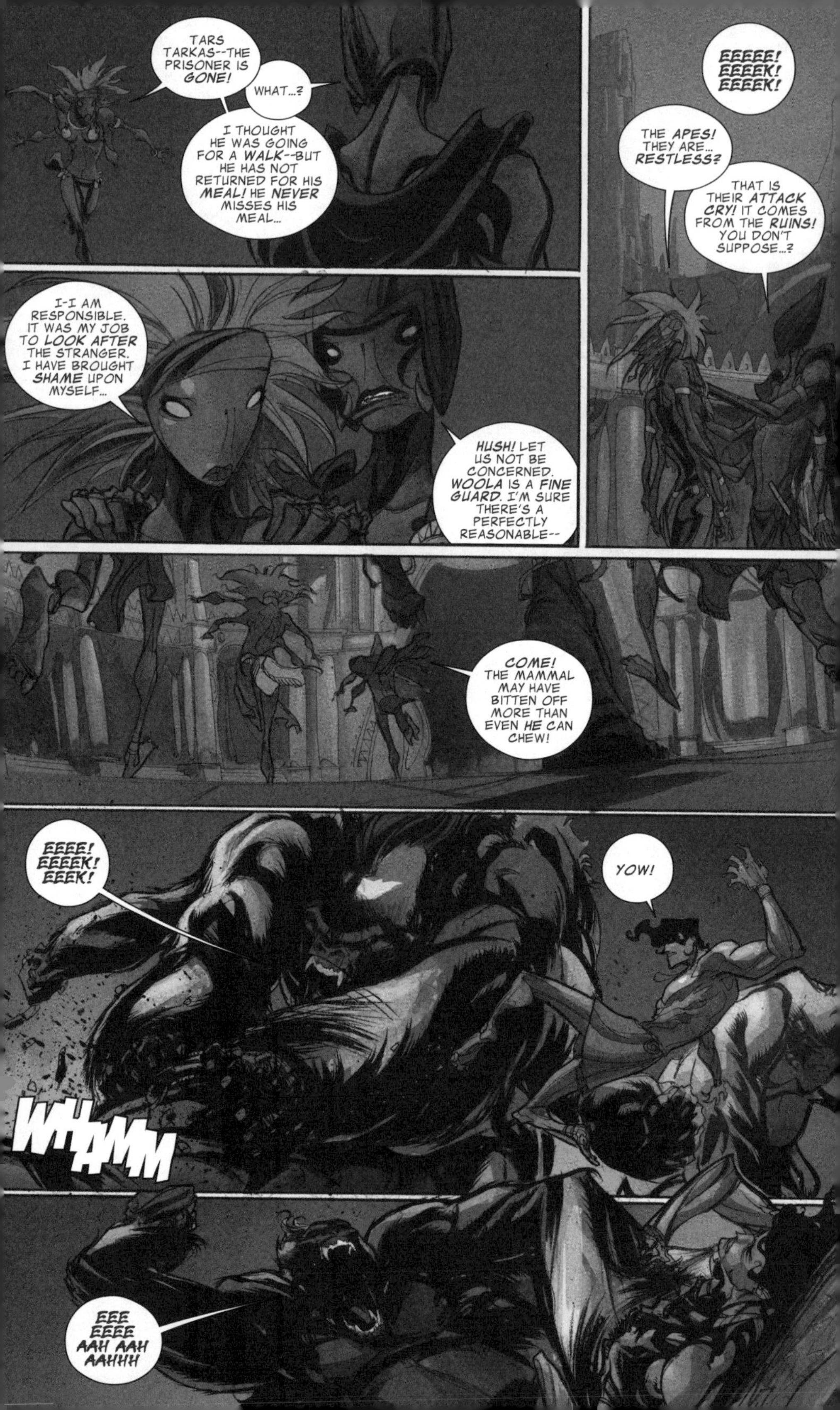
TARS TARKAS--THE PRISONER IS GONE!
WHAT...?
I THOUGHT HE WAS GOING FOR A WALK--BUT HE HAS NOT RETURNED FOR HIS MEAL! HE NEVER MISSES HIS MEAL...
EEEEE! EEEEK! EEEEK!
THE APES! THEY ARE... RESTLESS?
THAT IS THEIR ATTACK CRY! IT COMES FROM THE RUINS! YOU DON'T SUPPOSE...?
I-I AM RESPONSIBLE. IT WAS MY JOB TO LOOK AFTER THE STRANGER. I HAVE BROUGHT SHAME UPON MYSELF...
HUSH! LET US NOT BE CONCERNED. WOOLA IS A FINE GUARD. I'M SURE THERE'S A PERFECTLY REASONABLE--
COME! THE MAMMAL MAY HAVE BITTEN OFF MORE THAN EVEN HE CAN CHEW!
EEEE! EEEEK! EEEK!
YOW!
WHAMM
EEE EEEE AAH AAH AAHHH

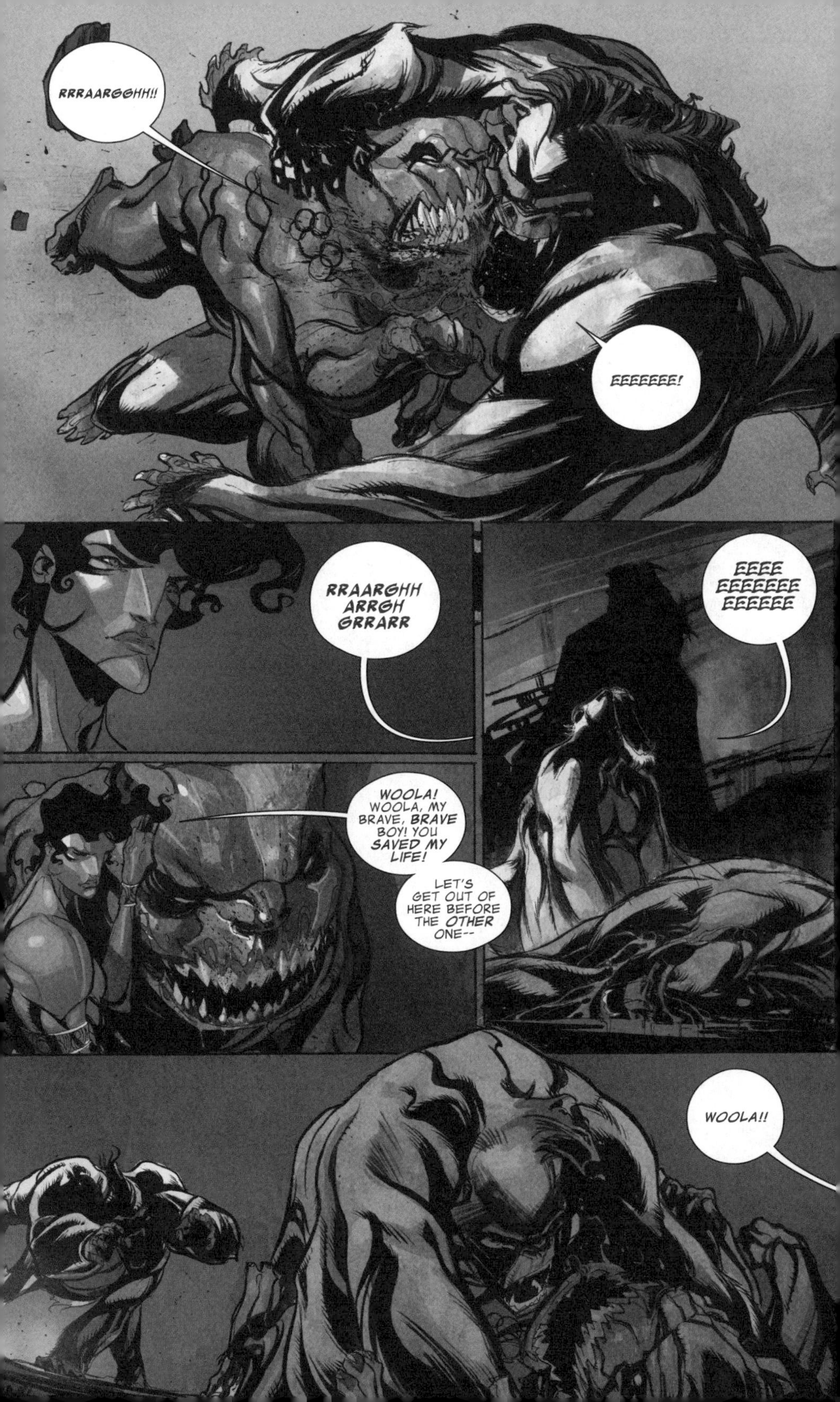
RRRAARGGHH!!
EEEEEEE!
RRAARGHH ARRGH GRRARR
EEEE EEEEEEE EEEEEE
WOOLA! WOOLA, MY BRAVE, BRAVE BOY! YOU SAVED MY LIFE!
LET'S GET OUT OF HERE BEFORE THE OTHER ONE--
WOOLA!!

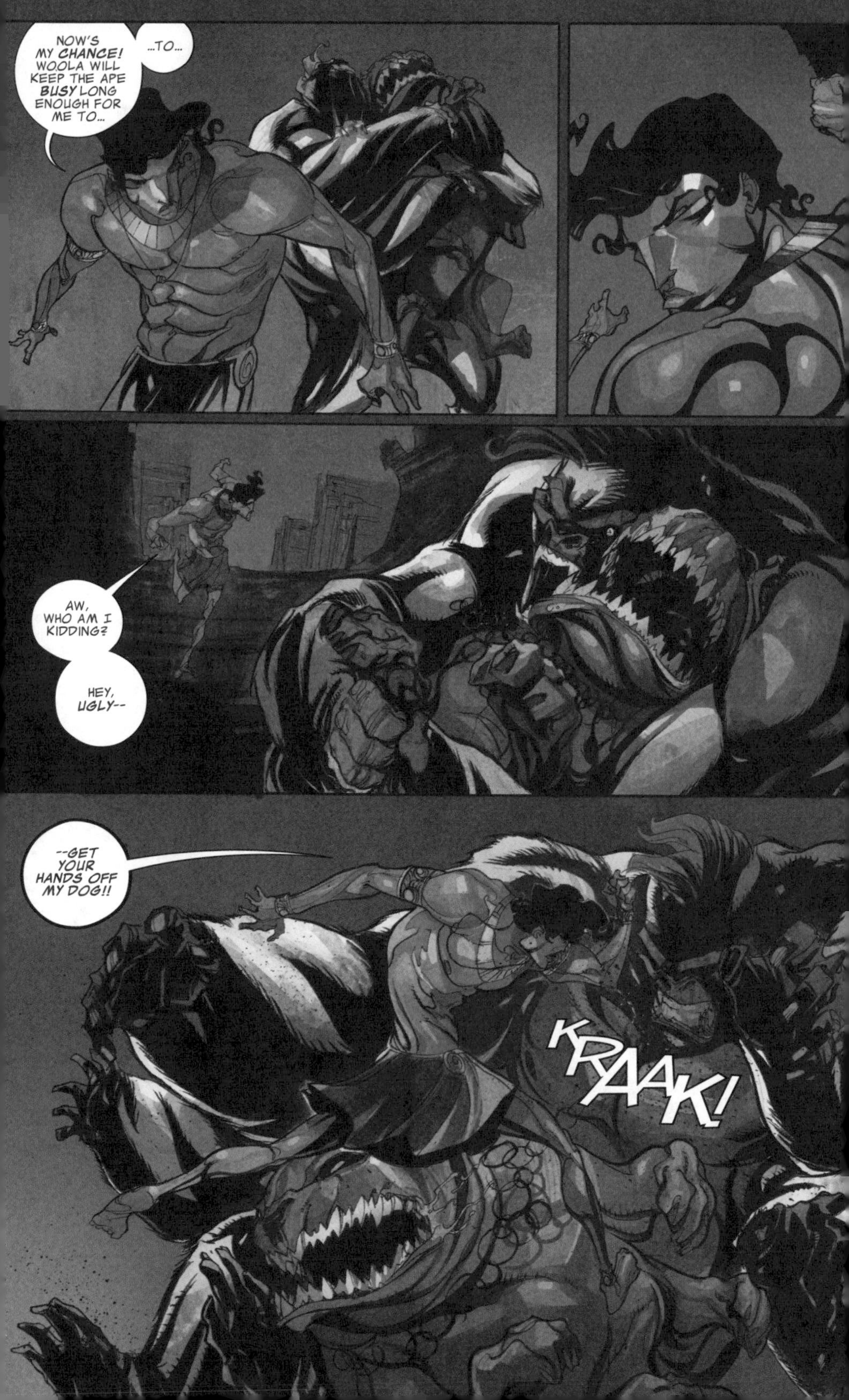
NOW'S MY CHANCE! WOOLA WILL KEEP THE APE BUSY LONG ENOUGH FOR ME TO...
...TO...
AW, WHO AM I KIDDING?
HEY, UGLY--
--GET YOUR HANDS OFF MY DOG!!
KRAAK!

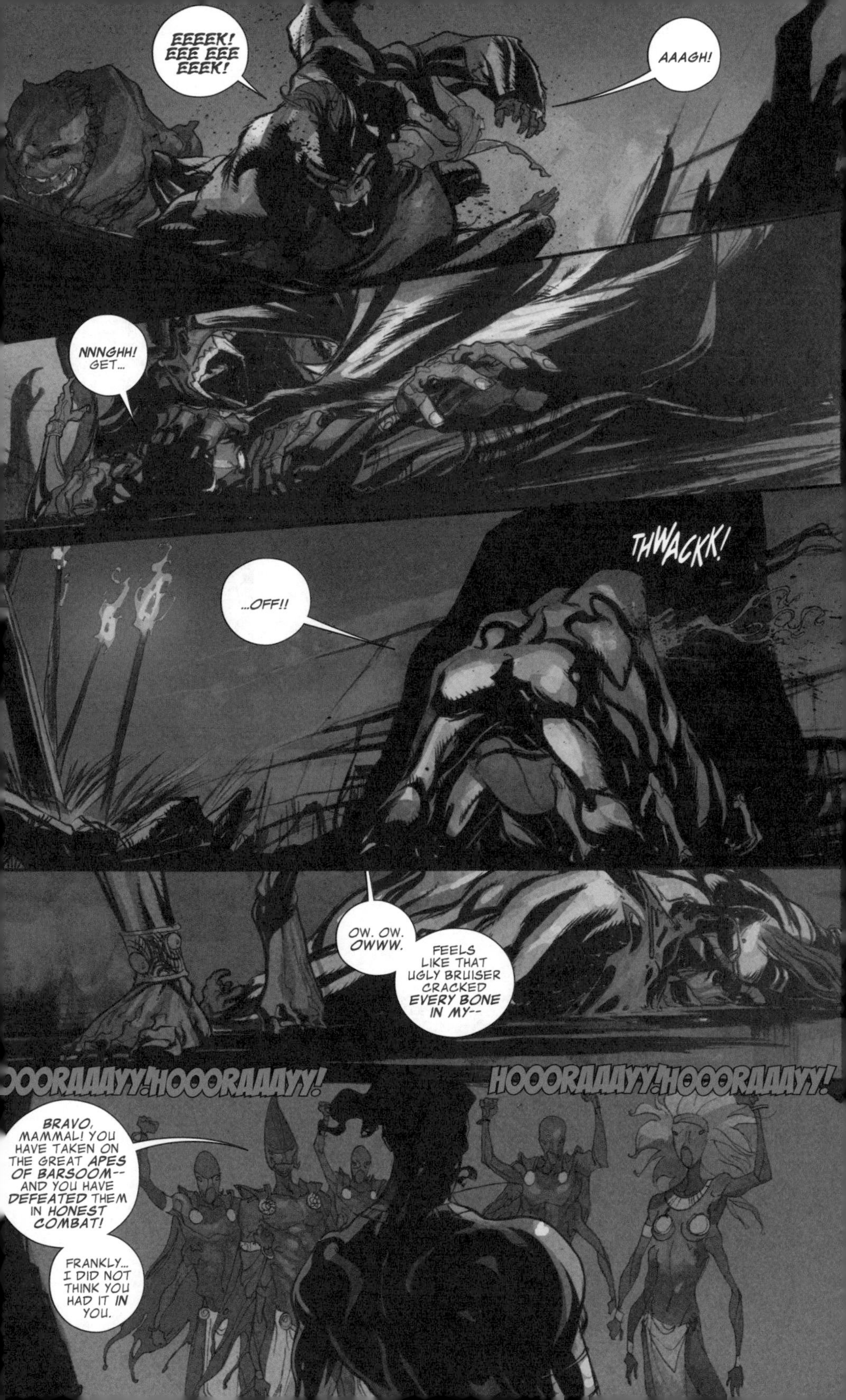
EEEEK! EEE EEE EEEK!
AAAGH!
NNNGHH! GET...
...OFF!!
THWACKK!
OW. OW. OWWW.
FEELS LIKE THAT UGLY BRUISER CRACKED EVERY BONE IN MY--
HOOORAAAYY! HOOORAAAYY!
HOOORAAAYY! HOOORAAAYY!
BRAVO, MAMMAL! YOU HAVE TAKEN ON THE GREAT APES OF BARSOOM-- AND YOU HAVE DEFEATED THEM IN HONEST COMBAT!
FRANKLY... I DID NOT THINK YOU HAD IT IN YOU.

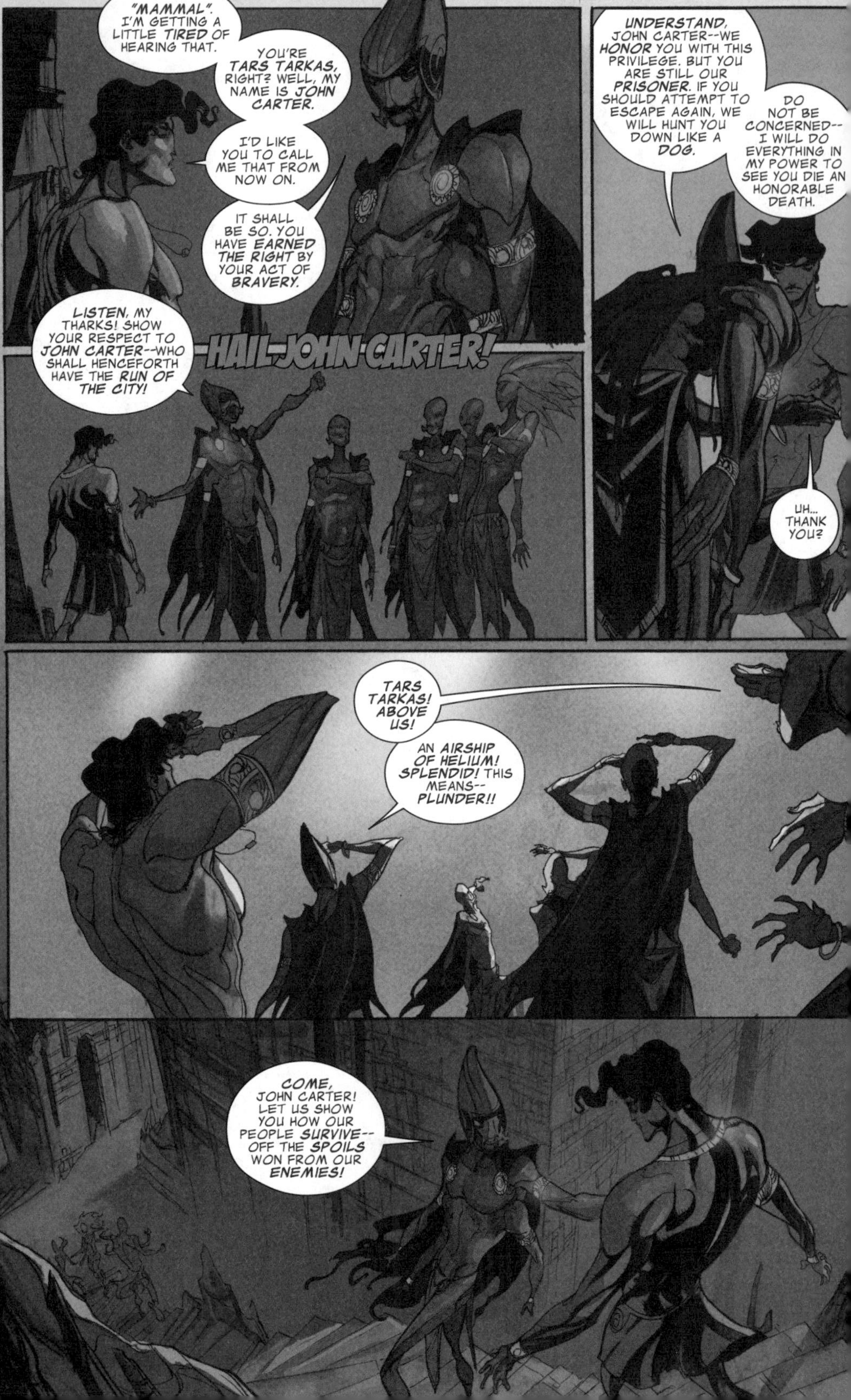

"MAMMAL". I'M GETTING A LITTLE TIRED OF HEARING THAT.
YOU'RE TARS TARKAS, RIGHT? WELL, MY NAME IS JOHN CARTER.
I'D LIKE YOU TO CALL ME THAT FROM NOW ON.
IT SHALL BE SO. YOU HAVE EARNED THE RIGHT BY YOUR ACT OF BRAVERY.
UNDERSTAND, JOHN CARTER--WE HONOR YOU WITH THIS PRIVILEGE. BUT YOU ARE STILL OUR PRISONER. IF YOU SHOULD ATTEMPT TO ESCAPE AGAIN, WE WILL HUNT YOU DOWN LIKE A DOG.
DO NOT BE CONCERNED--I WILL DO EVERYTHING IN MY POWER TO SEE YOU DIE AN HONORABLE DEATH.
UH... THANK YOU?
LISTEN, MY THARKS! SHOW YOUR RESPECT TO JOHN CARTER--WHO SHALL HENCEFORTH HAVE THE RUN OF THE CITY!
HAIL JOHN CARTER!
TARS TARKAS! ABOVE US!
AN AIRSHIP OF HELIUM! SPLENDID! THIS MEANS--PLUNDER!!
COME, JOHN CARTER! LET US SHOW YOU HOW OUR PEOPLE SURVIVE--OFF THE SPOILS WON FROM OUR ENEMIES!

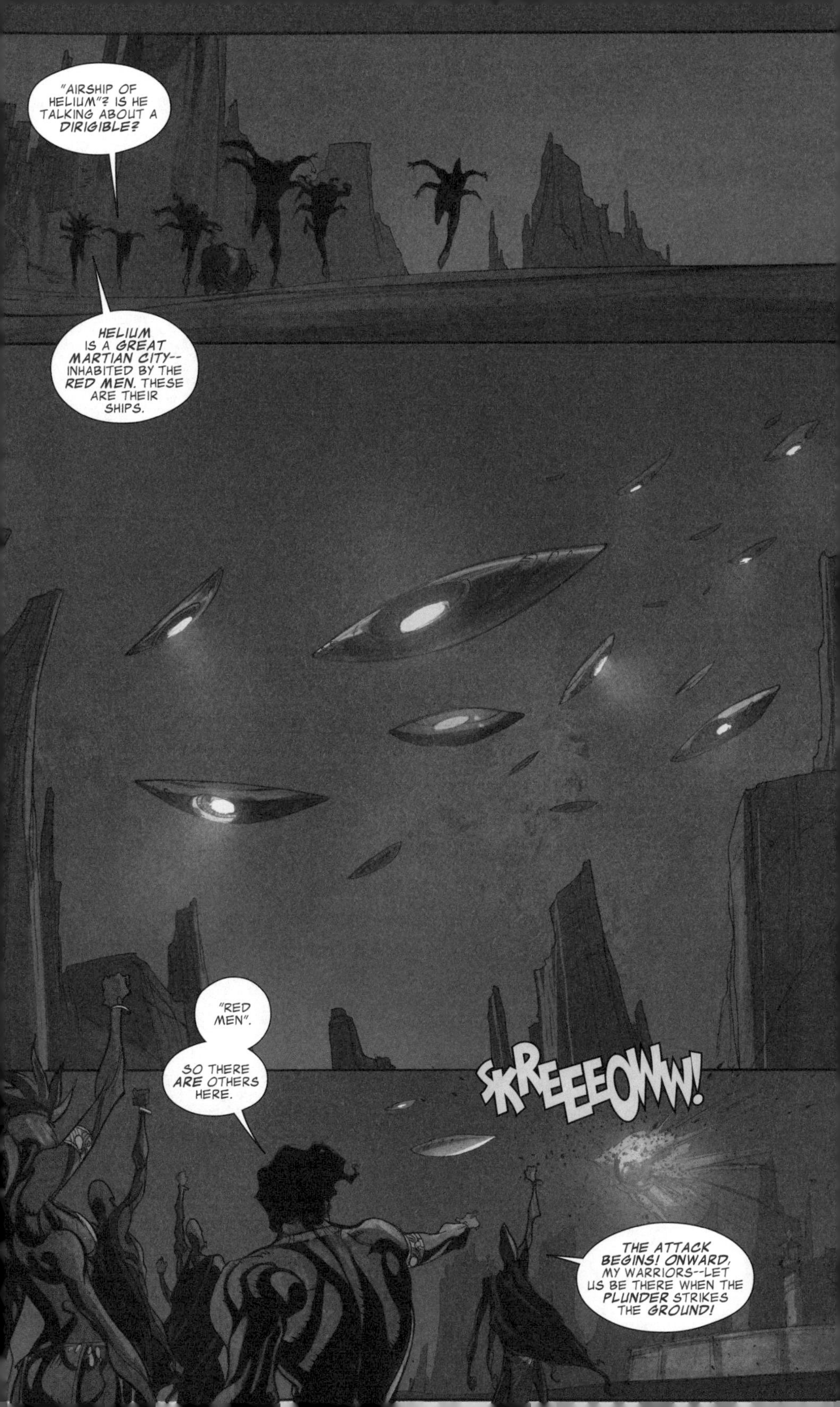
"AIRSHIP OF HELIUM"? IS HE TALKING ABOUT A DIRIGIBLE?
HELIUM IS A GREAT MARTIAN CITY--INHABITED BY THE RED MEN. THESE ARE THEIR SHIPS.
"RED MEN".
SO THERE ARE OTHERS HERE.
SKREEEEOWW!
THE ATTACK BEGINS! ONWARD, MY WARRIORS--LET US BE THERE WHEN THE PLUNDER STRIKES THE GROUND!

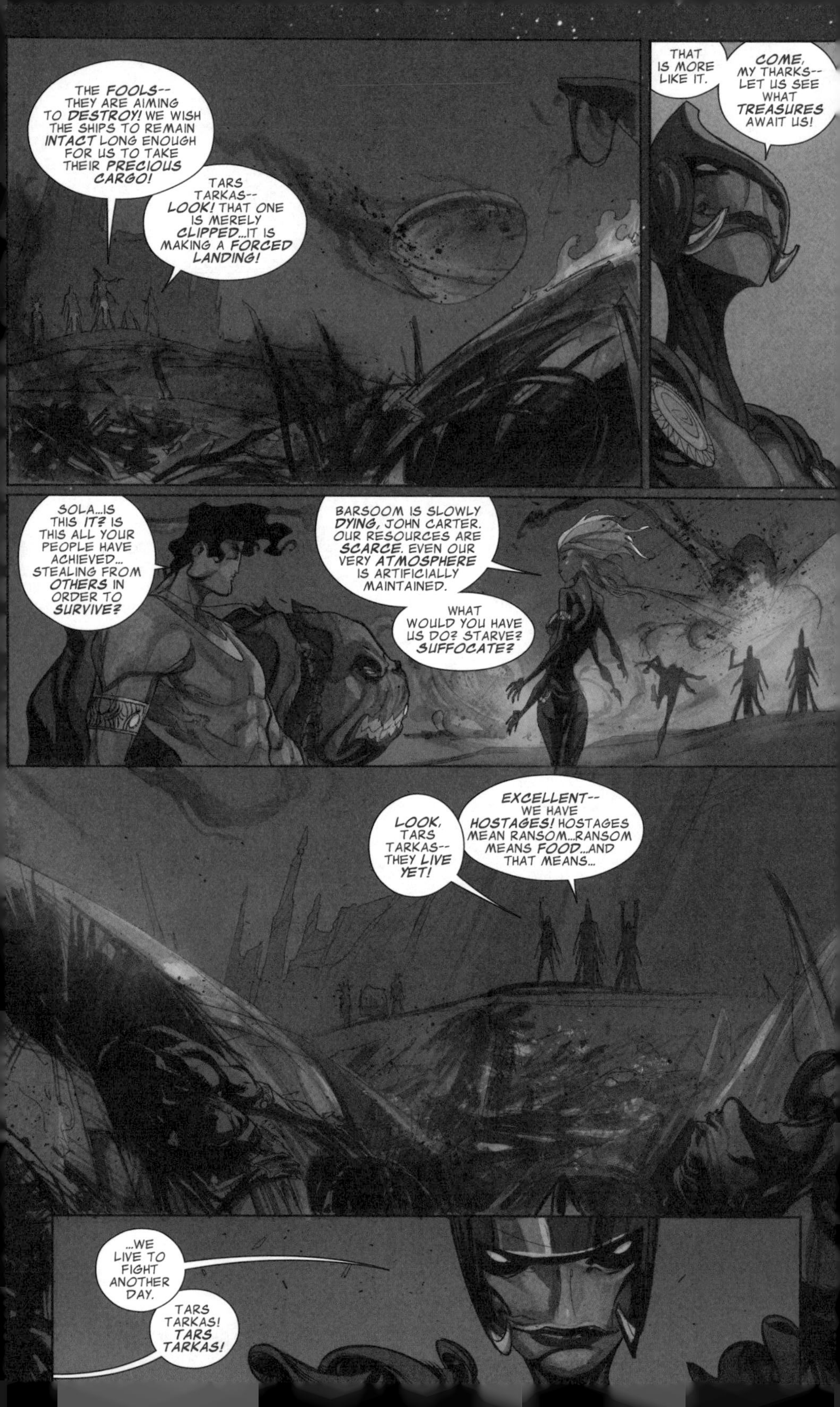

THE FOOLS-- THEY ARE AIMING TO DESTROY! WE WISH THE SHIPS TO REMAIN INTACT LONG ENOUGH FOR US TO TAKE THEIR PRECIOUS CARGO!
TARS TARKAS-- LOOK! THAT ONE IS MERELY CLIPPED...IT IS MAKING A FORCED LANDING!
THAT IS MORE LIKE IT.
COME, MY THARKS-- LET US SEE WHAT TREASURES AWAIT US!
SOLA...IS THIS IT? IS THIS ALL YOUR PEOPLE HAVE ACHIEVED... STEALING FROM OTHERS IN ORDER TO SURVIVE?
BARSOOM IS SLOWLY DYING, JOHN CARTER. OUR RESOURCES ARE SCARCE. EVEN OUR VERY ATMOSPHERE IS ARTIFICIALLY MAINTAINED.
WHAT WOULD YOU HAVE US DO? STARVE? SUFFOCATE?
LOOK, TARS TARKAS-- THEY LIVE YET!
EXCELLENT-- WE HAVE HOSTAGES! HOSTAGES MEAN RANSOM...RANSOM MEANS FOOD...AND THAT MEANS...
...WE LIVE TO FIGHT ANOTHER DAY.
TARS TARKAS! TARS TARKAS!

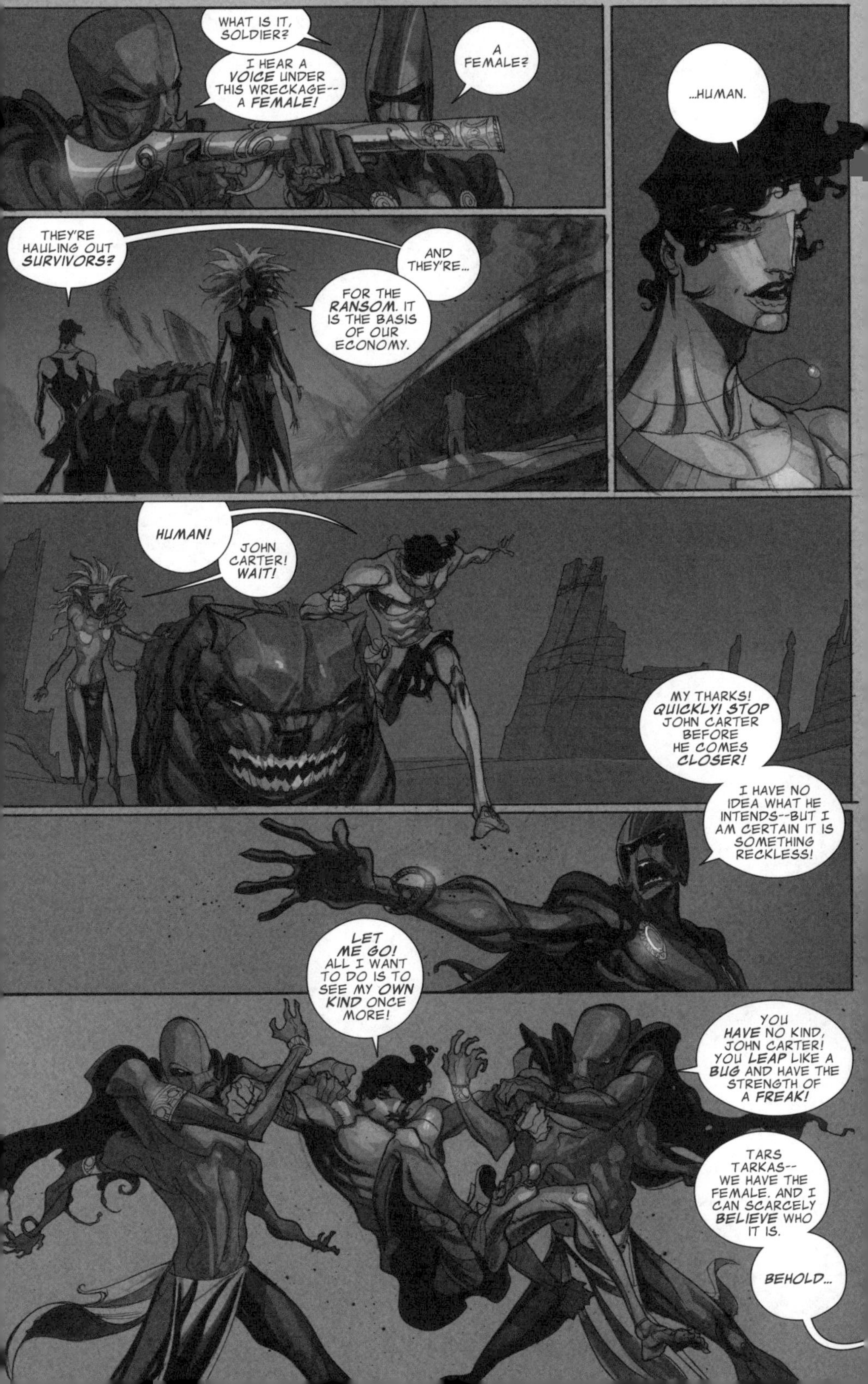
WHAT IS IT, SOLDIER?
I HEAR A VOICE UNDER THIS WRECKAGE-- A FEMALE!
A FEMALE?
...HUMAN.
THEY'RE HAULING OUT SURVIVORS?
AND THEY'RE...
FOR THE RANSOM. IT IS THE BASIS OF OUR ECONOMY.
HUMAN!
JOHN CARTER! WAIT!
MY THARKS! QUICKLY! STOP JOHN CARTER BEFORE HE COMES CLOSER!
I HAVE NO IDEA WHAT HE INTENDS--BUT I AM CERTAIN IT IS SOMETHING RECKLESS!
LET ME GO! ALL I WANT TO DO IS TO SEE MY OWN KIND ONCE MORE!
YOU HAVE NO KIND, JOHN CARTER! YOU LEAP LIKE A BUG AND HAVE THE STRENGTH OF A FREAK!
TARS TARKAS-- WE HAVE THE FEMALE. AND I CAN SCARCELY BELIEVE WHO IT IS.
BEHOLD...

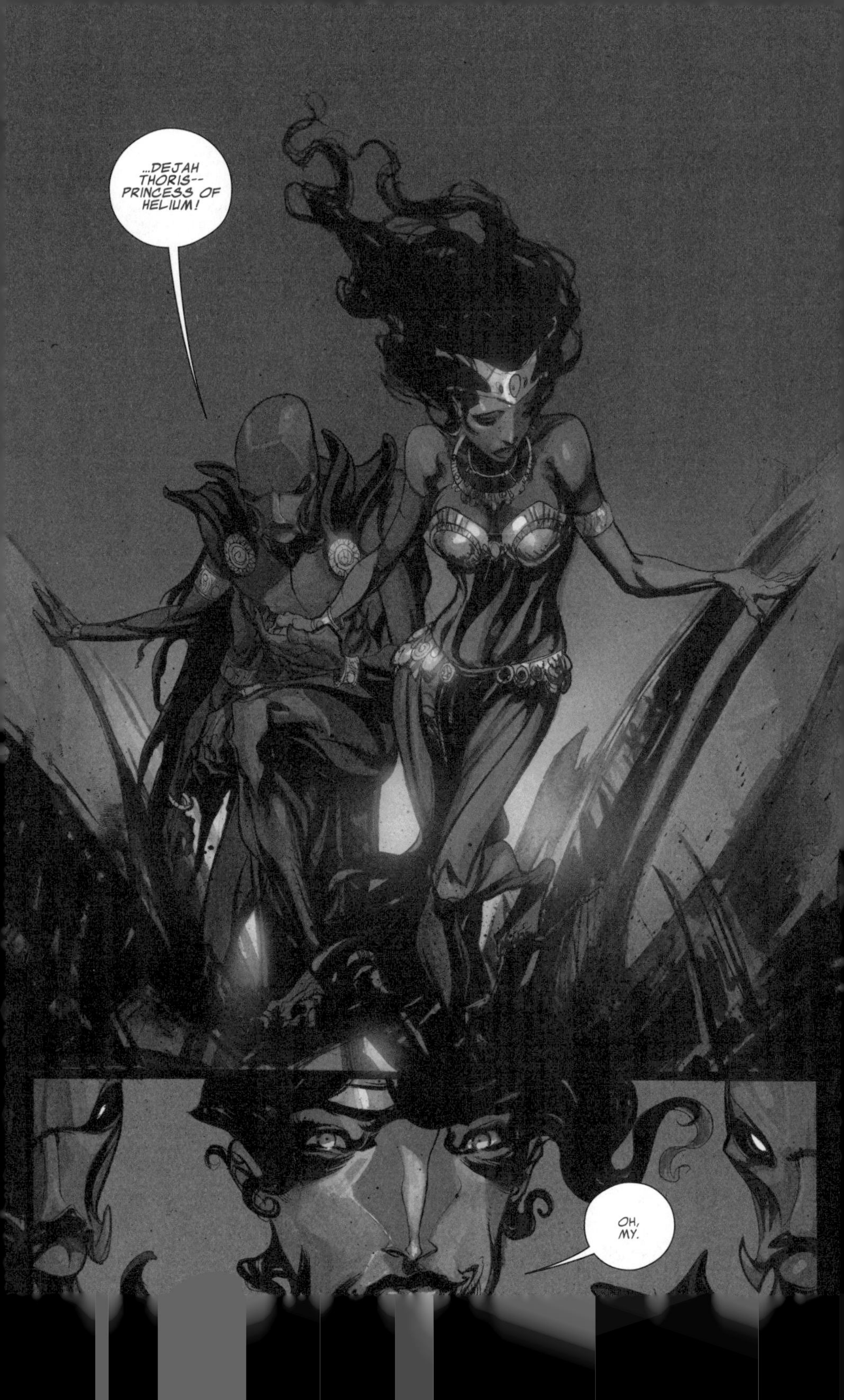
...DEJAH THORIS-- PRINCESS OF HELIUM!
OH, MY.

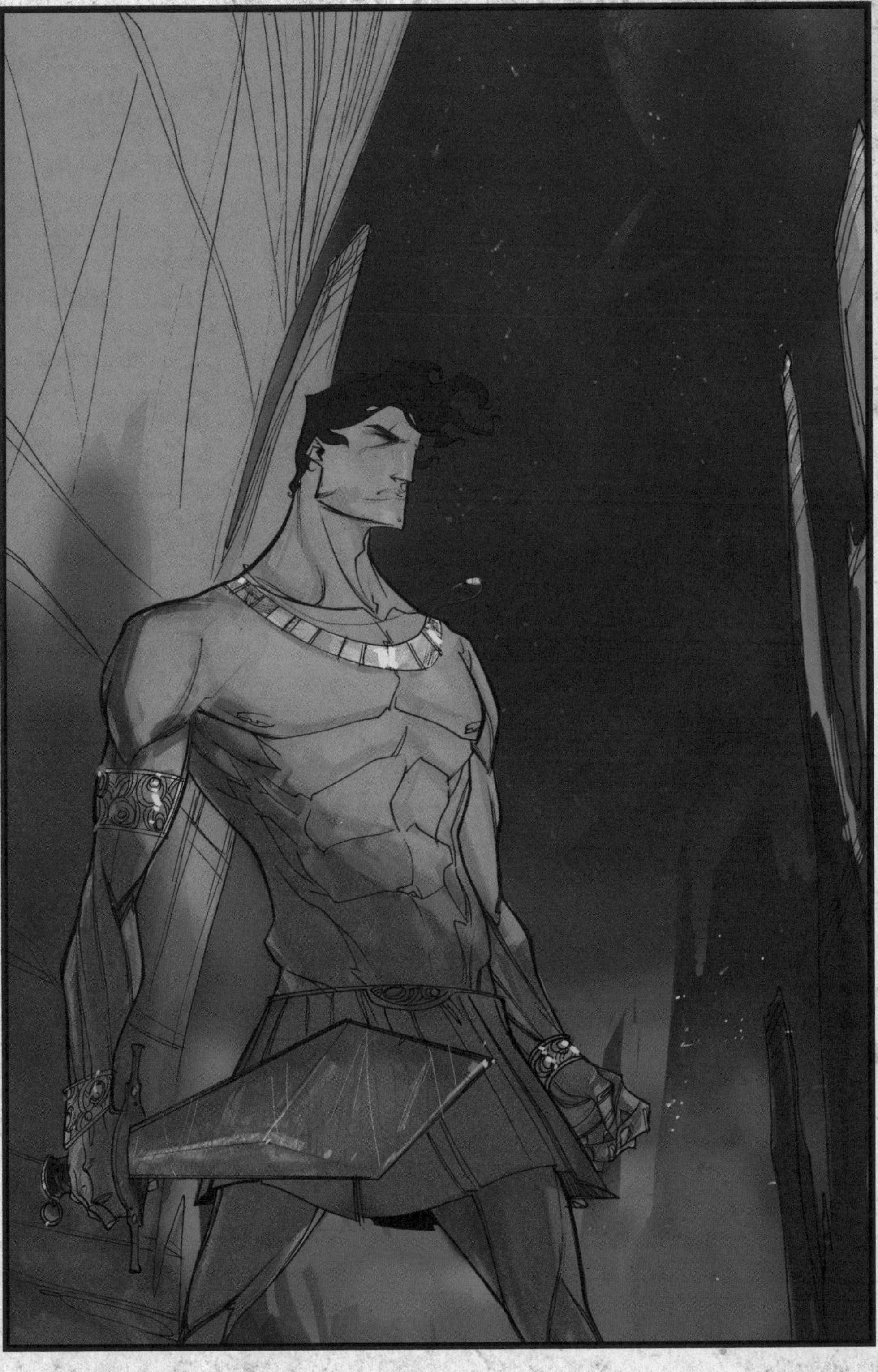

JOHN CARTER: A PRINCESS OF MARS #1 VARIANT BY FILIPE ANDRADE

– TWO –

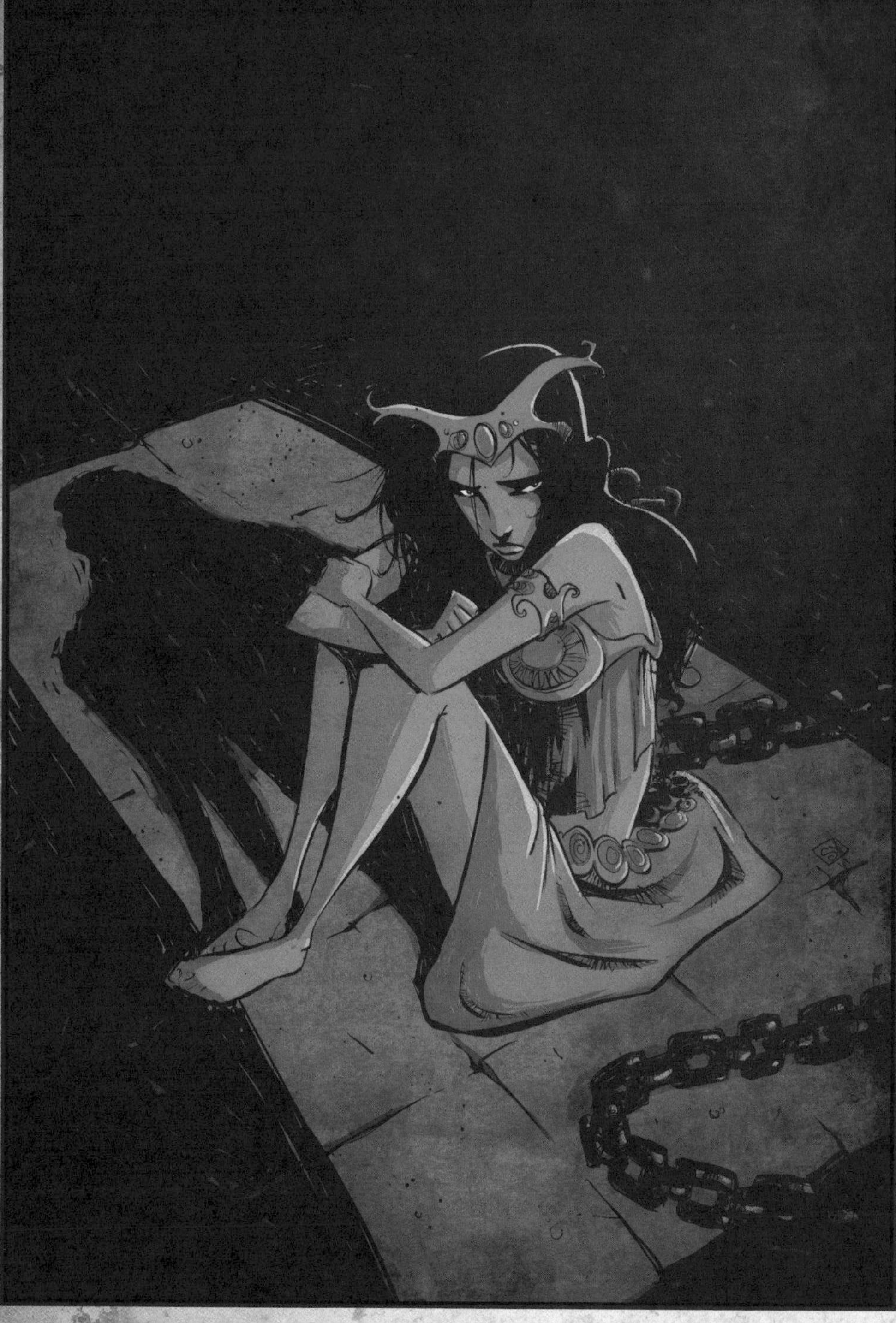

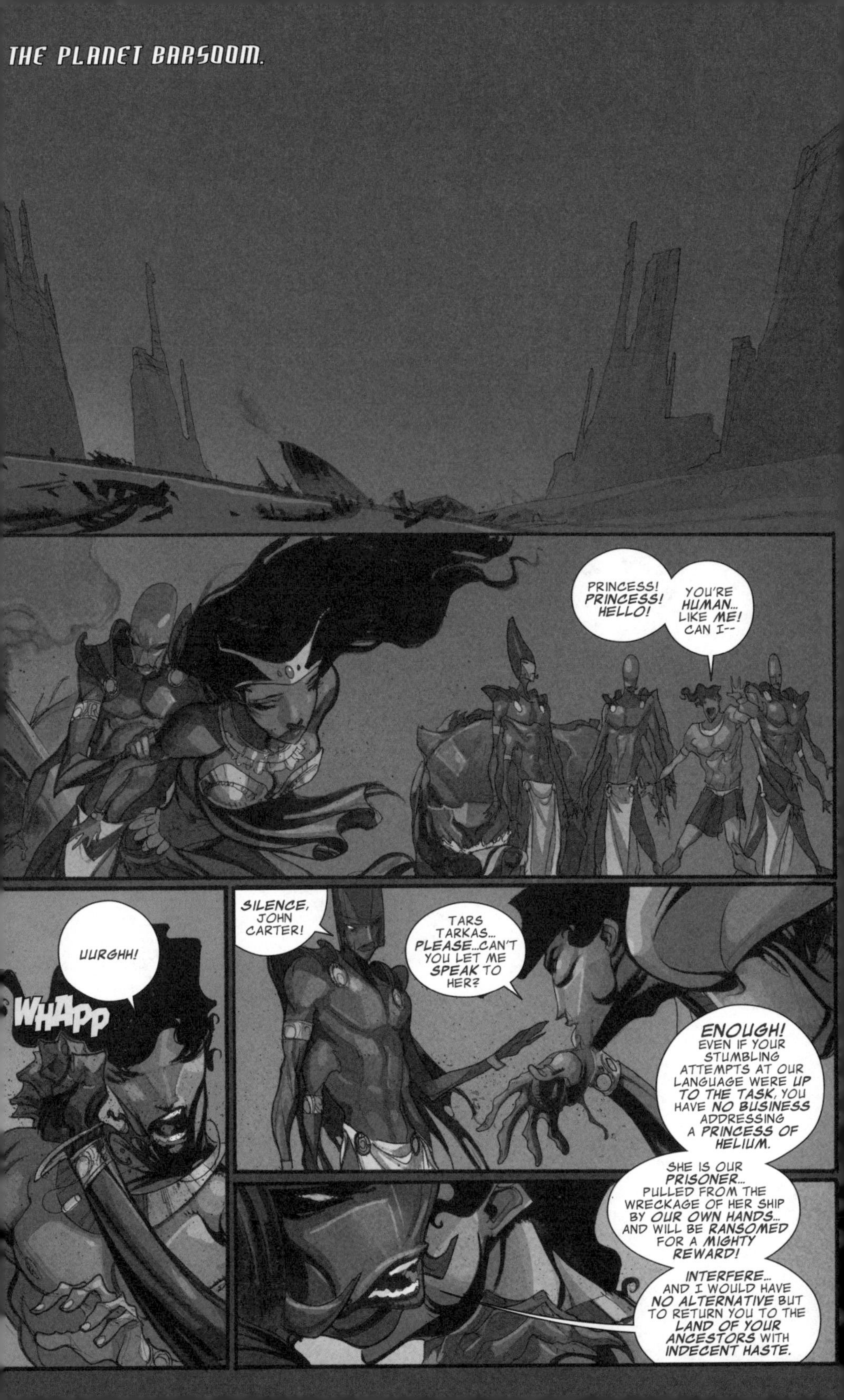
THE PLANET BARSOOM.
PRINCESS! PRINCESS! HELLO!
YOU'RE HUMAN... LIKE ME! CAN I--
UURGHH!
WHAPP
SILENCE, JOHN CARTER!
TARS TARKAS... PLEASE...CAN'T YOU LET ME SPEAK TO HER?
ENOUGH! EVEN IF YOUR STUMBLING ATTEMPTS AT OUR LANGUAGE WERE UP TO THE TASK, YOU HAVE NO BUSINESS ADDRESSING A PRINCESS OF HELIUM.
SHE IS OUR PRISONER... PULLED FROM THE WRECKAGE OF HER SHIP BY OUR OWN HANDS... AND WILL BE RANSOMED FOR A MIGHTY REWARD!
INTERFERE... AND I WOULD HAVE NO ALTERNATIVE BUT TO RETURN YOU TO THE LAND OF YOUR ANCESTORS WITH INDECENT HASTE.

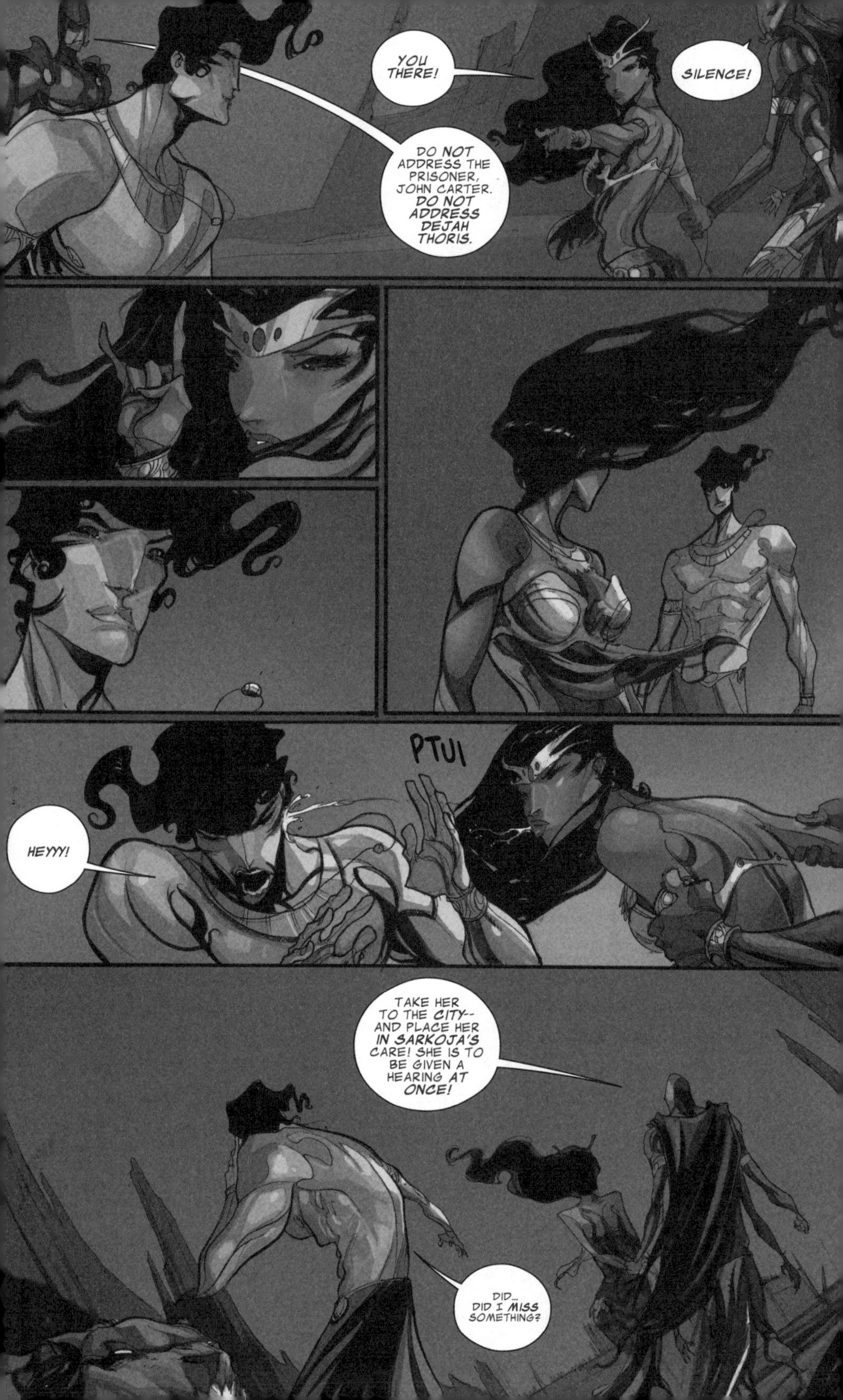
YOU THERE!
SILENCE!
DO NOT ADDRESS THE PRISONER, JOHN CARTER. DO NOT ADDRESS DEJAH THORIS.
PTUI
HEYYY!
TAKE HER TO THE CITY-- AND PLACE HER IN SARKOJA'S CARE! SHE IS TO BE GIVEN A HEARING AT ONCE!
DID... DID I MISS SOMETHING?

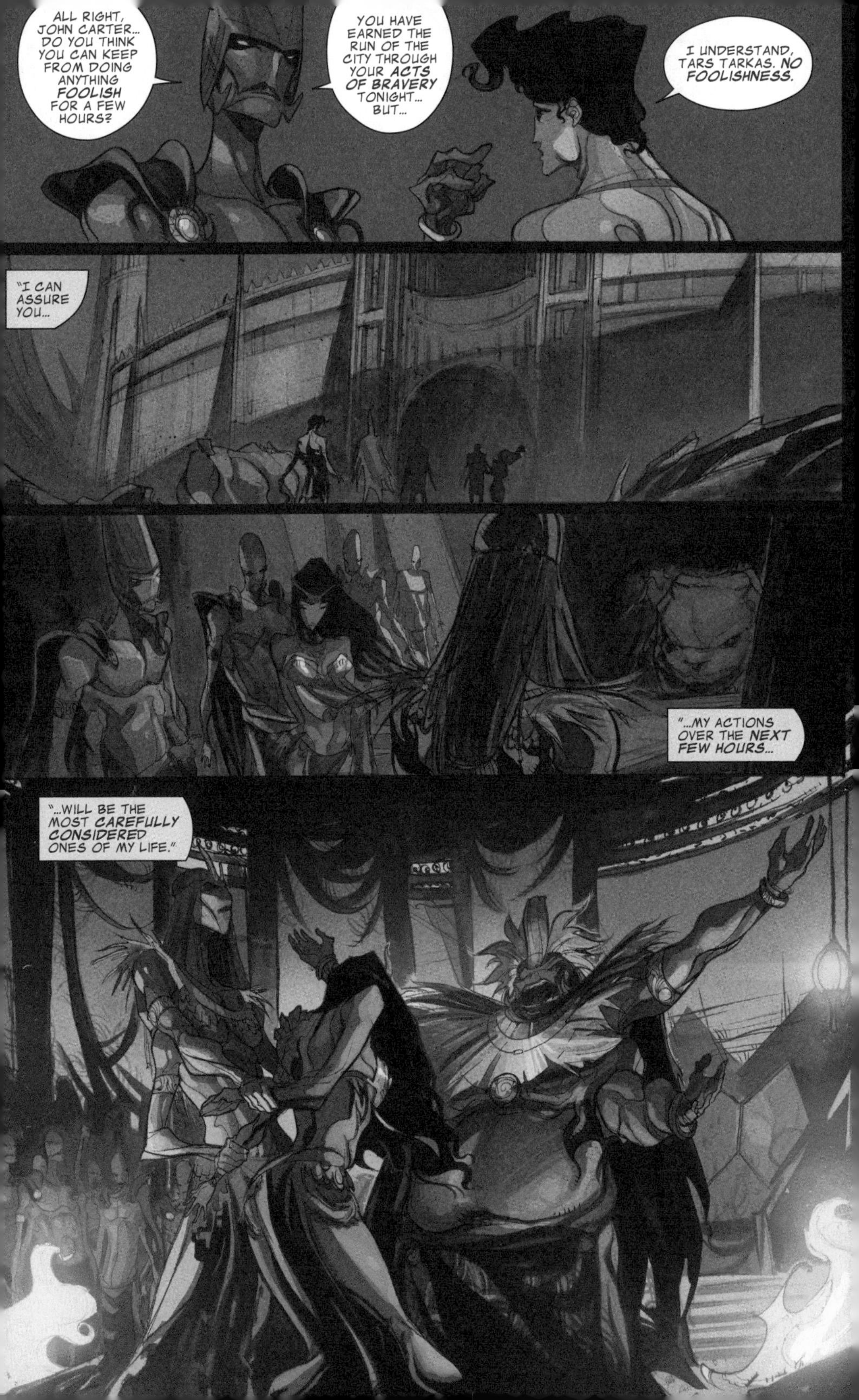
ALL RIGHT, JOHN CARTER... DO YOU THINK YOU CAN KEEP FROM DOING ANYTHING FOOLISH FOR A FEW HOURS?
YOU HAVE EARNED THE RUN OF THE CITY THROUGH YOUR ACTS OF BRAVERY TONIGHT... BUT...
I UNDERSTAND, TARS TARKAS. NO FOOLISHNESS.
"I CAN ASSURE YOU...
"...MY ACTIONS OVER THE NEXT FEW HOURS...
"...WILL BE THE MOST CAREFULLY CONSIDERED ONES OF MY LIFE."

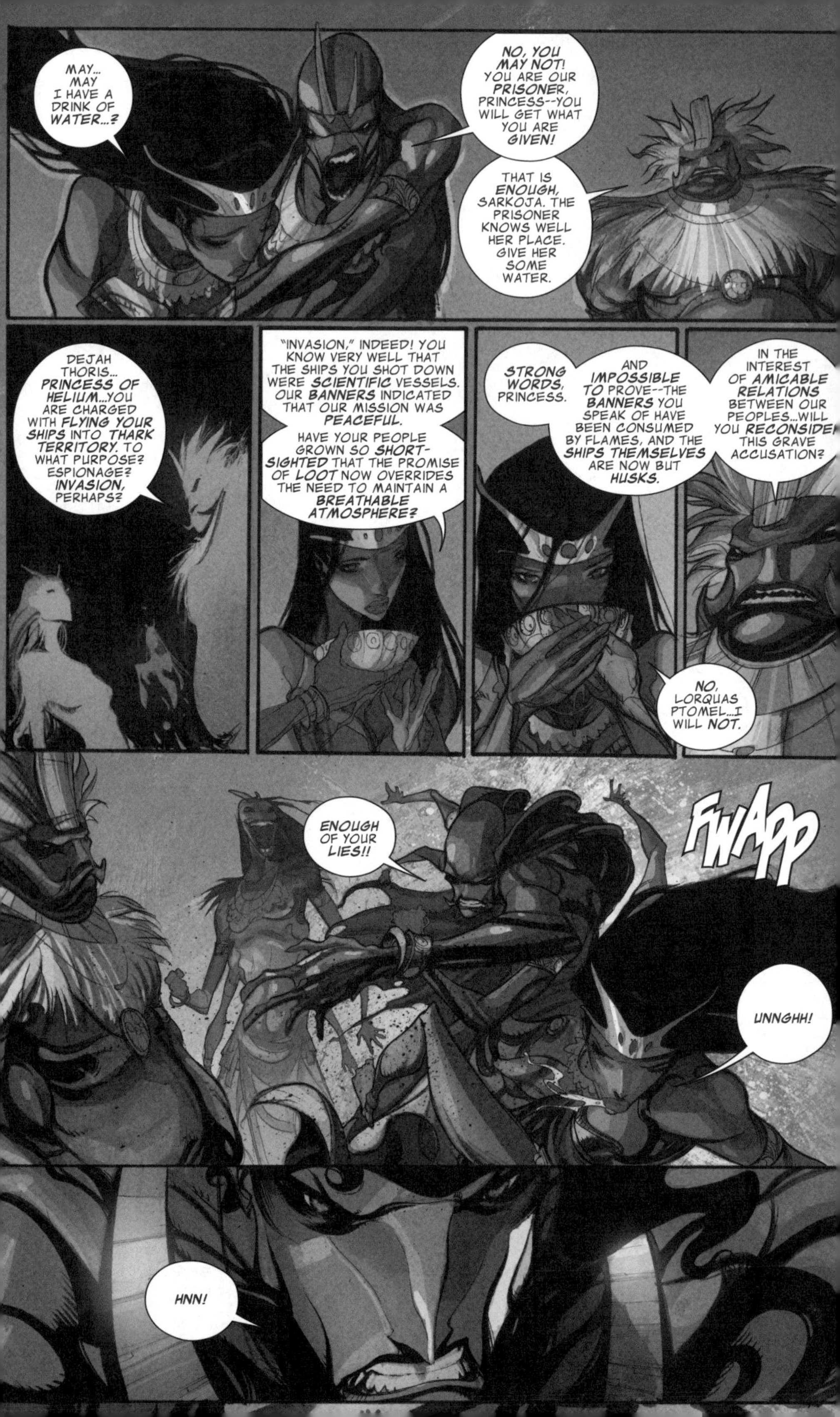

MAY... MAY I HAVE A DRINK OF WATER...?
NO, YOU MAY NOT! YOU ARE OUR PRISONER, PRINCESS--YOU WILL GET WHAT YOU ARE GIVEN!
THAT IS ENOUGH, SARKOJA. THE PRISONER KNOWS WELL HER PLACE. GIVE HER SOME WATER.
DEJAH THORIS... PRINCESS OF HELIUM...YOU ARE CHARGED WITH FLYING YOUR SHIPS INTO THARK TERRITORY. TO WHAT PURPOSE? ESPIONAGE? INVASION, PERHAPS?
"INVASION," INDEED! YOU KNOW VERY WELL THAT THE SHIPS YOU SHOT DOWN WERE SCIENTIFIC VESSELS. OUR BANNERS INDICATED THAT OUR MISSION WAS PEACEFUL.
HAVE YOUR PEOPLE GROWN SO SHORT-SIGHTED THAT THE PROMISE OF LOOT NOW OVERRIDES THE NEED TO MAINTAIN A BREATHABLE ATMOSPHERE?
STRONG WORDS, PRINCESS.
AND IMPOSSIBLE TO PROVE--THE BANNERS YOU SPEAK OF HAVE BEEN CONSUMED BY FLAMES, AND THE SHIPS THEMSELVES ARE NOW BUT HUSKS.
IN THE INTEREST OF AMICABLE RELATIONS BETWEEN OUR PEOPLES...WILL YOU RECONSIDE THIS GRAVE ACCUSATION?
NO, LORQUAS PTOMEL...I WILL NOT.
ENOUGH OF YOUR LIES!!
FWAPP
UNNGHH!
HNN!

THE PRISONER AND THE PRINCESS!

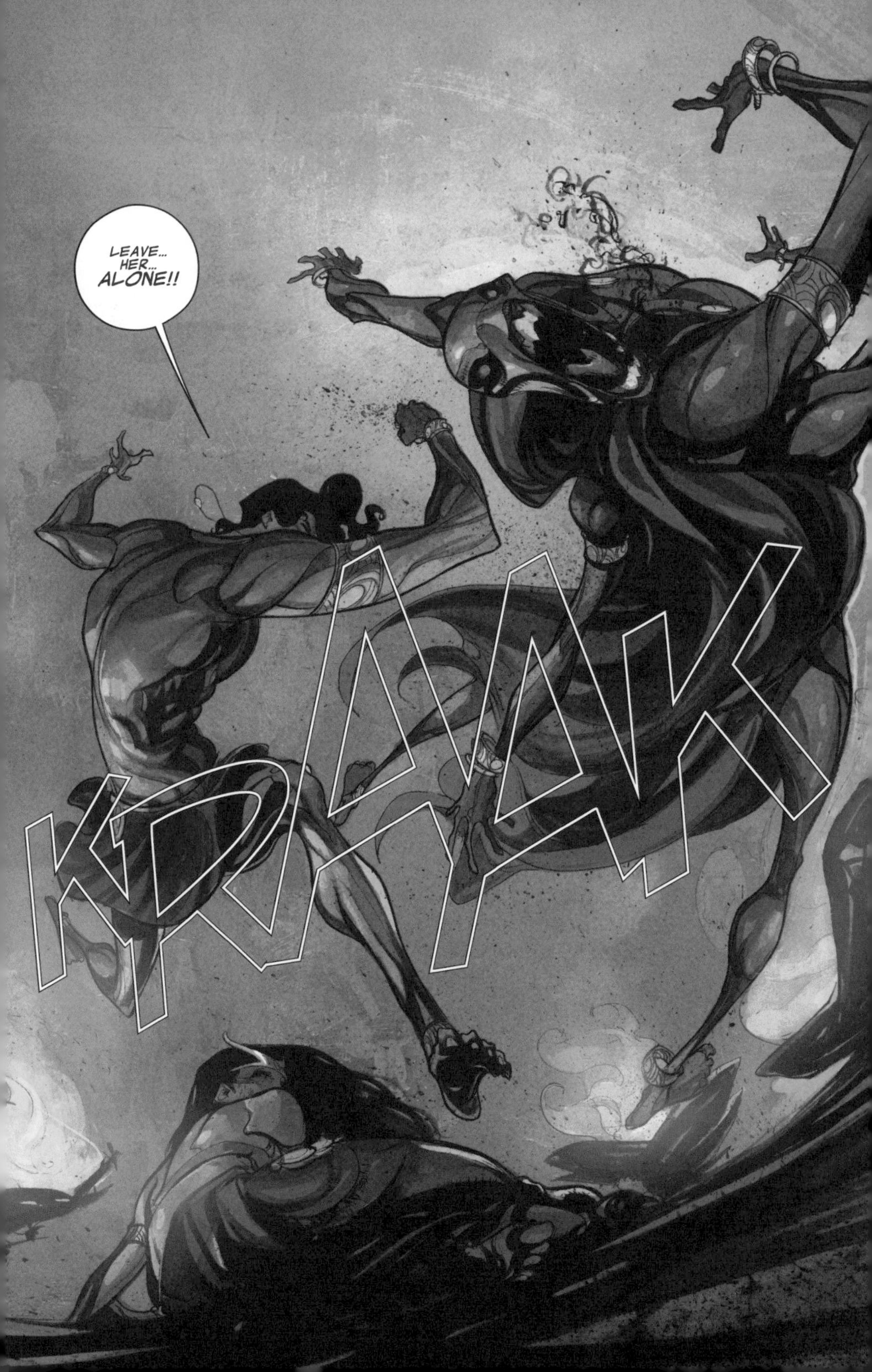
LEAVE... HER... ALONE!!
KRAAK

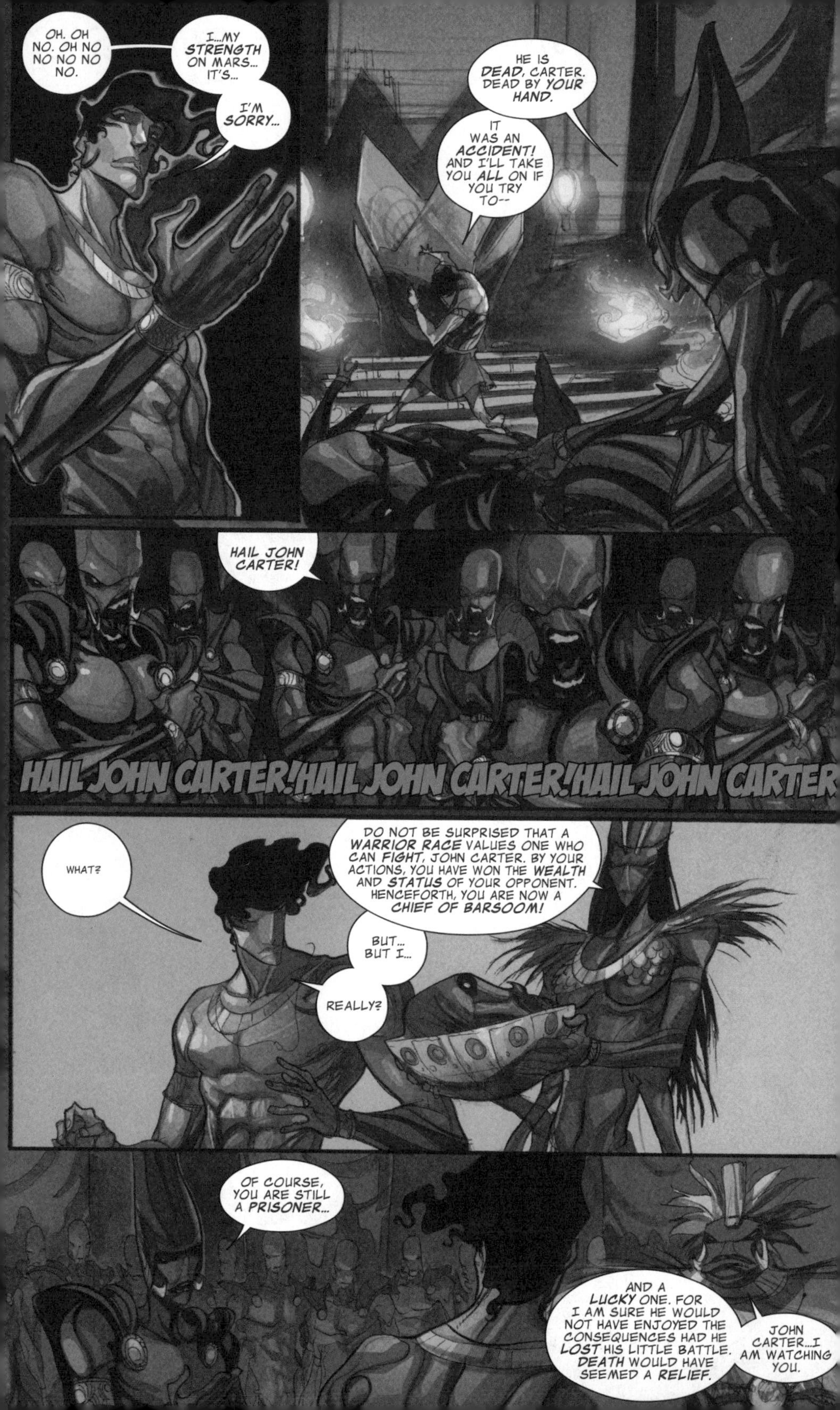
OH. OH NO. OH NO NO NO NO NO.
I...MY STRENGTH ON MARS... IT'S...
I'M SORRY...
HE IS DEAD, CARTER. DEAD BY YOUR HAND.
IT WAS AN ACCIDENT! AND I'LL TAKE YOU ALL ON IF YOU TRY TO--
HAIL JOHN CARTER!
HAIL JOHN CARTER! HAIL JOHN CARTER! HAIL JOHN CARTER
WHAT?
DO NOT BE SURPRISED THAT A WARRIOR RACE VALUES ONE WHO CAN FIGHT, JOHN CARTER. BY YOUR ACTIONS, YOU HAVE WON THE WEALTH AND STATUS OF YOUR OPPONENT. HENCEFORTH, YOU ARE NOW A CHIEF OF BARSOOM!
BUT... BUT I...
REALLY?
OF COURSE, YOU ARE STILL A PRISONER...
AND A LUCKY ONE. FOR I AM SURE HE WOULD NOT HAVE ENJOYED THE CONSEQUENCES HAD HE LOST HIS LITTLE BATTLE. DEATH WOULD HAVE SEEMED A RELIEF.
JOHN CARTER...I AM WATCHING YOU.

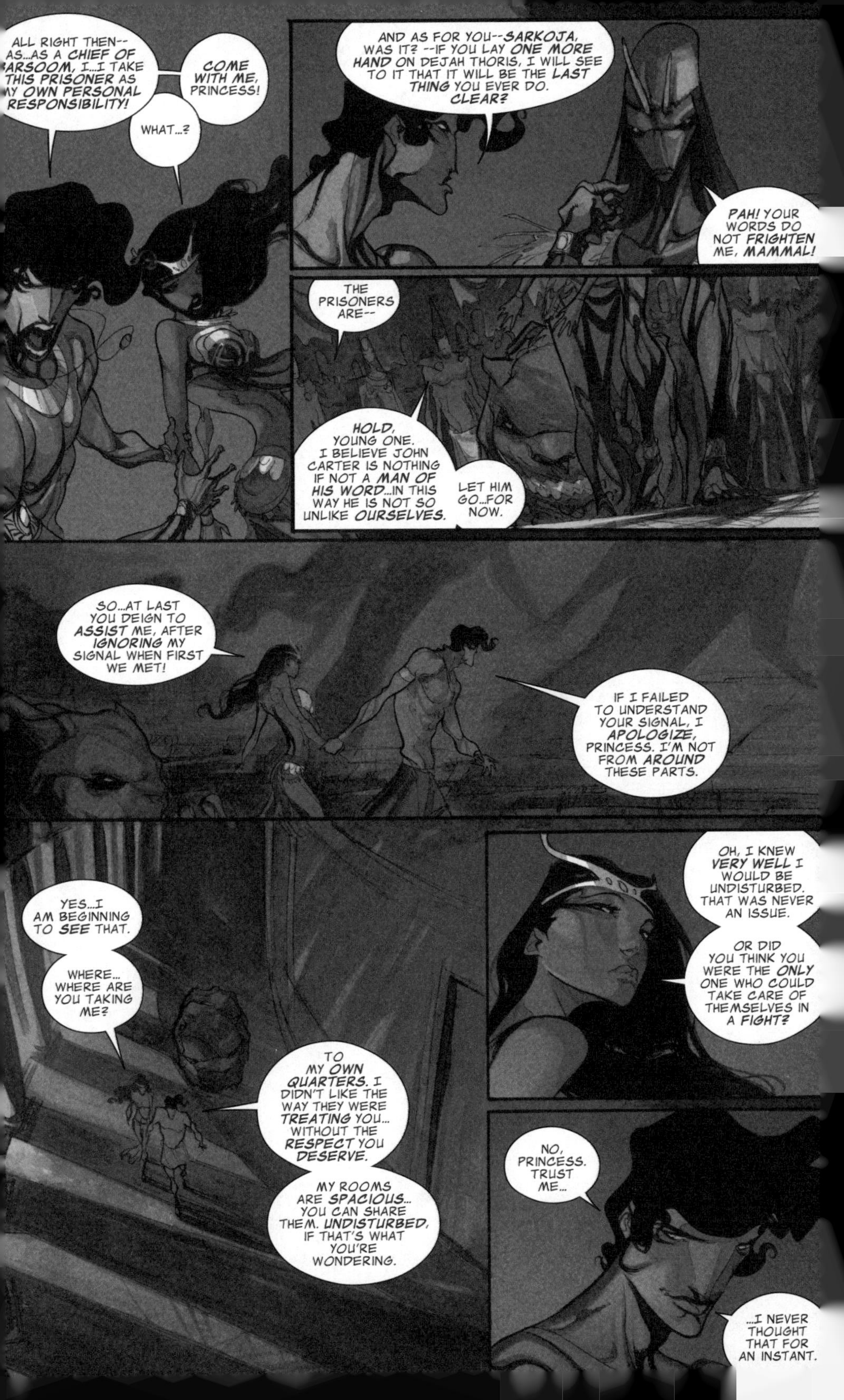
ALL RIGHT THEN-- AS...AS A CHIEF OF BARSOOM, I...I TAKE THIS PRISONER AS MY OWN PERSONAL RESPONSIBILITY!
COME WITH ME, PRINCESS!
WHAT...?
AND AS FOR YOU--SARKOJA, WAS IT? --IF YOU LAY ONE MORE HAND ON DEJAH THORIS, I WILL SEE TO IT THAT IT WILL BE THE LAST THING YOU EVER DO. CLEAR?
PAH! YOUR WORDS DO NOT FRIGHTEN ME, MAMMAL!
THE PRISONERS ARE--
HOLD, YOUNG ONE. I BELIEVE JOHN CARTER IS NOTHING IF NOT A MAN OF HIS WORD...IN THIS WAY HE IS NOT SO UNLIKE OURSELVES.
LET HIM GO...FOR NOW.
SO...AT LAST YOU DEIGN TO ASSIST ME, AFTER IGNORING MY SIGNAL WHEN FIRST WE MET!
IF I FAILED TO UNDERSTAND YOUR SIGNAL, I APOLOGIZE, PRINCESS. I'M NOT FROM AROUND THESE PARTS.
YES...I AM BEGINNING TO SEE THAT.
WHERE... WHERE ARE YOU TAKING ME?
TO MY OWN QUARTERS. I DIDN'T LIKE THE WAY THEY WERE TREATING YOU... WITHOUT THE RESPECT YOU DESERVE.
MY ROOMS ARE SPACIOUS... YOU CAN SHARE THEM. UNDISTURBED, IF THAT'S WHAT YOU'RE WONDERING.
OH, I KNEW VERY WELL I WOULD BE UNDISTURBED. THAT WAS NEVER AN ISSUE.
OR DID YOU THINK YOU WERE THE ONLY ONE WHO COULD TAKE CARE OF THEMSELVES IN A FIGHT?
NO, PRINCESS. TRUST ME...
...I NEVER THOUGHT THAT FOR AN INSTANT.

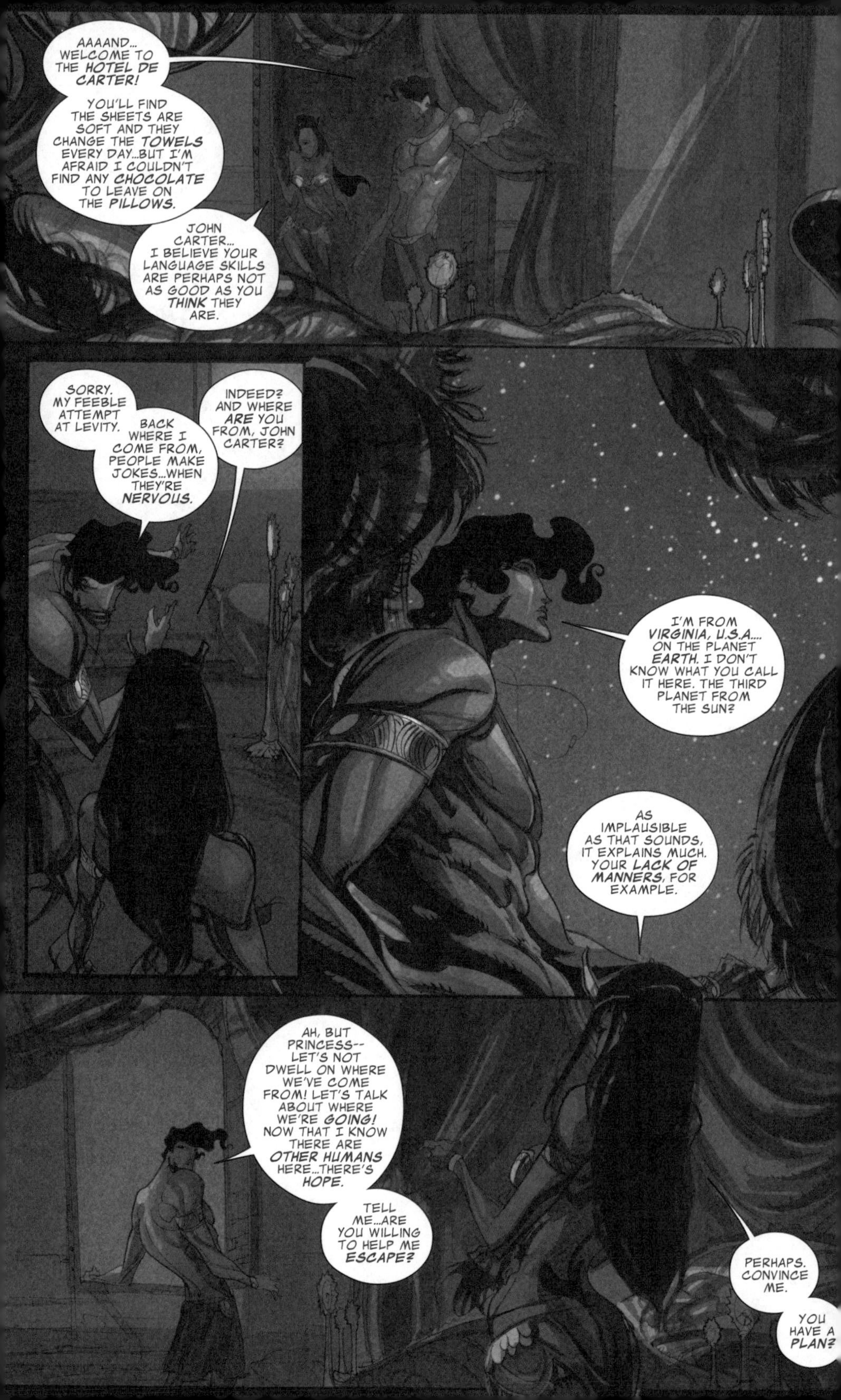
AAAAND... WELCOME TO THE HOTEL DE CARTER!
YOU'LL FIND THE SHEETS ARE SOFT AND THEY CHANGE THE TOWELS EVERY DAY...BUT I'M AFRAID I COULDN'T FIND ANY CHOCOLATE TO LEAVE ON THE PILLOWS.
JOHN CARTER... I BELIEVE YOUR LANGUAGE SKILLS ARE PERHAPS NOT AS GOOD AS YOU THINK THEY ARE.
SORRY. MY FEEBLE ATTEMPT AT LEVITY.
BACK WHERE I COME FROM, PEOPLE MAKE JOKES...WHEN THEY'RE NERVOUS.
INDEED? AND WHERE ARE YOU FROM, JOHN CARTER?
I'M FROM VIRGINIA, U.S.A.... ON THE PLANET EARTH. I DON'T KNOW WHAT YOU CALL IT HERE. THE THIRD PLANET FROM THE SUN?
AS IMPLAUSIBLE AS THAT SOUNDS, IT EXPLAINS MUCH. YOUR LACK OF MANNERS, FOR EXAMPLE.
AH, BUT PRINCESS-- LET'S NOT DWELL ON WHERE WE'VE COME FROM! LET'S TALK ABOUT WHERE WE'RE GOING! NOW THAT I KNOW THERE ARE OTHER HUMANS HERE...THERE'S HOPE.
TELL ME...ARE YOU WILLING TO HELP ME ESCAPE?
PERHAPS. CONVINCE ME.
YOU HAVE A PLAN?

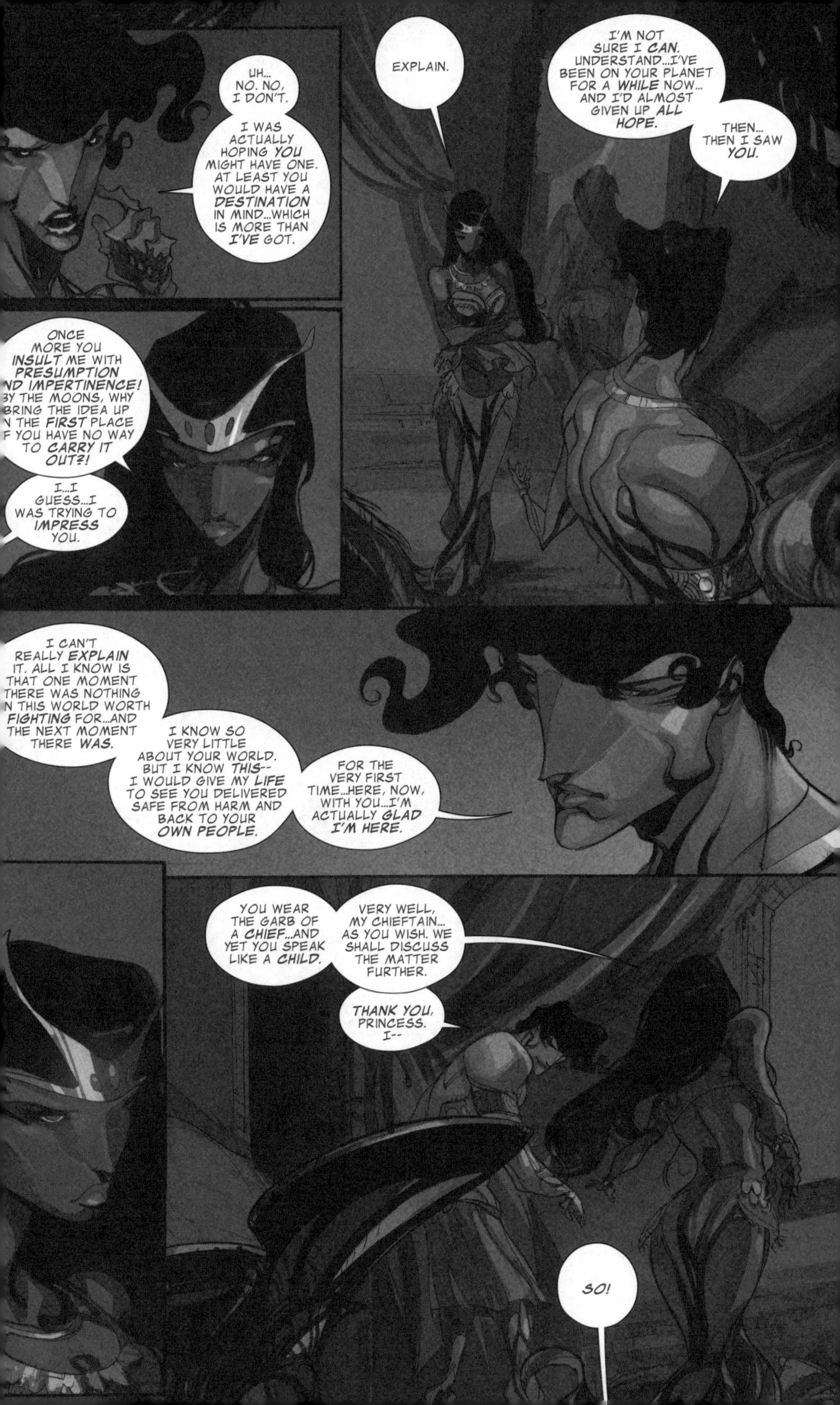
UH... NO. NO, I DON'T.
I WAS ACTUALLY HOPING YOU MIGHT HAVE ONE. AT LEAST YOU WOULD HAVE A DESTINATION IN MIND...WHICH IS MORE THAN I'VE GOT.
EXPLAIN.
I'M NOT SURE I CAN. UNDERSTAND...I'VE BEEN ON YOUR PLANET FOR A WHILE NOW... AND I'D ALMOST GIVEN UP ALL HOPE.
THEN... THEN I SAW YOU.
ONCE MORE YOU INSULT ME WITH PRESUMPTION ND IMPERTINENCE! BY THE MOONS, WHY BRING THE IDEA UP N THE FIRST PLACE F YOU HAVE NO WAY TO CARRY IT OUT?!
I...I GUESS...I WAS TRYING TO IMPRESS YOU.
I CAN'T REALLY EXPLAIN IT. ALL I KNOW IS THAT ONE MOMENT THERE WAS NOTHING N THIS WORLD WORTH FIGHTING FOR...AND THE NEXT MOMENT THERE WAS.
I KNOW SO VERY LITTLE ABOUT YOUR WORLD. BUT I KNOW THIS-- I WOULD GIVE MY LIFE TO SEE YOU DELIVERED SAFE FROM HARM AND BACK TO YOUR OWN PEOPLE.
FOR THE VERY FIRST TIME...HERE, NOW, WITH YOU...I'M ACTUALLY GLAD I'M HERE.
YOU WEAR THE GARB OF A CHIEF...AND YET YOU SPEAK LIKE A CHILD.
VERY WELL, MY CHIEFTAIN... AS YOU WISH. WE SHALL DISCUSS THE MATTER FURTHER.
THANK YOU, PRINCESS. I--
SO!

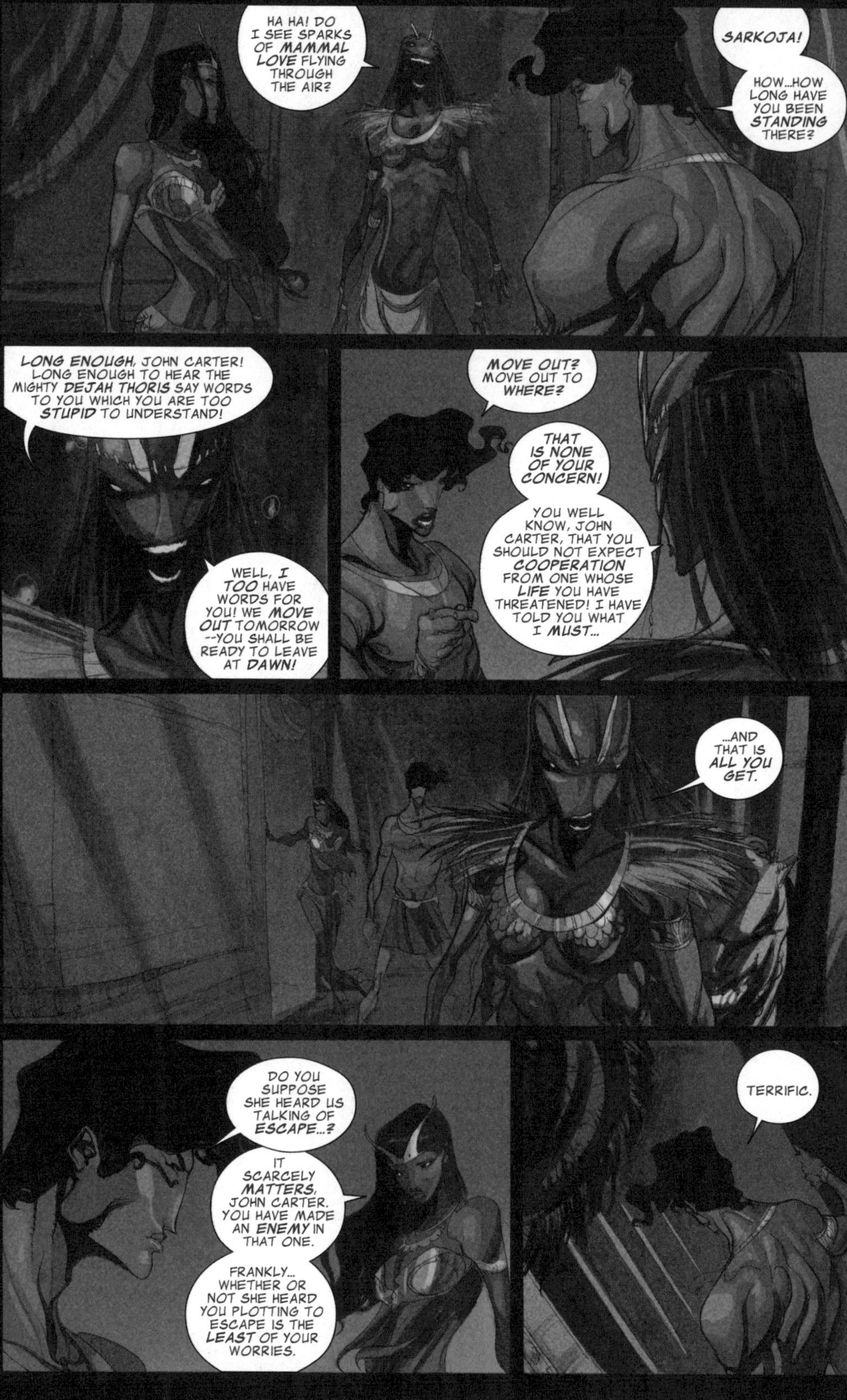

HA HA! DO I SEE SPARKS OF MAMMAL LOVE FLYING THROUGH THE AIR?
SARKOJA!
HOW...HOW LONG HAVE YOU BEEN STANDING THERE?
LONG ENOUGH, JOHN CARTER! LONG ENOUGH TO HEAR THE MIGHTY DEJAH THORIS SAY WORDS TO YOU WHICH YOU ARE TOO STUPID TO UNDERSTAND!
WELL, I TOO HAVE WORDS FOR YOU! WE MOVE OUT TOMORROW --YOU SHALL BE READY TO LEAVE AT DAWN!
MOVE OUT? MOVE OUT TO WHERE?
THAT IS NONE OF YOUR CONCERN!
YOU WELL KNOW, JOHN CARTER, THAT YOU SHOULD NOT EXPECT COOPERATION FROM ONE WHOSE LIFE YOU HAVE THREATENED! I HAVE TOLD YOU WHAT I MUST...
...AND THAT IS ALL YOU GET.
DO YOU SUPPOSE SHE HEARD US TALKING OF ESCAPE...?
IT SCARCELY MATTERS, JOHN CARTER. YOU HAVE MADE AN ENEMY IN THAT ONE.
FRANKLY... WHETHER OR NOT SHE HEARD YOU PLOTTING TO ESCAPE IS THE LEAST OF YOUR WORRIES.
TERRIFIC.

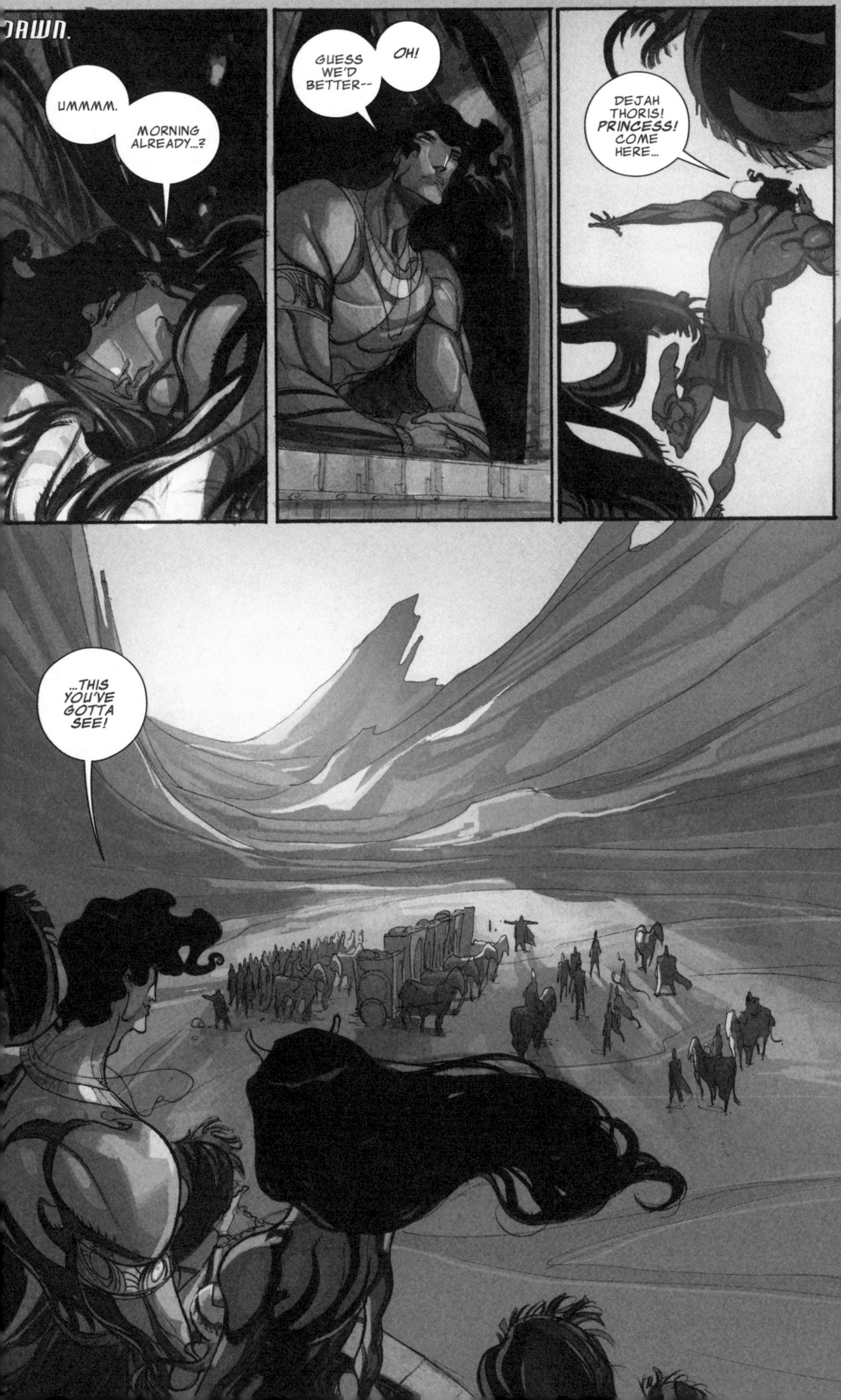
DAWN.
UMMMM.
MORNING ALREADY...?
GUESS WE'D BETTER--
OH!
DEJAH THORIS! PRINCESS! COME HERE...
...THIS YOU'VE GOTTA SEE!

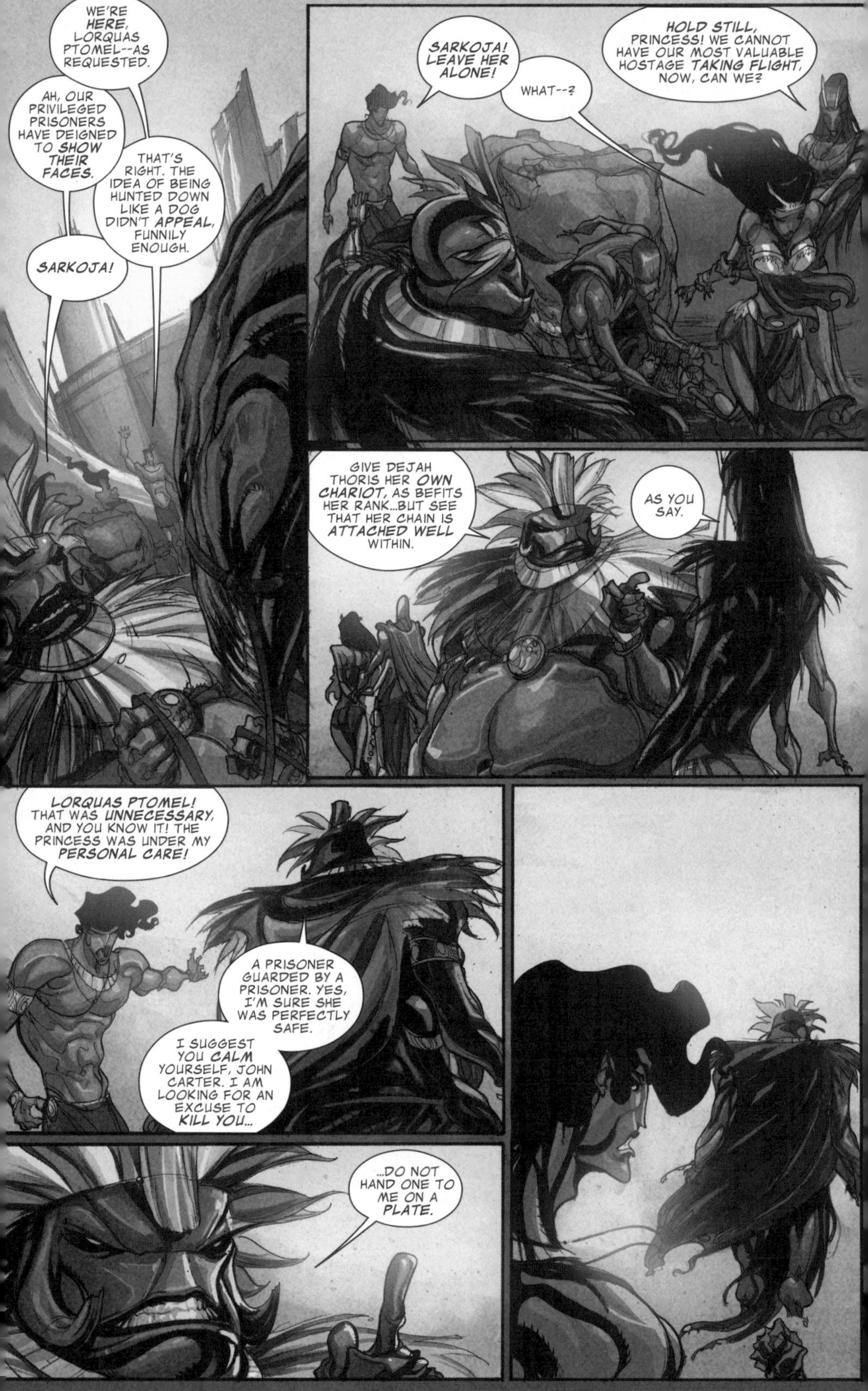
WE'RE HERE, LORQUAS PTOMEL--AS REQUESTED.
AH, OUR PRIVILEGED PRISONERS HAVE DEIGNED TO SHOW THEIR FACES.
THAT'S RIGHT. THE IDEA OF BEING HUNTED DOWN LIKE A DOG DIDN'T APPEAL, FUNNILY ENOUGH.
SARKOJA!
SARKOJA! LEAVE HER ALONE!
WHAT--?
HOLD STILL, PRINCESS! WE CANNOT HAVE OUR MOST VALUABLE HOSTAGE TAKING FLIGHT, NOW, CAN WE?
GIVE DEJAH THORIS HER OWN CHARIOT, AS BEFITS HER RANK...BUT SEE THAT HER CHAIN IS ATTACHED WELL WITHIN.
AS YOU SAY.
LORQUAS PTOMEL! THAT WAS UNNECESSARY, AND YOU KNOW IT! THE PRINCESS WAS UNDER MY PERSONAL CARE!
A PRISONER GUARDED BY A PRISONER. YES, I'M SURE SHE WAS PERFECTLY SAFE.
I SUGGEST YOU CALM YOURSELF, JOHN CARTER. I AM LOOKING FOR AN EXCUSE TO KILL YOU...
...DO NOT HAND ONE TO ME ON A PLATE.

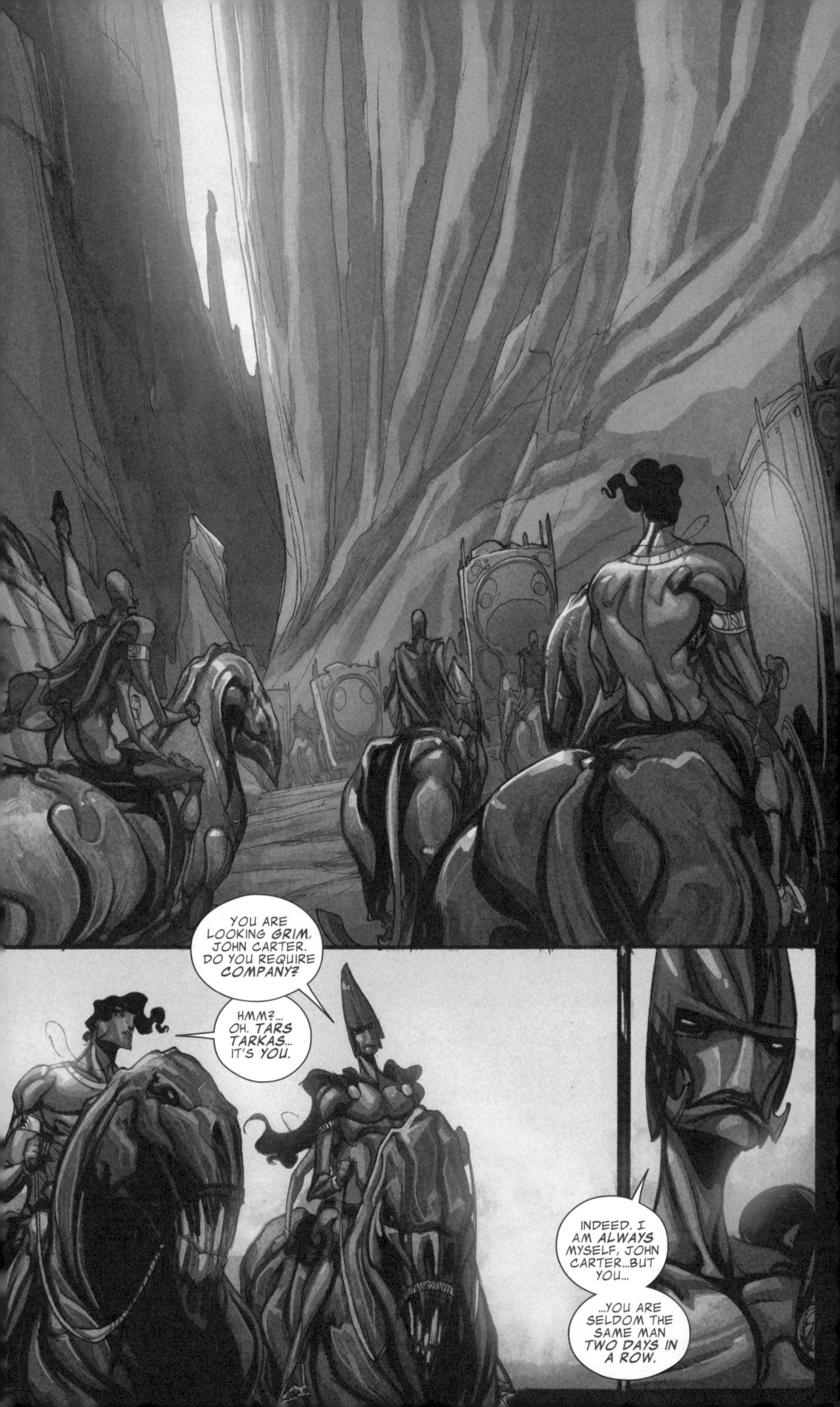
YOU ARE LOOKING GRIM, JOHN CARTER. DO YOU REQUIRE COMPANY?
HMM?... OH. TARS TARKAS... IT'S YOU.
INDEED. I AM ALWAYS MYSELF, JOHN CARTER...BUT YOU...
...YOU ARE SELDOM THE SAME MAN TWO DAYS IN A ROW.

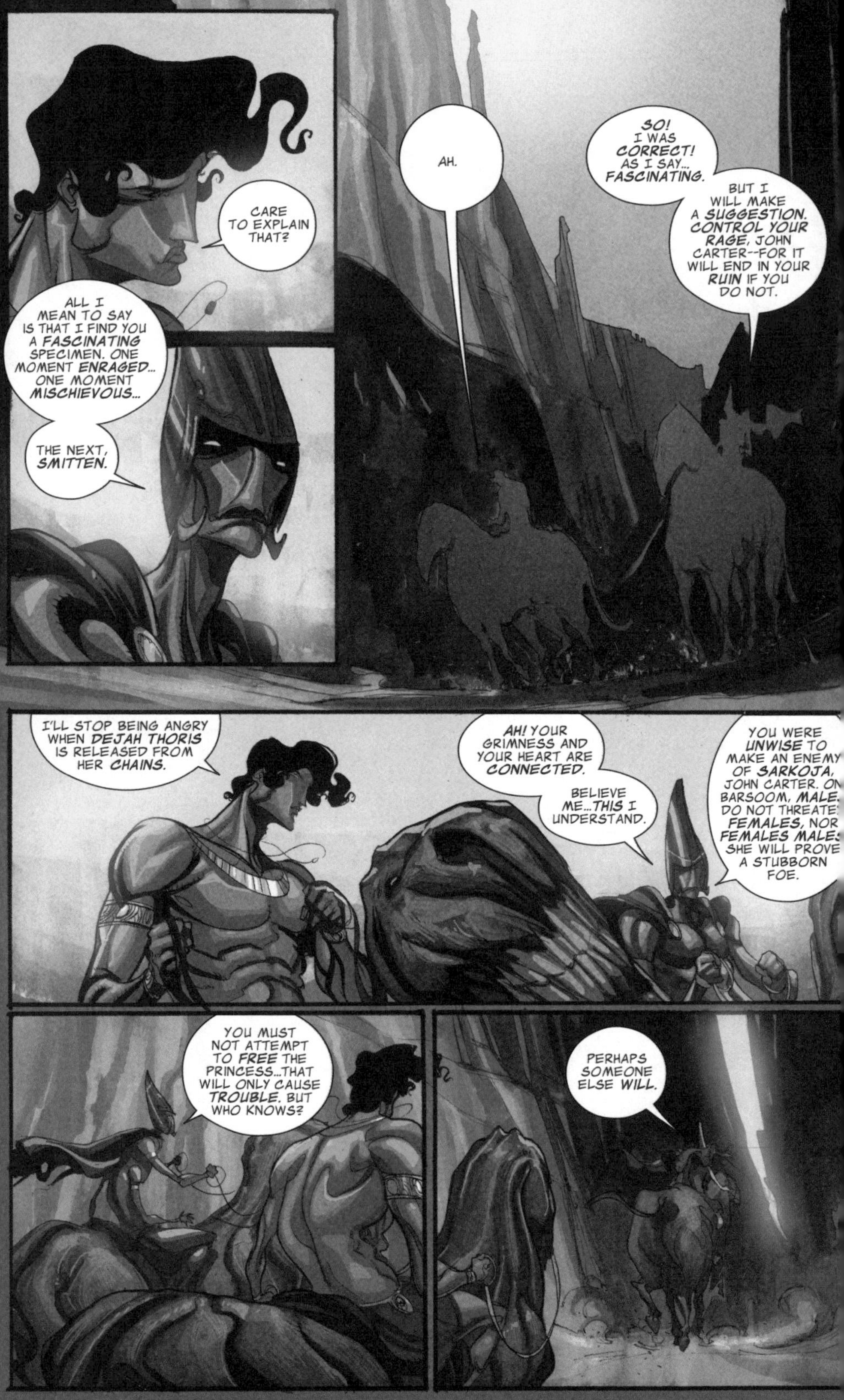
CARE TO EXPLAIN THAT?
ALL I MEAN TO SAY IS THAT I FIND YOU A FASCINATING SPECIMEN. ONE MOMENT ENRAGED... ONE MOMENT MISCHIEVOUS...
THE NEXT, SMITTEN.
AH.
SO! I WAS CORRECT! AS I SAY... FASCINATING.
BUT I WILL MAKE A SUGGESTION. CONTROL YOUR RAGE, JOHN CARTER--FOR IT WILL END IN YOUR RUIN IF YOU DO NOT.
I'LL STOP BEING ANGRY WHEN DEJAH THORIS IS RELEASED FROM HER CHAINS.
AH! YOUR GRIMNESS AND YOUR HEART ARE CONNECTED.
BELIEVE ME...THIS I UNDERSTAND.
YOU WERE UNWISE TO MAKE AN ENEMY OF SARKOJA, JOHN CARTER. ON BARSOOM, MALE DO NOT THREATE FEMALES, NOR FEMALES MALES SHE WILL PROVE A STUBBORN FOE.
YOU MUST NOT ATTEMPT TO FREE THE PRINCESS...THAT WILL ONLY CAUSE TROUBLE. BUT WHO KNOWS?
PERHAPS SOMEONE ELSE WILL.

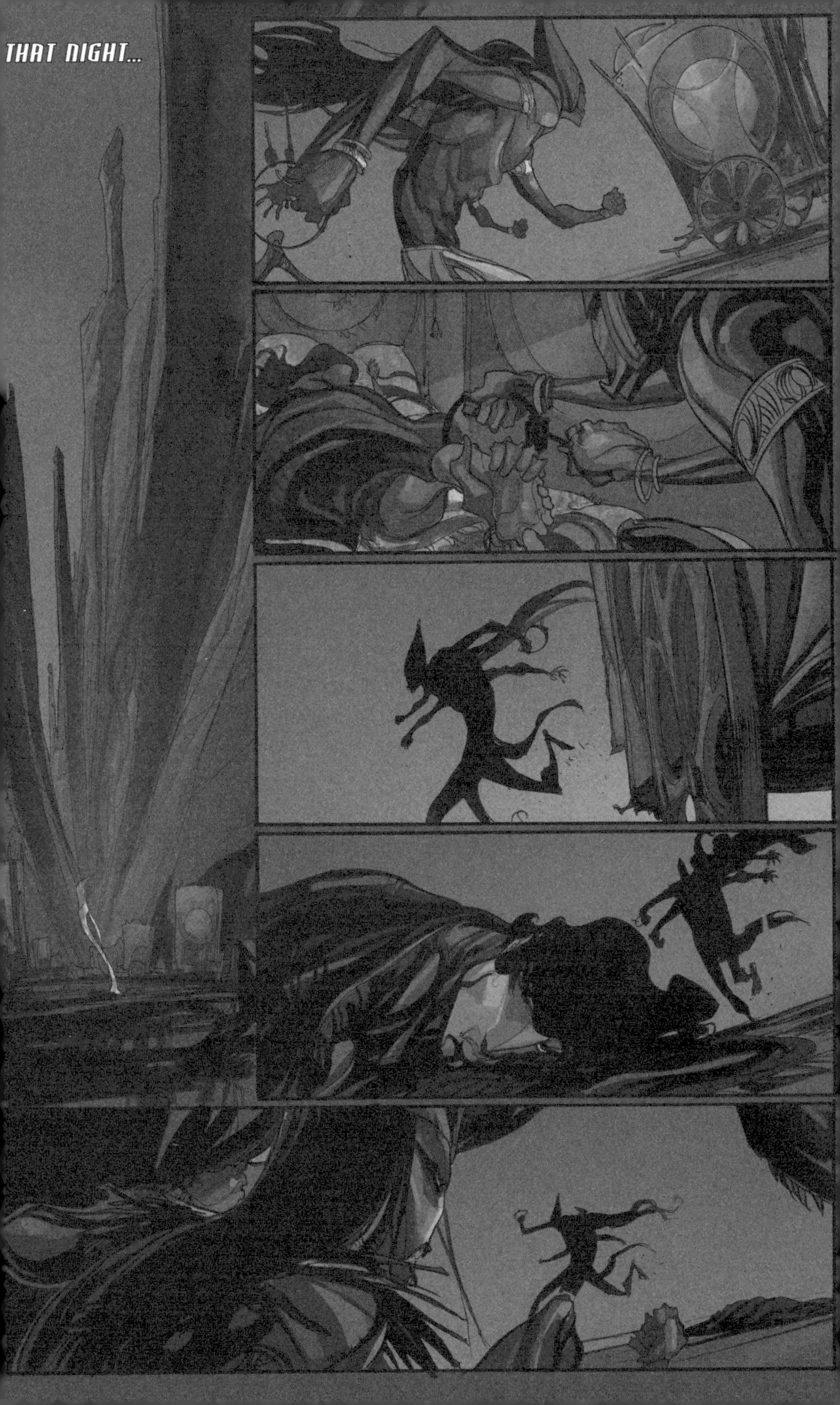
THAT NIGHT...

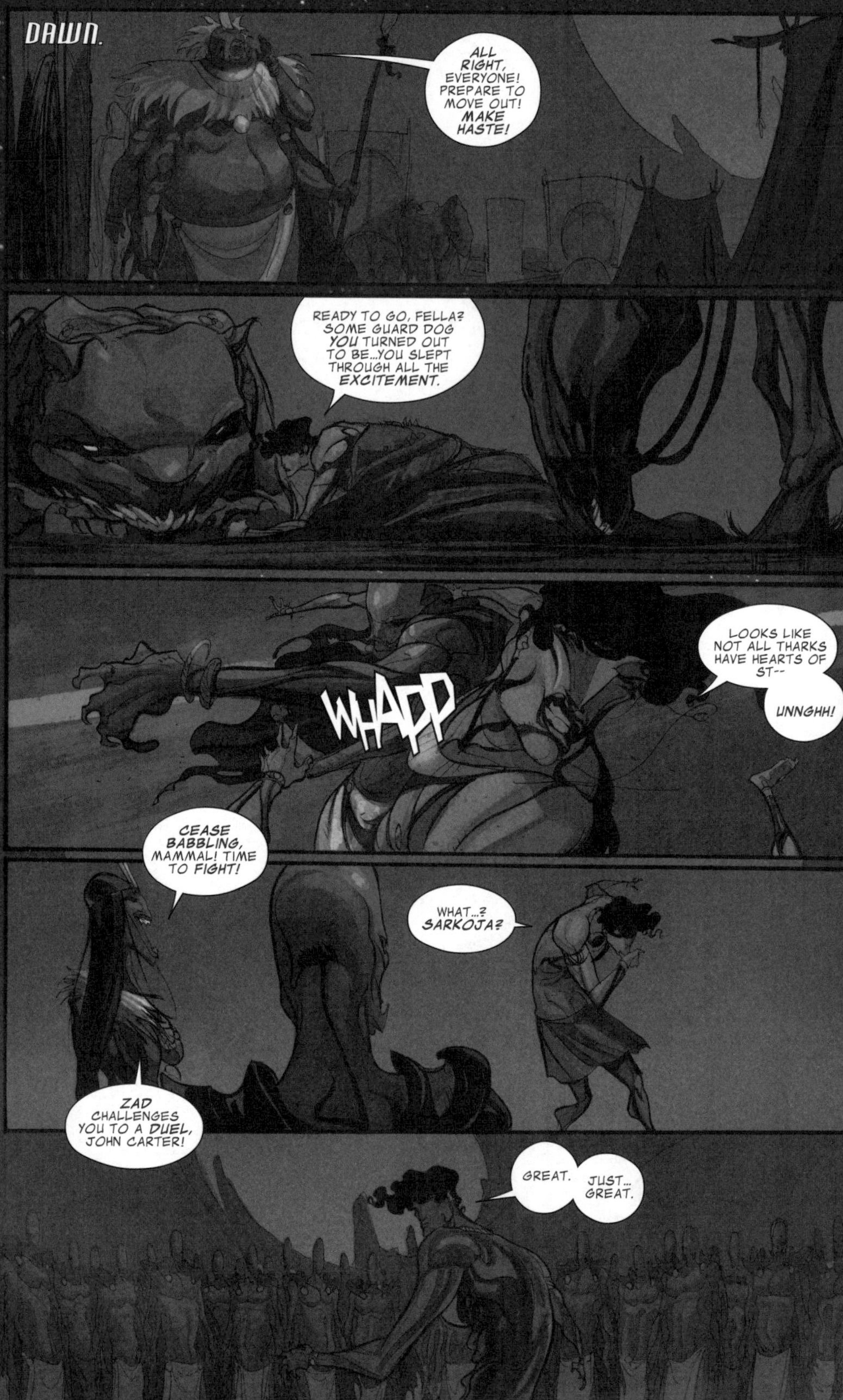
DAWN.
ALL RIGHT, EVERYONE! PREPARE TO MOVE OUT! MAKE HASTE!
READY TO GO, FELLA? SOME GUARD DOG YOU TURNED OUT TO BE...YOU SLEPT THROUGH ALL THE EXCITEMENT.
WHAPP
LOOKS LIKE NOT ALL THARKS HAVE HEARTS OF ST--
UNNGHH!
CEASE BABBLING, MAMMAL! TIME TO FIGHT!
WHAT...? SARKOJA?
ZAD CHALLENGES YOU TO A DUEL, JOHN CARTER!
GREAT.
JUST... GREAT.

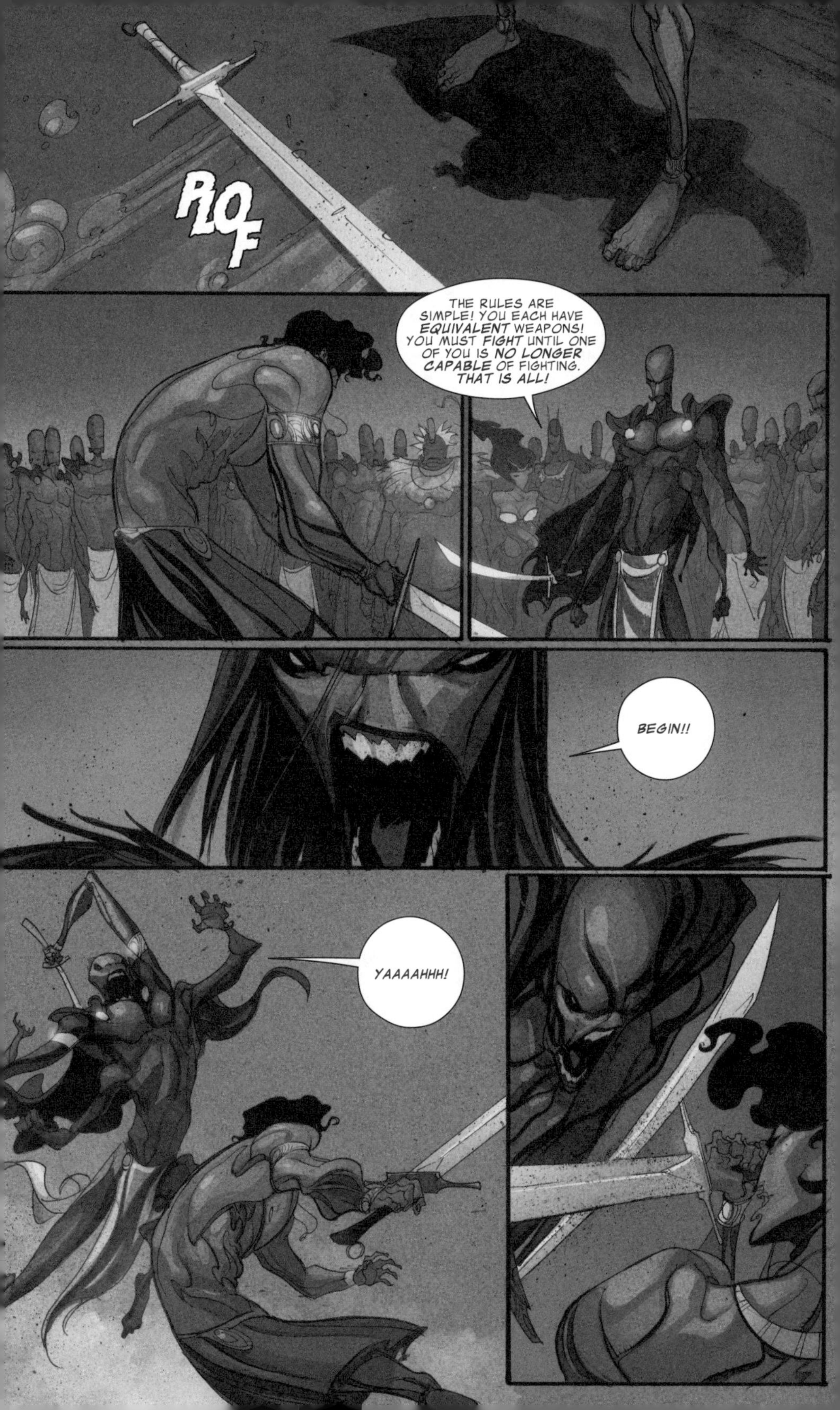
PLOF
THE RULES ARE SIMPLE! YOU EACH HAVE EQUIVALENT WEAPONS! YOU MUST FIGHT UNTIL ONE OF YOU IS NO LONGER CAPABLE OF FIGHTING. THAT IS ALL!
BEGIN!!
YAAAAHHH!

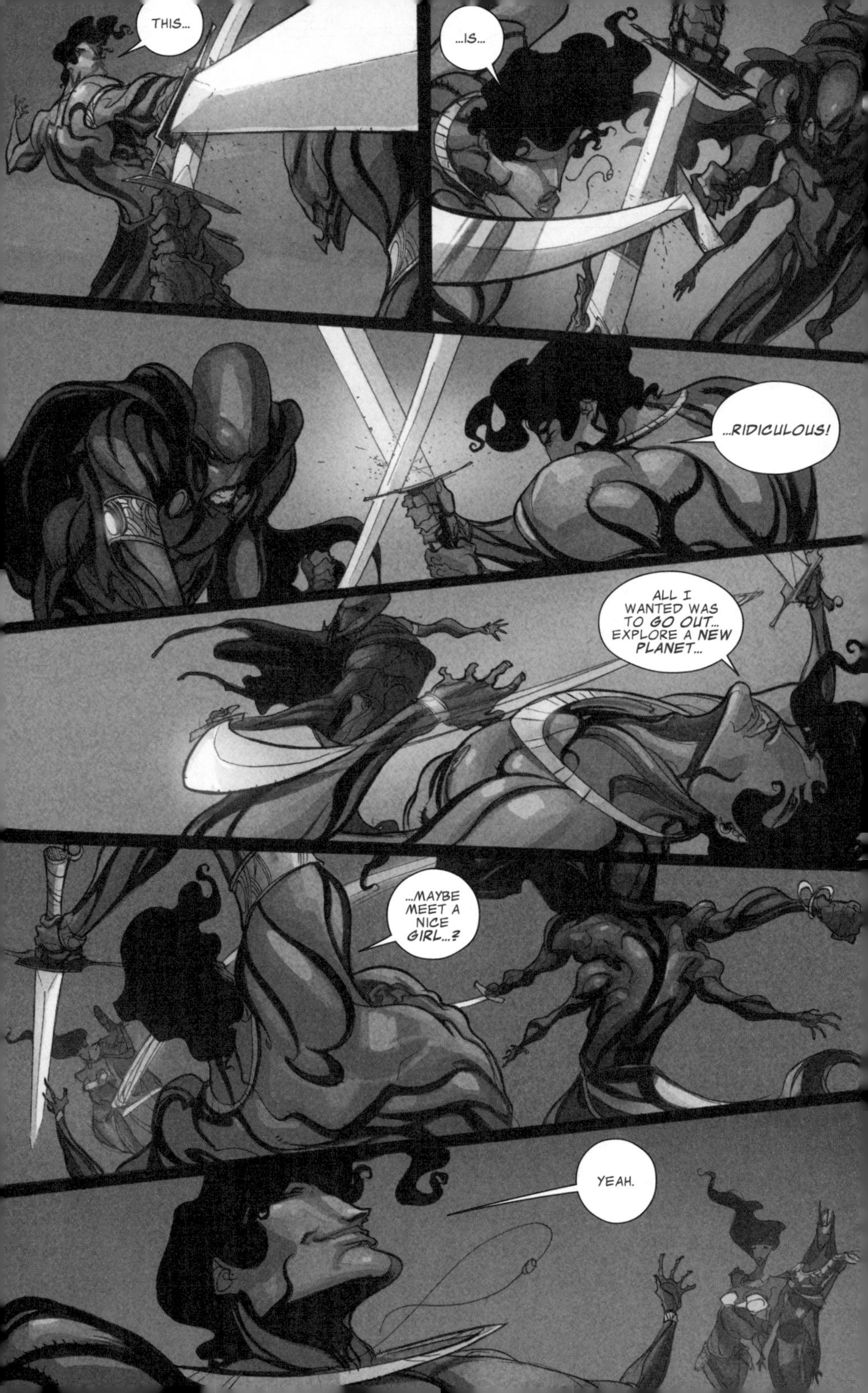
THIS...
...IS...
...RIDICULOUS!
ALL I WANTED WAS TO GO OUT... EXPLORE A NEW PLANET...
...MAYBE MEET A NICE GIRL...?
YEAH.

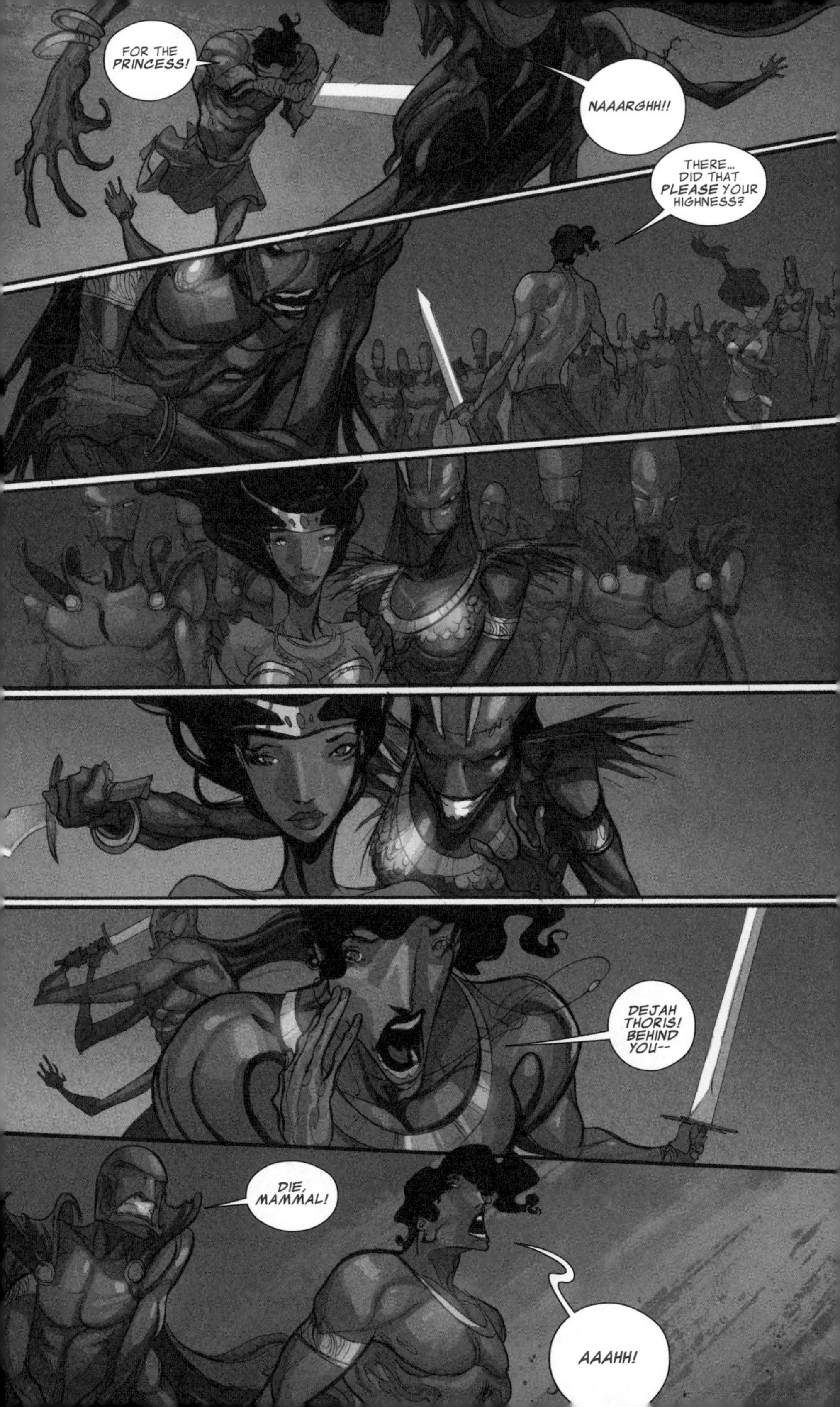
FOR THE PRINCESS!
NAAARGHH!!
THERE... DID THAT PLEASE YOUR HIGHNESS?
DEJAH THORIS! BEHIND YOU--
DIE, MAMMAL!
AAAHH!

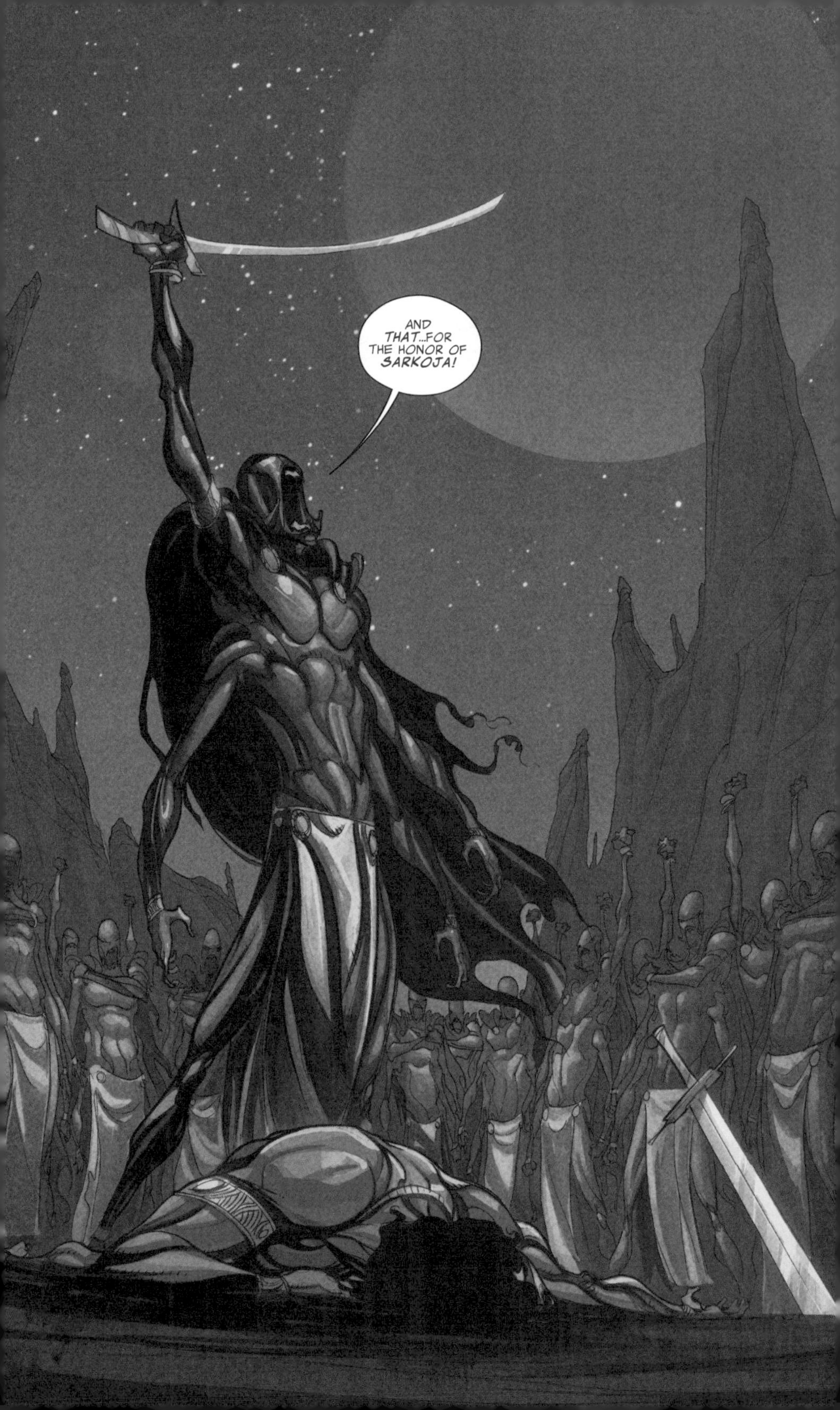
AND THAT...FOR THE HONOR OF SARKOJA!

– THREE –

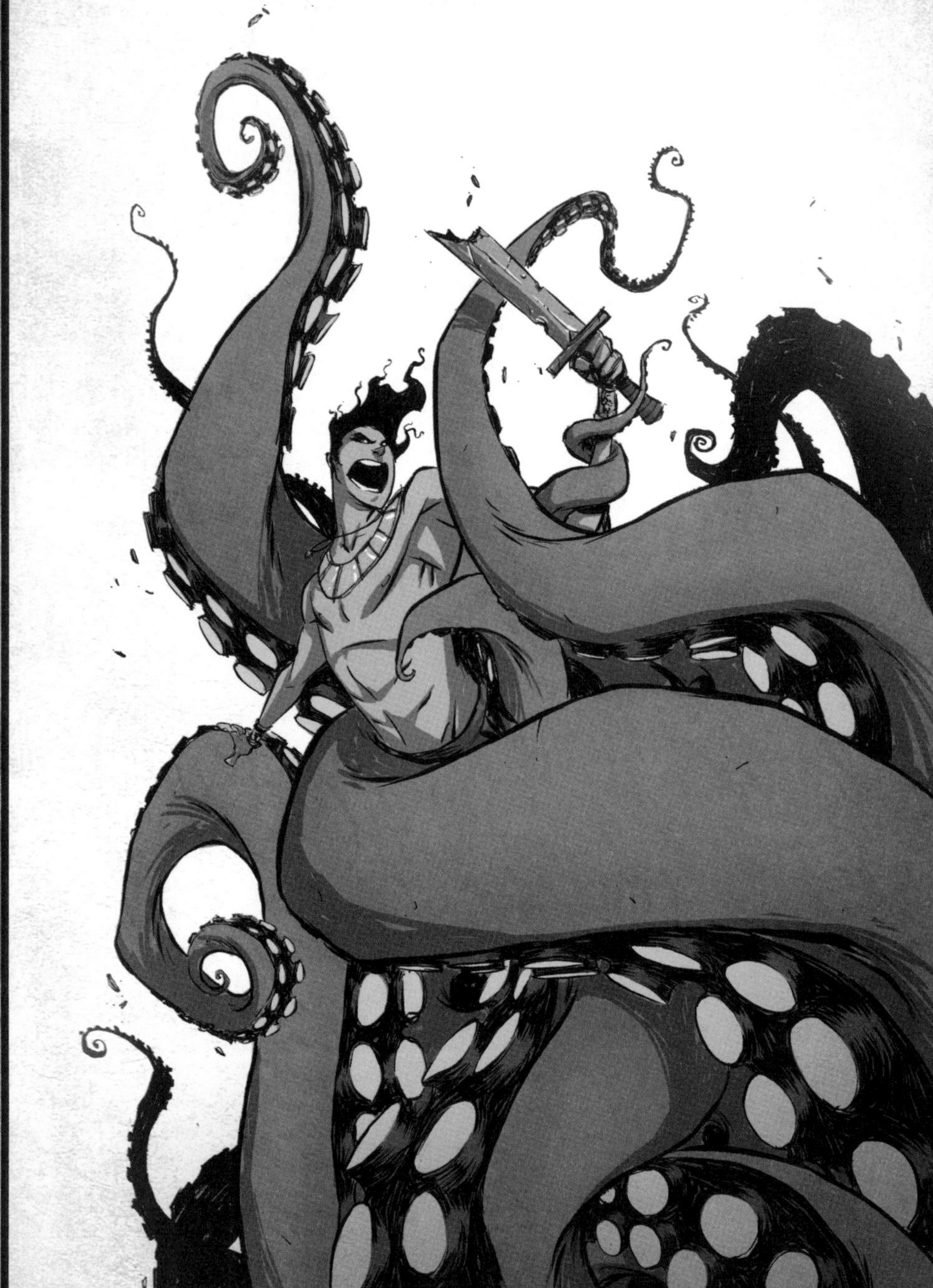

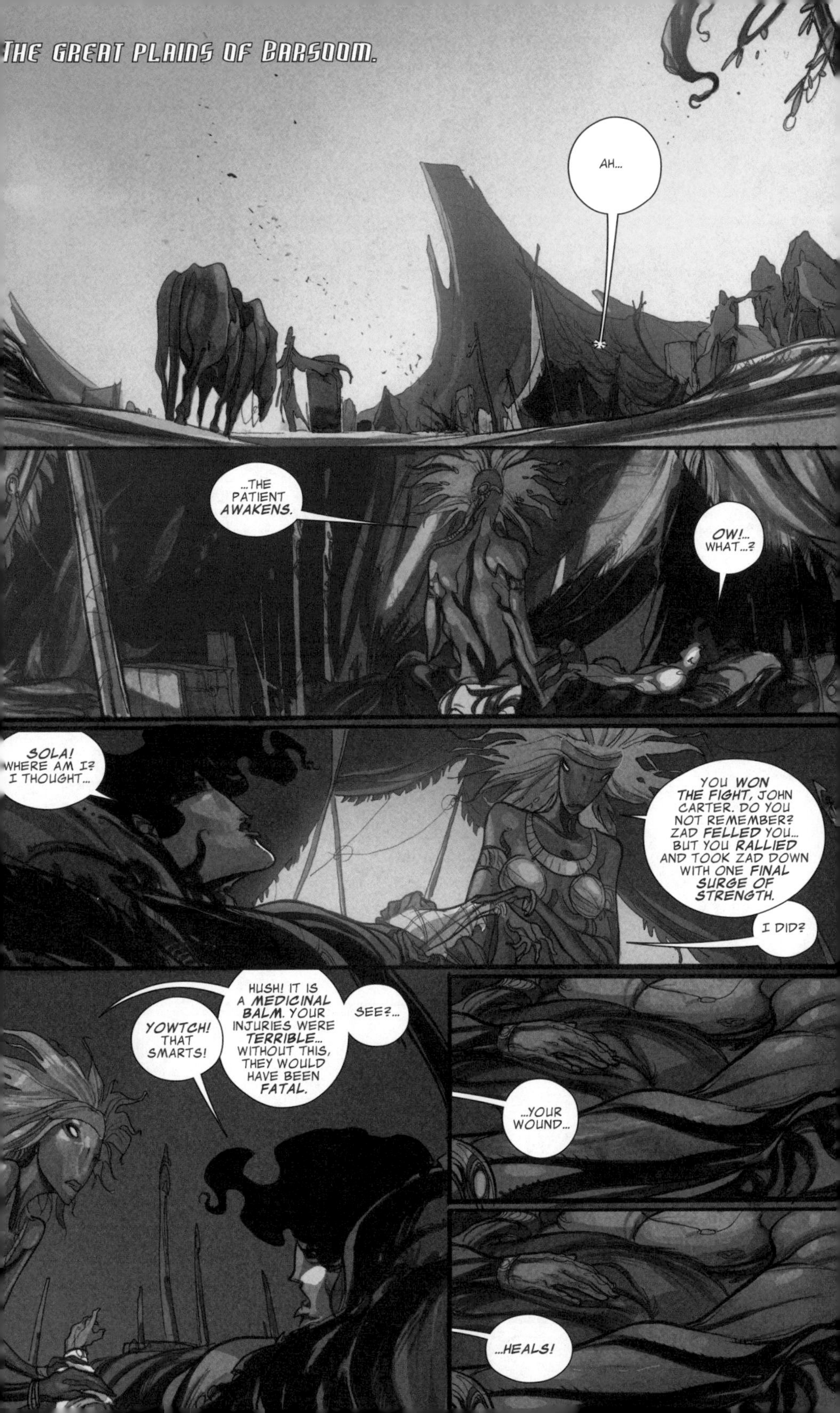
THE GREAT PLAINS OF BARSOOM.
AH...
...THE PATIENT AWAKENS.
OW!... WHAT...?
SOLA! WHERE AM I? I THOUGHT...
YOU WON THE FIGHT, JOHN CARTER. DO YOU NOT REMEMBER? ZAD FELLED YOU... BUT YOU RALLIED AND TOOK ZAD DOWN WITH ONE FINAL SURGE OF STRENGTH.
I DID?
YOWTCH! THAT SMARTS!
HUSH! IT IS A MEDICINAL BALM. YOUR INJURIES WERE TERRIBLE... WITHOUT THIS, THEY WOULD HAVE BEEN FATAL.
SEE?...
...YOUR WOUND...
...HEALS!

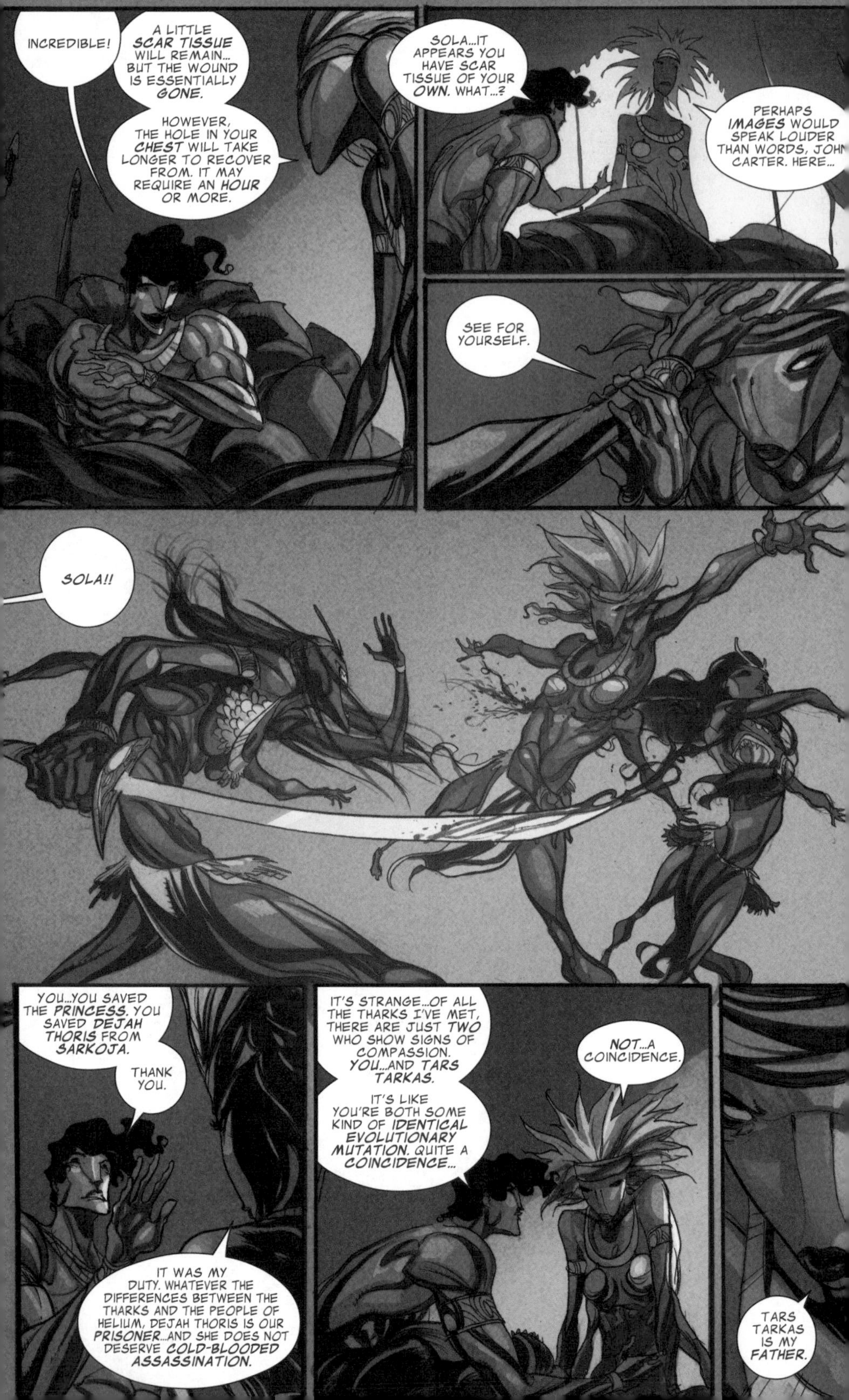
INCREDIBLE!
A LITTLE SCAR TISSUE WILL REMAIN... BUT THE WOUND IS ESSENTIALLY GONE.
HOWEVER, THE HOLE IN YOUR CHEST WILL TAKE LONGER TO RECOVER FROM. IT MAY REQUIRE AN HOUR OR MORE.
SOLA...IT APPEARS YOU HAVE SCAR TISSUE OF YOUR OWN. WHAT...?
PERHAPS IMAGES WOULD SPEAK LOUDER THAN WORDS, JOHN CARTER. HERE...
SEE FOR YOURSELF.
SOLA!!
YOU...YOU SAVED THE PRINCESS. YOU SAVED DEJAH THORIS FROM SARKOJA.
THANK YOU.
IT WAS MY DUTY. WHATEVER THE DIFFERENCES BETWEEN THE THARKS AND THE PEOPLE OF HELIUM, DEJAH THORIS IS OUR PRISONER...AND SHE DOES NOT DESERVE COLD-BLOODED ASSASSINATION.
IT'S STRANGE...OF ALL THE THARKS I'VE MET, THERE ARE JUST TWO WHO SHOW SIGNS OF COMPASSION. YOU...AND TARS TARKAS.
IT'S LIKE YOU'RE BOTH SOME KIND OF IDENTICAL EVOLUTIONARY MUTATION. QUITE A COINCIDENCE...
NOT...A COINCIDENCE.
TARS TARKAS IS MY FATHER.

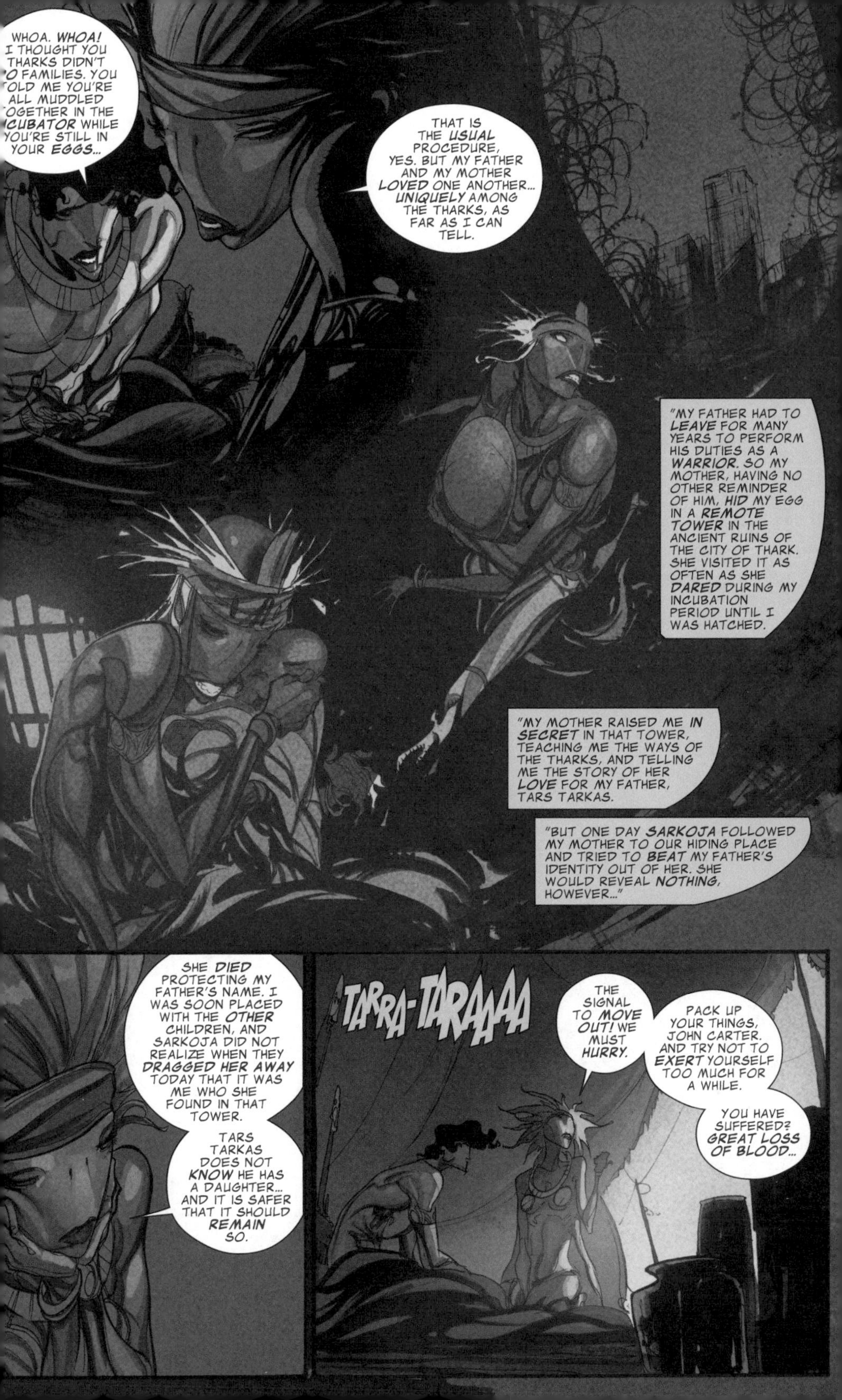

WHOA. WHOA! I THOUGHT YOU THARKS DIDN'T O FAMILIES. YOU OLD ME YOU'RE ALL MUDDLED OGETHER IN THE CUBATOR WHILE YOU'RE STILL IN YOUR EGGS...
THAT IS THE USUAL PROCEDURE, YES. BUT MY FATHER AND MY MOTHER LOVED ONE ANOTHER... UNIQUELY AMONG THE THARKS, AS FAR AS I CAN TELL.
"MY FATHER HAD TO LEAVE FOR MANY YEARS TO PERFORM HIS DUTIES AS A WARRIOR. SO MY MOTHER, HAVING NO OTHER REMINDER OF HIM, HID MY EGG IN A REMOTE TOWER IN THE ANCIENT RUINS OF THE CITY OF THARK. SHE VISITED IT AS OFTEN AS SHE DARED DURING MY INCUBATION PERIOD UNTIL I WAS HATCHED.
"MY MOTHER RAISED ME IN SECRET IN THAT TOWER, TEACHING ME THE WAYS OF THE THARKS, AND TELLING ME THE STORY OF HER LOVE FOR MY FATHER, TARS TARKAS.
"BUT ONE DAY SARKOJA FOLLOWED MY MOTHER TO OUR HIDING PLACE AND TRIED TO BEAT MY FATHER'S IDENTITY OUT OF HER. SHE WOULD REVEAL NOTHING, HOWEVER..."
SHE DIED PROTECTING MY FATHER'S NAME. I WAS SOON PLACED WITH THE OTHER CHILDREN, AND SARKOJA DID NOT REALIZE WHEN THEY DRAGGED HER AWAY TODAY THAT IT WAS ME WHO SHE FOUND IN THAT TOWER.
TARS TARKAS DOES NOT KNOW HE HAS A DAUGHTER... AND IT IS SAFER THAT IT SHOULD REMAIN SO.
TARRA-TARAAAA
THE SIGNAL TO MOVE OUT! WE MUST HURRY.
PACK UP YOUR THINGS, JOHN CARTER. AND TRY NOT TO EXERT YOURSELF TOO MUCH FOR A WHILE.
YOU HAVE SUFFERED? GREAT LOSS OF BLOOD...

THE GREAT GAMES!

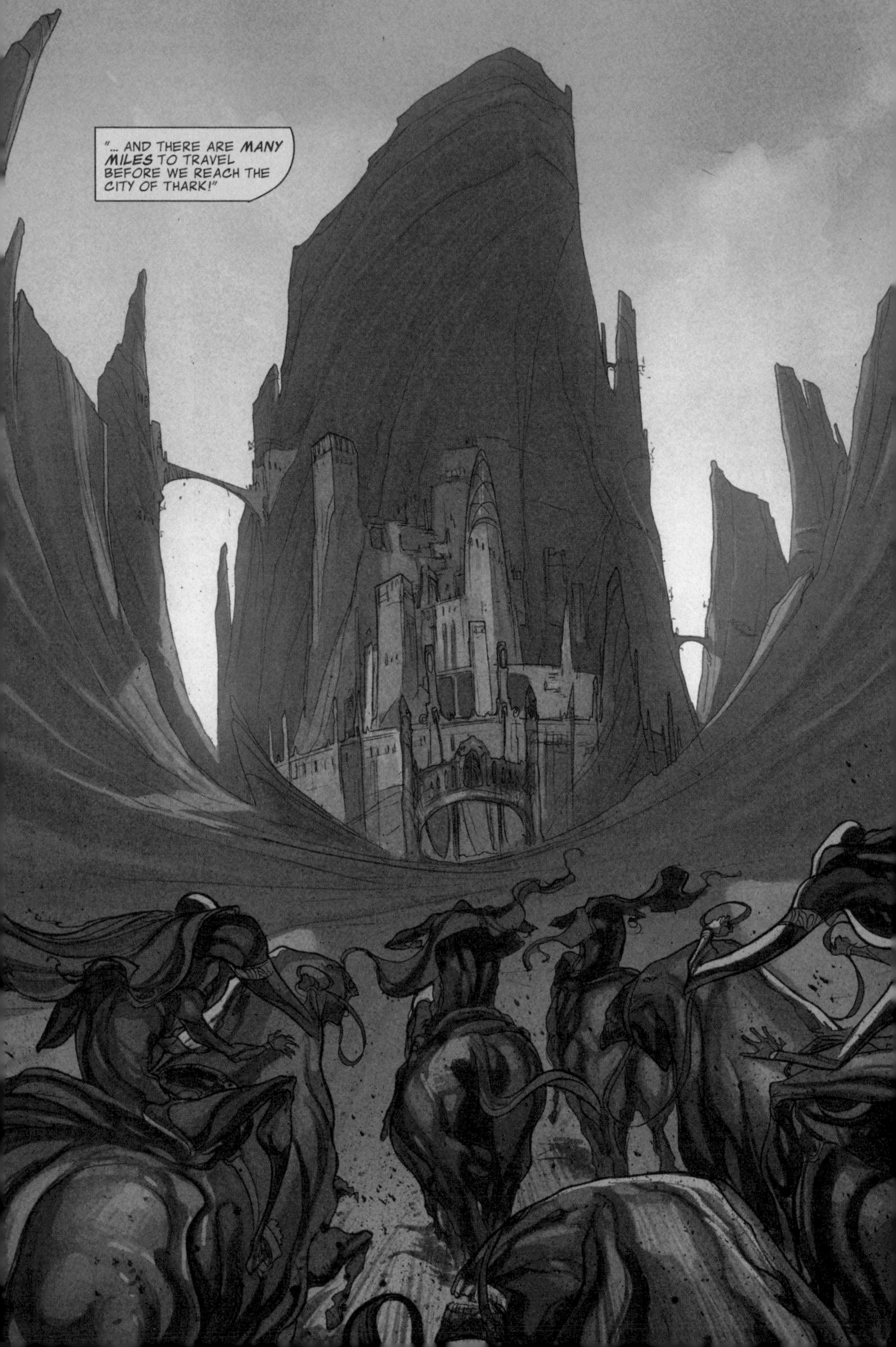
"... AND THERE ARE MANY MILES TO TRAVEL BEFORE WE REACH THE CITY OF THARK!"

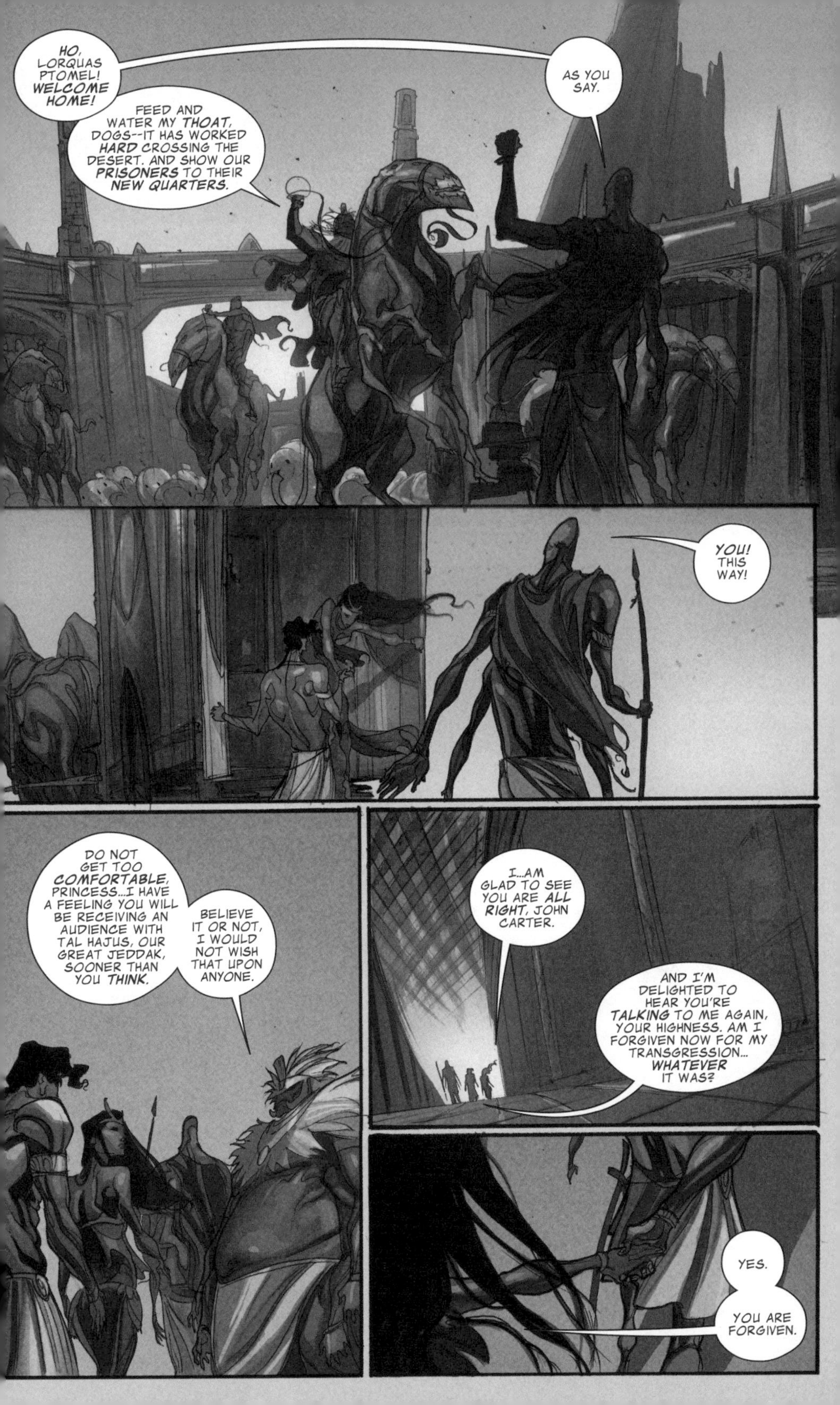
HO, LORQUAS PTOMEL! WELCOME HOME!
AS YOU SAY.
FEED AND WATER MY THOAT, DOGS--IT HAS WORKED HARD CROSSING THE DESERT. AND SHOW OUR PRISONERS TO THEIR NEW QUARTERS.
YOU! THIS WAY!
DO NOT GET TOO COMFORTABLE, PRINCESS...I HAVE A FEELING YOU WILL BE RECEIVING AN AUDIENCE WITH TAL HAJUS, OUR GREAT JEDDAK, SOONER THAN YOU THINK.
BELIEVE IT OR NOT, I WOULD NOT WISH THAT UPON ANYONE.
I...AM GLAD TO SEE YOU ARE ALL RIGHT, JOHN CARTER.
AND I'M DELIGHTED TO HEAR YOU'RE TALKING TO ME AGAIN, YOUR HIGHNESS. AM I FORGIVEN NOW FOR MY TRANSGRESSION... WHATEVER IT WAS?
YES.
YOU ARE FORGIVEN.

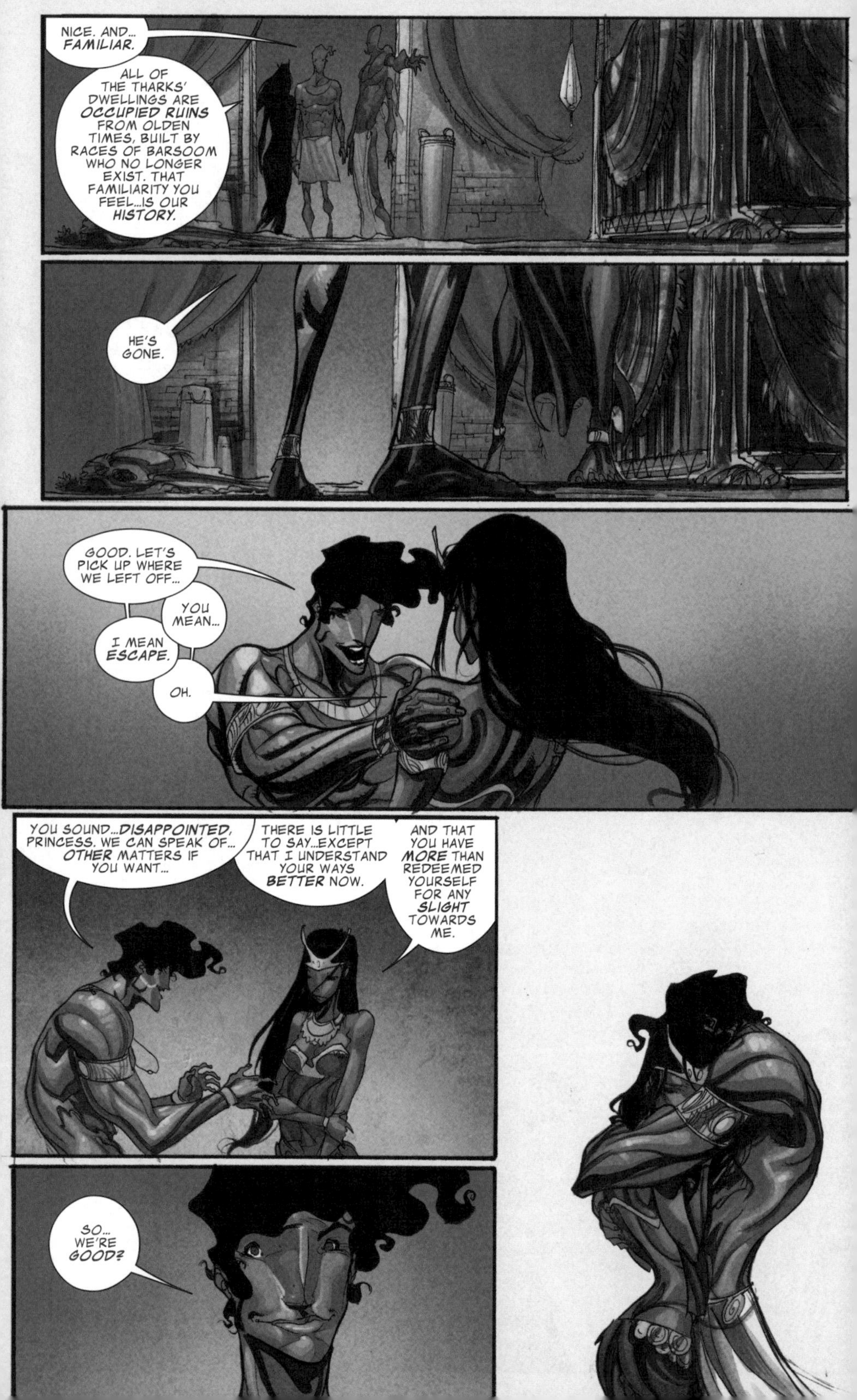

NICE. AND... FAMILIAR.
ALL OF THE THARKS' DWELLINGS ARE OCCUPIED RUINS FROM OLDEN TIMES, BUILT BY RACES OF BARSOOM WHO NO LONGER EXIST. THAT FAMILIARITY YOU FEEL...IS OUR HISTORY.
HE'S GONE.
GOOD. LET'S PICK UP WHERE WE LEFT OFF...
YOU MEAN...
I MEAN ESCAPE.
OH.
YOU SOUND...DISAPPOINTED, PRINCESS. WE CAN SPEAK OF... OTHER MATTERS IF YOU WANT...
THERE IS LITTLE TO SAY...EXCEPT THAT I UNDERSTAND YOUR WAYS BETTER NOW.
AND THAT YOU HAVE MORE THAN REDEEMED YOURSELF FOR ANY SLIGHT TOWARDS ME.
SO... WE'RE GOOD?

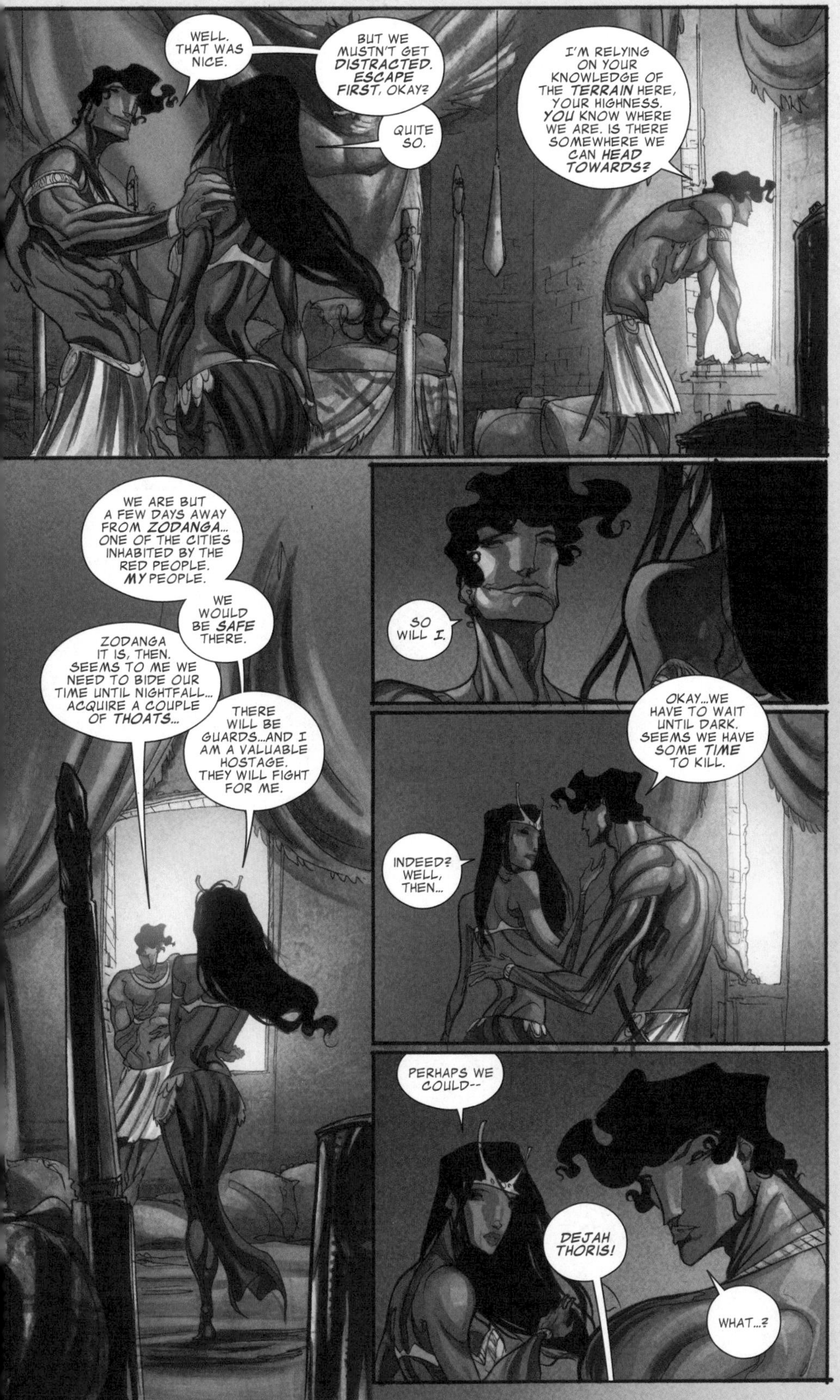
WELL. THAT WAS NICE.
BUT WE MUSTN'T GET DISTRACTED. ESCAPE FIRST, OKAY?
QUITE SO.
I'M RELYING ON YOUR KNOWLEDGE OF THE TERRAIN HERE, YOUR HIGHNESS. YOU KNOW WHERE WE ARE. IS THERE SOMEWHERE WE CAN HEAD TOWARDS?
WE ARE BUT A FEW DAYS AWAY FROM ZODANGA... ONE OF THE CITIES INHABITED BY THE RED PEOPLE. MY PEOPLE.
WE WOULD BE SAFE THERE.
ZODANGA IT IS, THEN. SEEMS TO ME WE NEED TO BIDE OUR TIME UNTIL NIGHTFALL... ACQUIRE A COUPLE OF THOATS...
THERE WILL BE GUARDS...AND I AM A VALUABLE HOSTAGE. THEY WILL FIGHT FOR ME.
SO WILL I.
OKAY...WE HAVE TO WAIT UNTIL DARK. SEEMS WE HAVE SOME TIME TO KILL.
INDEED? WELL, THEN...
PERHAPS WE COULD--
DEJAH THORIS!
WHAT...?

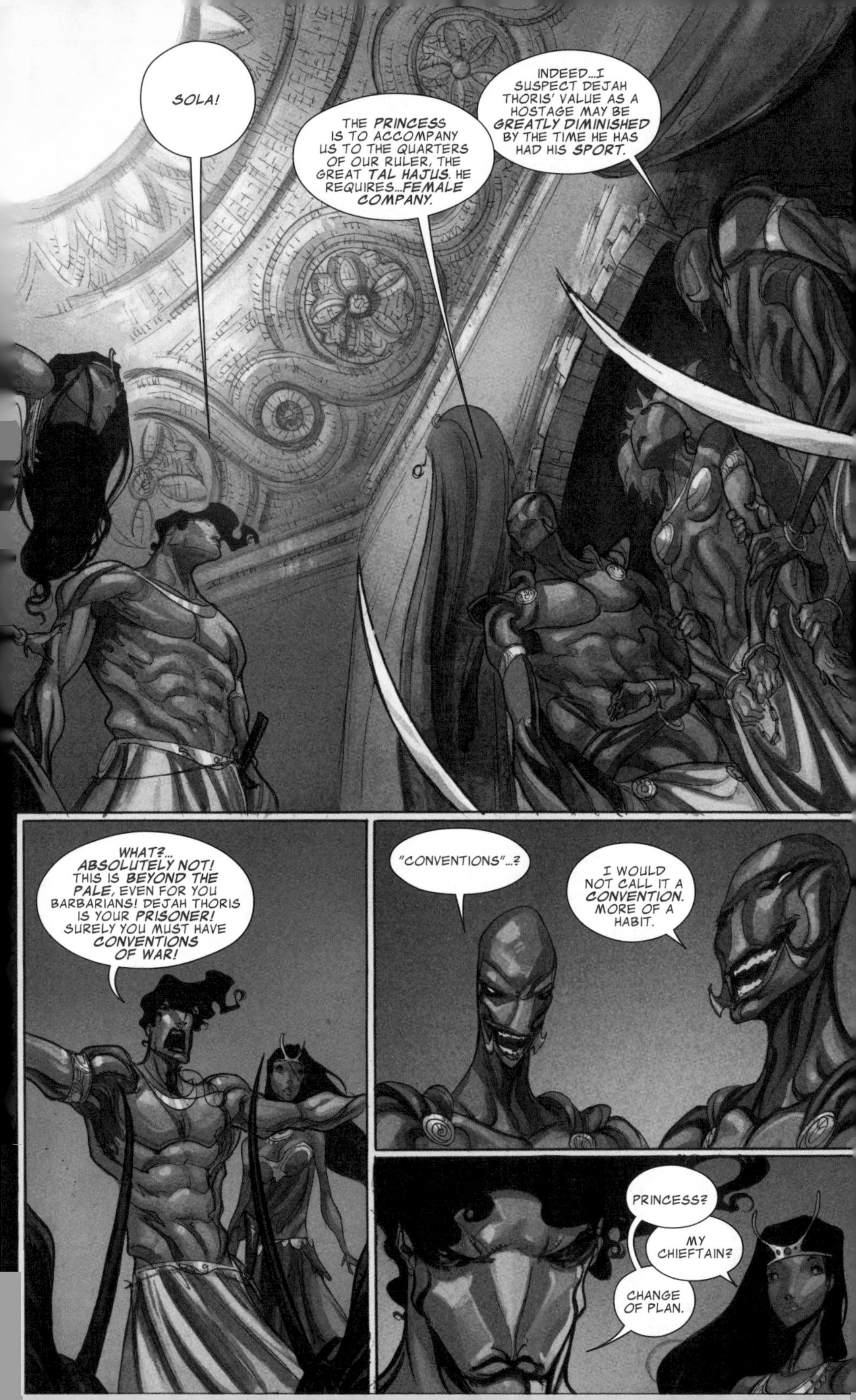
SOLA!
THE PRINCESS IS TO ACCOMPANY US TO THE QUARTERS OF OUR RULER, THE GREAT TAL HAJUS. HE REQUIRES...FEMALE COMPANY.
INDEED...I SUSPECT DEJAH THORIS' VALUE AS A HOSTAGE MAY BE GREATLY DIMINISHED BY THE TIME HE HAS HAD HIS SPORT.
WHAT?... ABSOLUTELY NOT! THIS IS BEYOND THE PALE, EVEN FOR YOU BARBARIANS! DEJAH THORIS IS YOUR PRISONER! SURELY YOU MUST HAVE CONVENTIONS OF WAR!
"CONVENTIONS"...?
I WOULD NOT CALL IT A CONVENTION. MORE OF A HABIT.
PRINCESS?
MY CHIEFTAIN?
CHANGE OF PLAN.

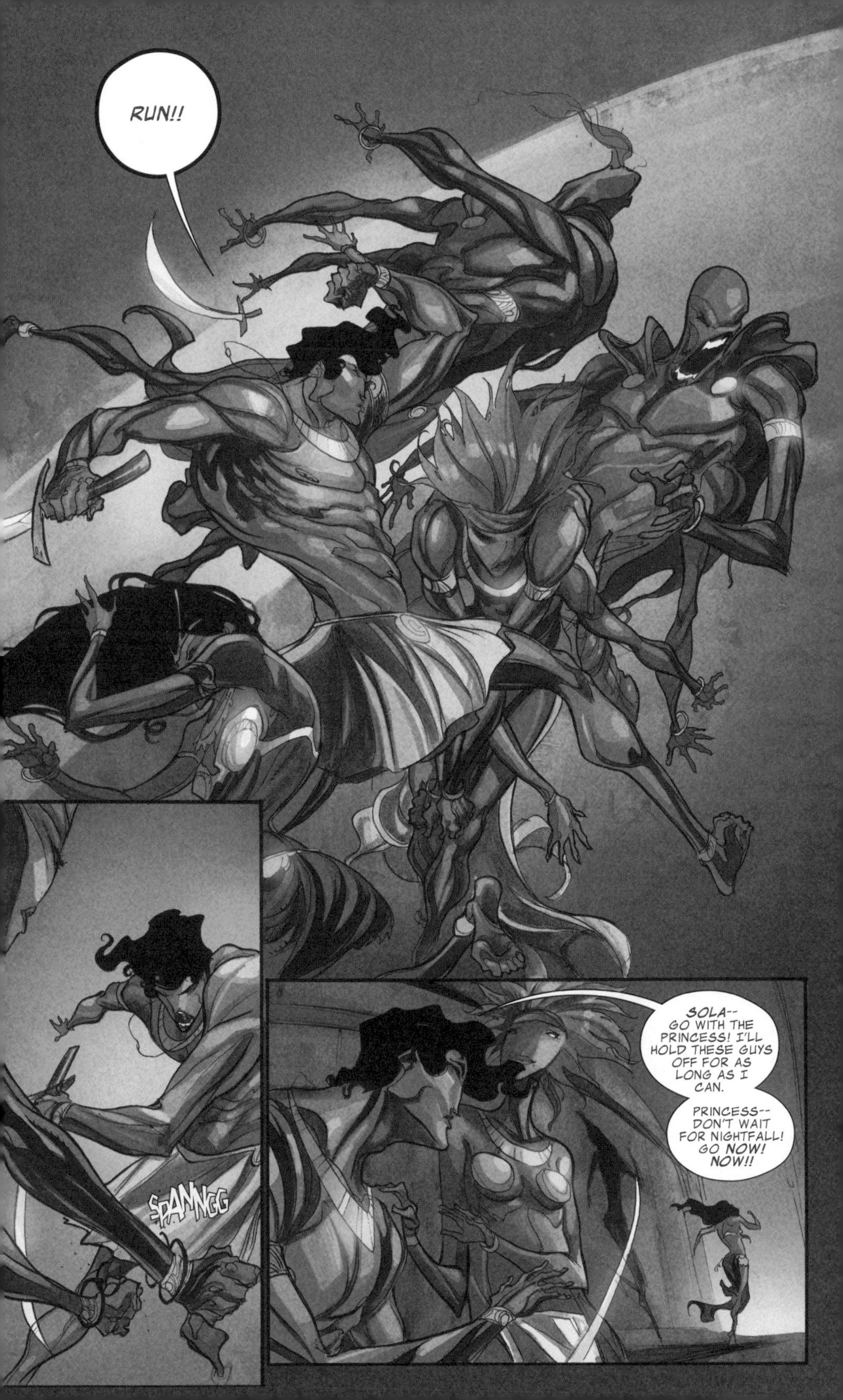
RUN!!
SPANNGG
SOLA-- GO WITH THE PRINCESS! I'LL HOLD THESE GUYS OFF FOR AS LONG AS I CAN.
PRINCESS-- DON'T WAIT FOR NIGHTFALL! GO NOW! NOW!!

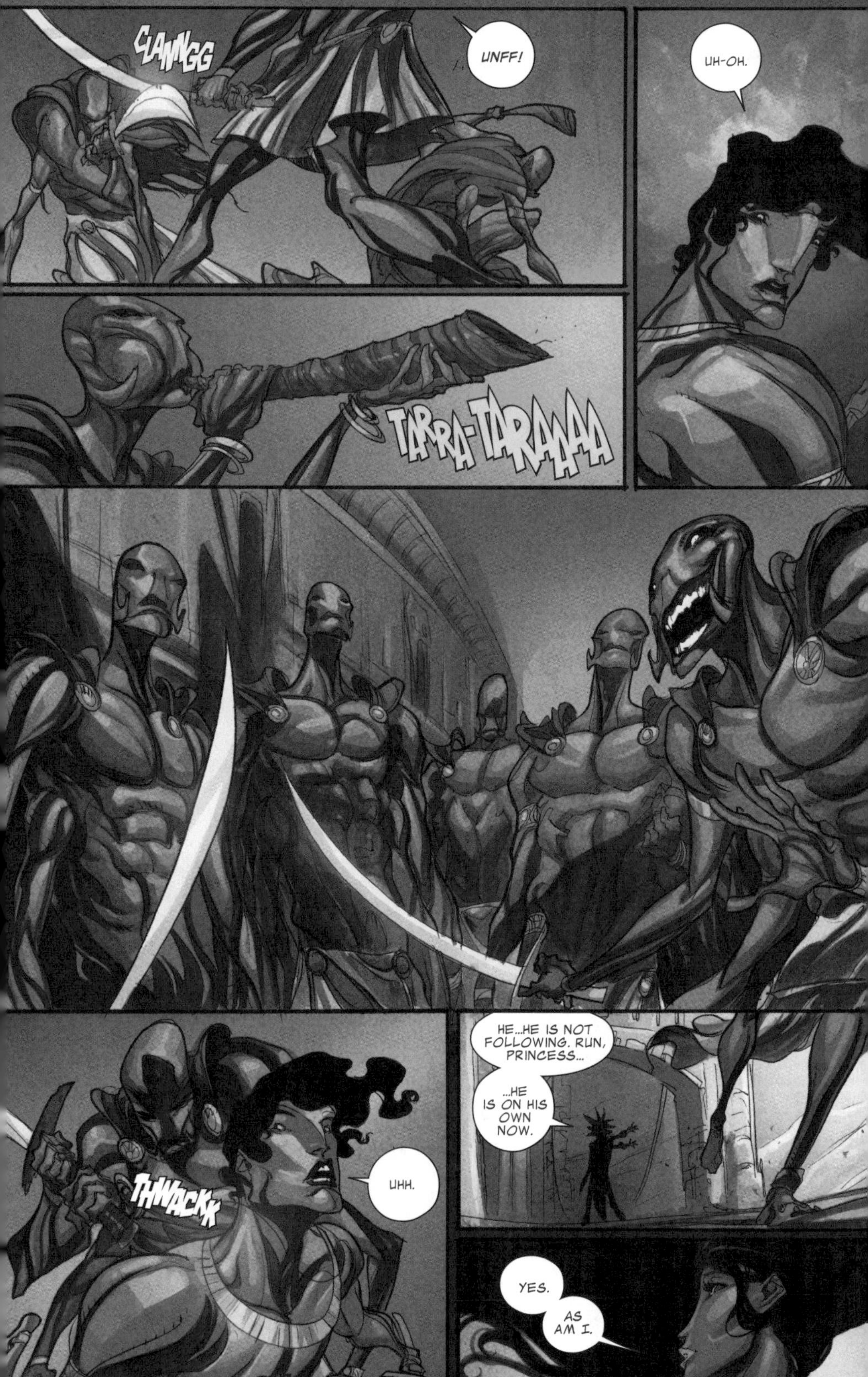
CLANNGG
UNFF!
UH-OH.
TARRA-TARAAAA
THWACKK
UHH.
HE...HE IS NOT FOLLOWING. RUN, PRINCESS...
...HE IS ON HIS OWN NOW.
YES.
AS AM I.

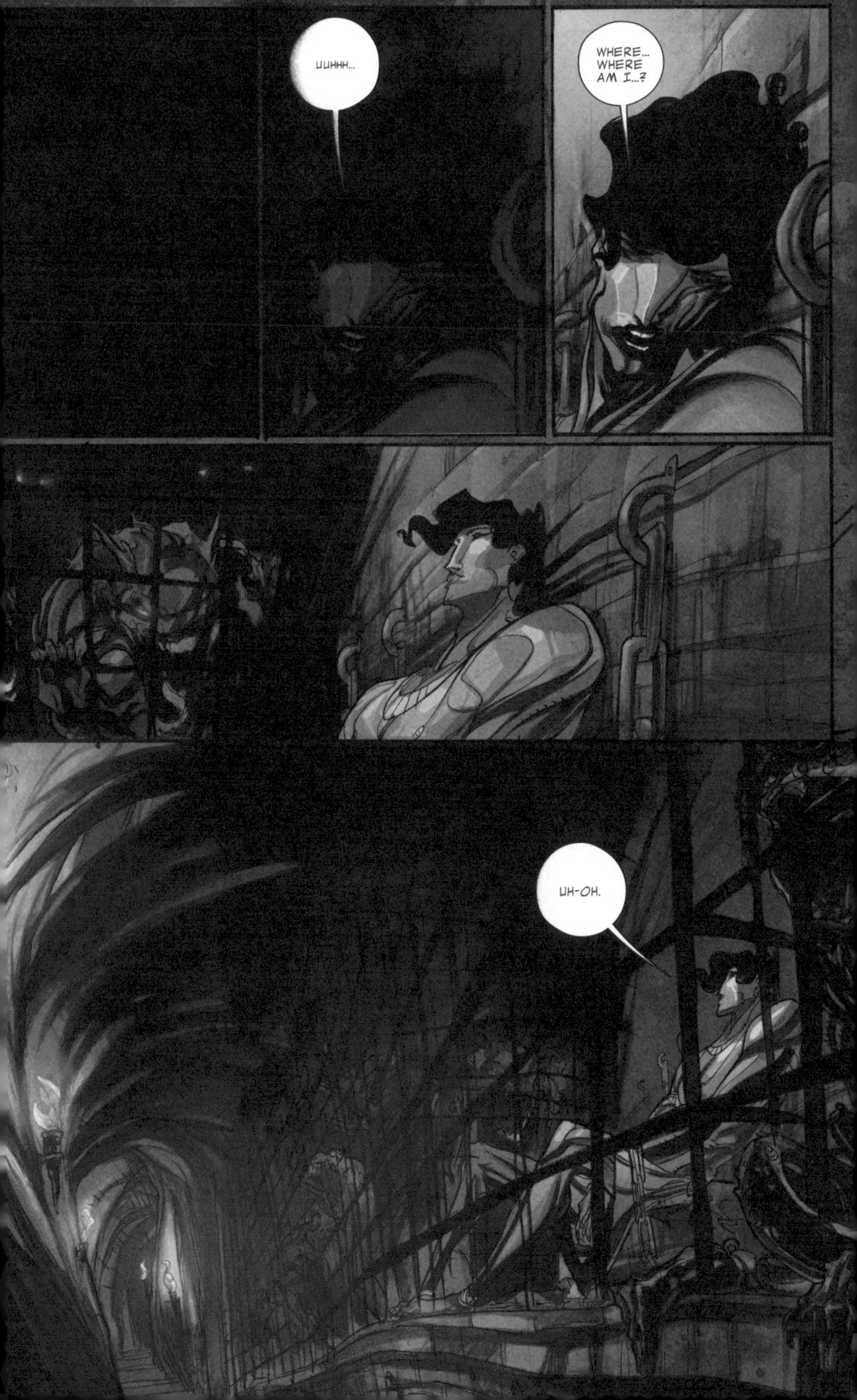
UUHHH...
WHERE... WHERE AM I...?
UH-OH.

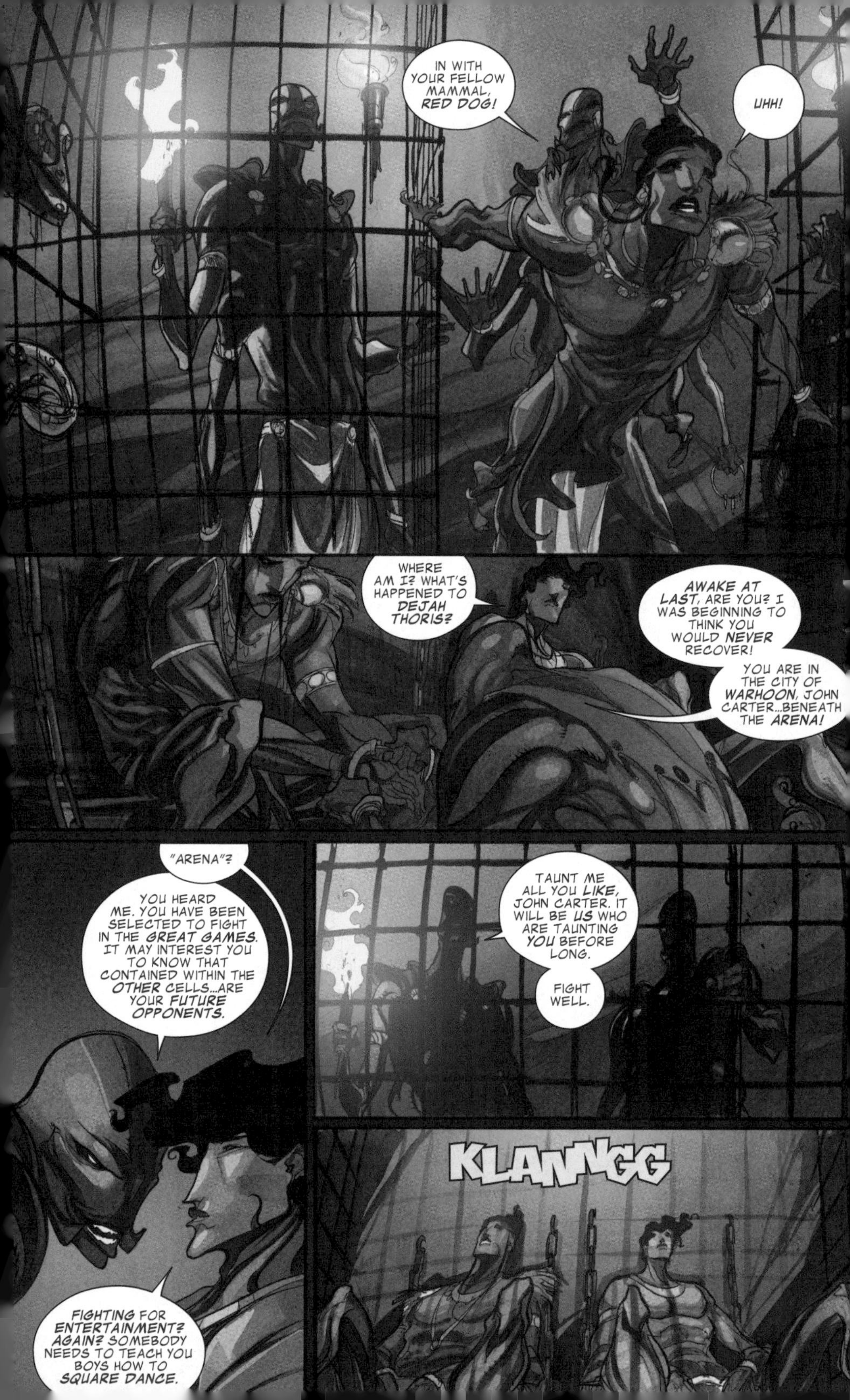
IN WITH YOUR FELLOW MAMMAL, RED DOG!
UHH!
WHERE AM I? WHAT'S HAPPENED TO DEJAH THORIS?
AWAKE AT LAST, ARE YOU? I WAS BEGINNING TO THINK YOU WOULD NEVER RECOVER!
YOU ARE IN THE CITY OF WARHOON, JOHN CARTER...BENEATH THE ARENA!
"ARENA"?
YOU HEARD ME. YOU HAVE BEEN SELECTED TO FIGHT IN THE GREAT GAMES. IT MAY INTEREST YOU TO KNOW THAT CONTAINED WITHIN THE OTHER CELLS...ARE YOUR FUTURE OPPONENTS.
FIGHTING FOR ENTERTAINMENT? AGAIN? SOMEBODY NEEDS TO TEACH YOU BOYS HOW TO SQUARE DANCE.
TAUNT ME ALL YOU LIKE, JOHN CARTER. IT WILL BE US WHO ARE TAUNTING YOU BEFORE LONG.
FIGHT WELL.
KLANNGG

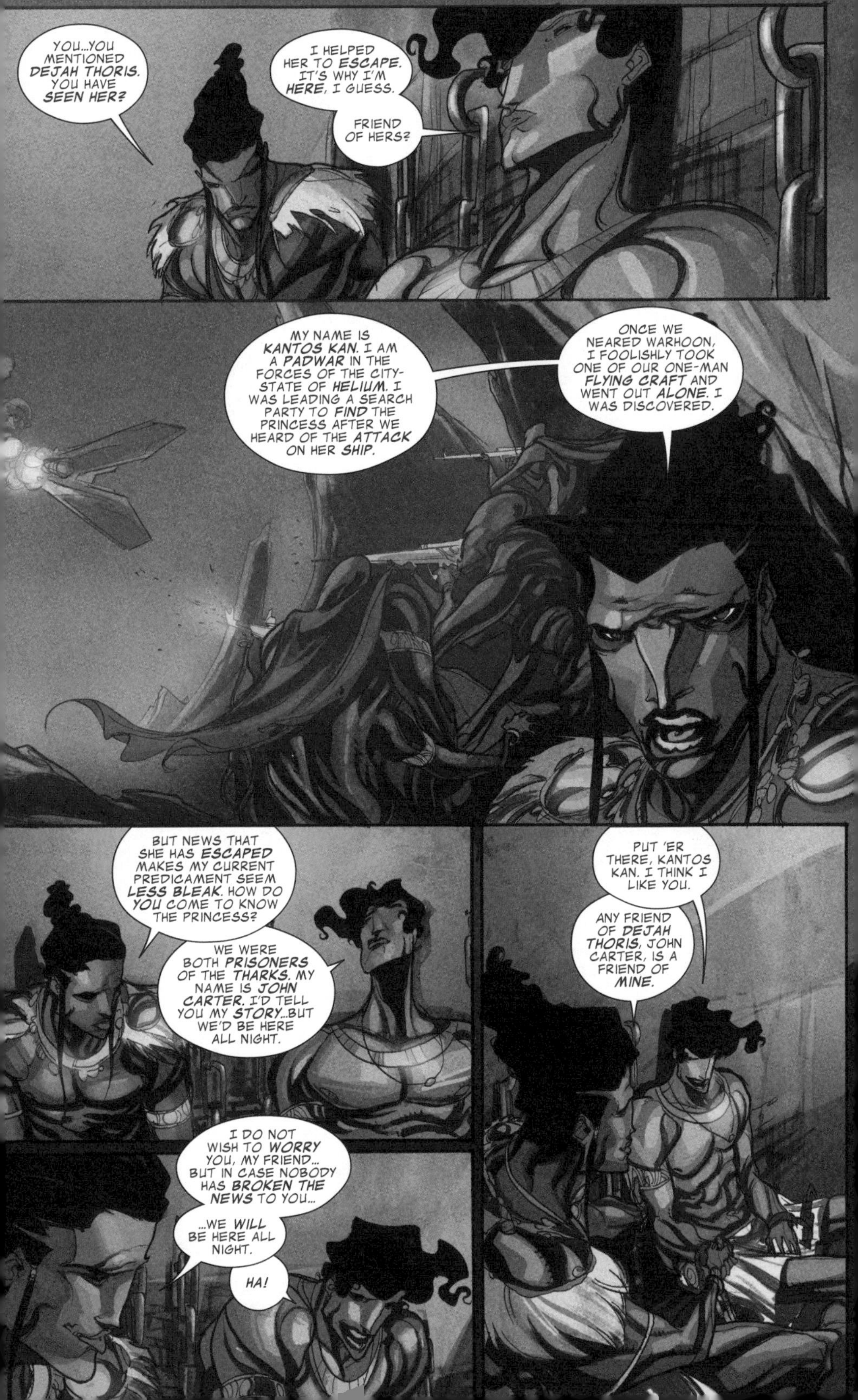

YOU...YOU MENTIONED DEJAH THORIS. YOU HAVE SEEN HER?
I HELPED HER TO ESCAPE. IT'S WHY I'M HERE, I GUESS.
FRIEND OF HERS?
MY NAME IS KANTOS KAN. I AM A PADWAR IN THE FORCES OF THE CITY-STATE OF HELIUM. I WAS LEADING A SEARCH PARTY TO FIND THE PRINCESS AFTER WE HEARD OF THE ATTACK ON HER SHIP.
ONCE WE NEARED WARHOON, I FOOLISHLY TOOK ONE OF OUR ONE-MAN FLYING CRAFT AND WENT OUT ALONE. I WAS DISCOVERED.
BUT NEWS THAT SHE HAS ESCAPED MAKES MY CURRENT PREDICAMENT SEEM LESS BLEAK. HOW DO YOU COME TO KNOW THE PRINCESS?
WE WERE BOTH PRISONERS OF THE THARKS. MY NAME IS JOHN CARTER. I'D TELL YOU MY STORY...BUT WE'D BE HERE ALL NIGHT.
I DO NOT WISH TO WORRY YOU, MY FRIEND... BUT IN CASE NOBODY HAS BROKEN THE NEWS TO YOU...
...WE WILL BE HERE ALL NIGHT.
HA!
PUT 'ER THERE, KANTOS KAN. I THINK I LIKE YOU.
ANY FRIEND OF DEJAH THORIS, JOHN CARTER, IS A FRIEND OF MINE.

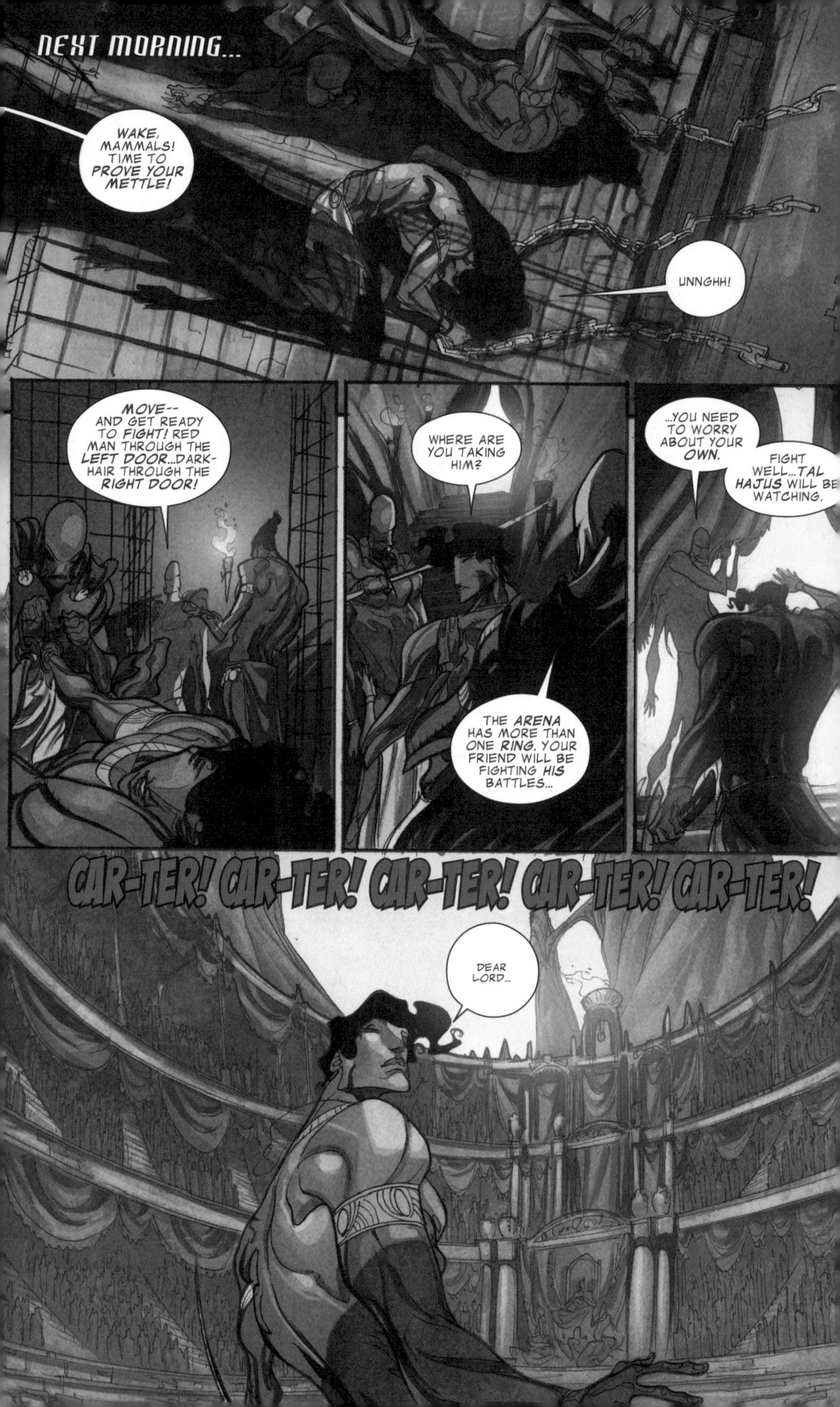
NEXT MORNING...
WAKE, MAMMALS! TIME TO PROVE YOUR METTLE!
UNNGHH!
MOVE-- AND GET READY TO FIGHT! RED MAN THROUGH THE LEFT DOOR...DARK-HAIR THROUGH THE RIGHT DOOR!
WHERE ARE YOU TAKING HIM?
THE ARENA HAS MORE THAN ONE RING. YOUR FRIEND WILL BE FIGHTING HIS BATTLES...
...YOU NEED TO WORRY ABOUT YOUR OWN.
FIGHT WELL...TAL HAJUS WILL BE WATCHING.
CAR-TER! CAR-TER! CAR-TER! CAR-TER! CAR-TER!
DEAR LORD...

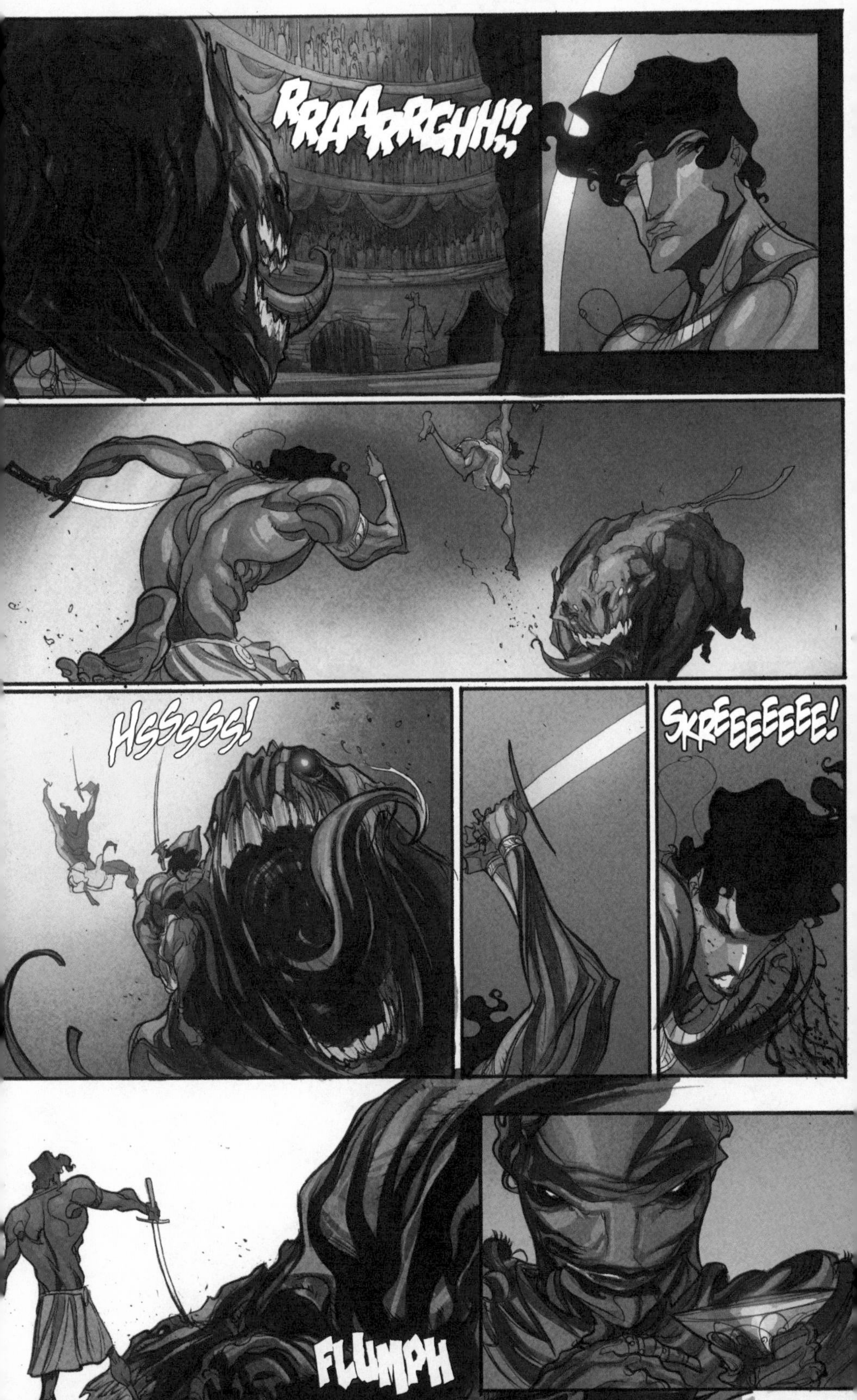
RRAARRGHH!!
HSSSSS!
SKREEEEEEE!
FLUMPH

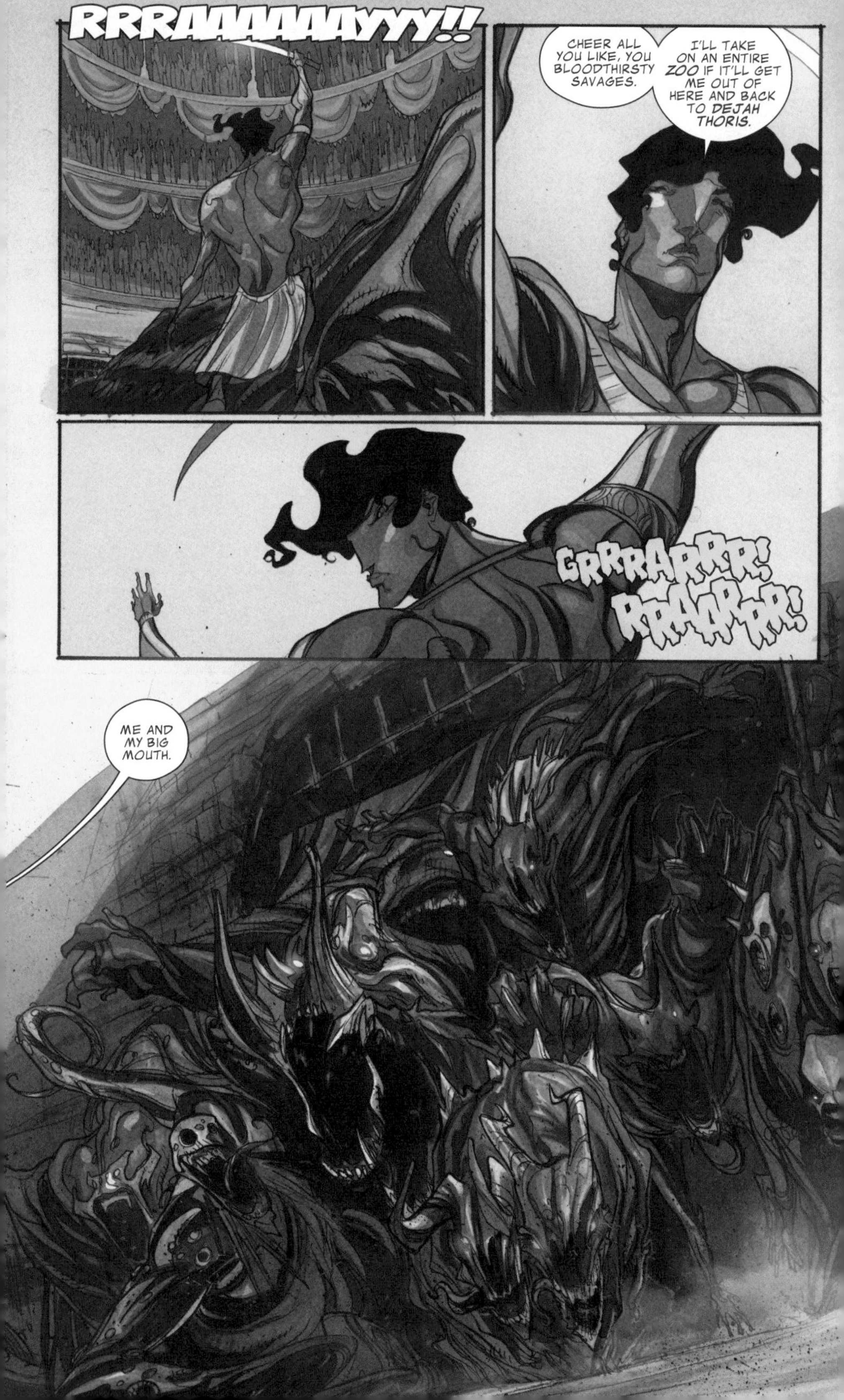
RRRAAAAAAYYY!!
CHEER ALL YOU LIKE, YOU BLOODTHIRSTY SAVAGES.
I'LL TAKE ON AN ENTIRE ZOO IF IT'LL GET ME OUT OF HERE AND BACK TO DEJAH THORIS.
GRRRARRR! RRRAARRR!
ME AND MY BIG MOUTH.

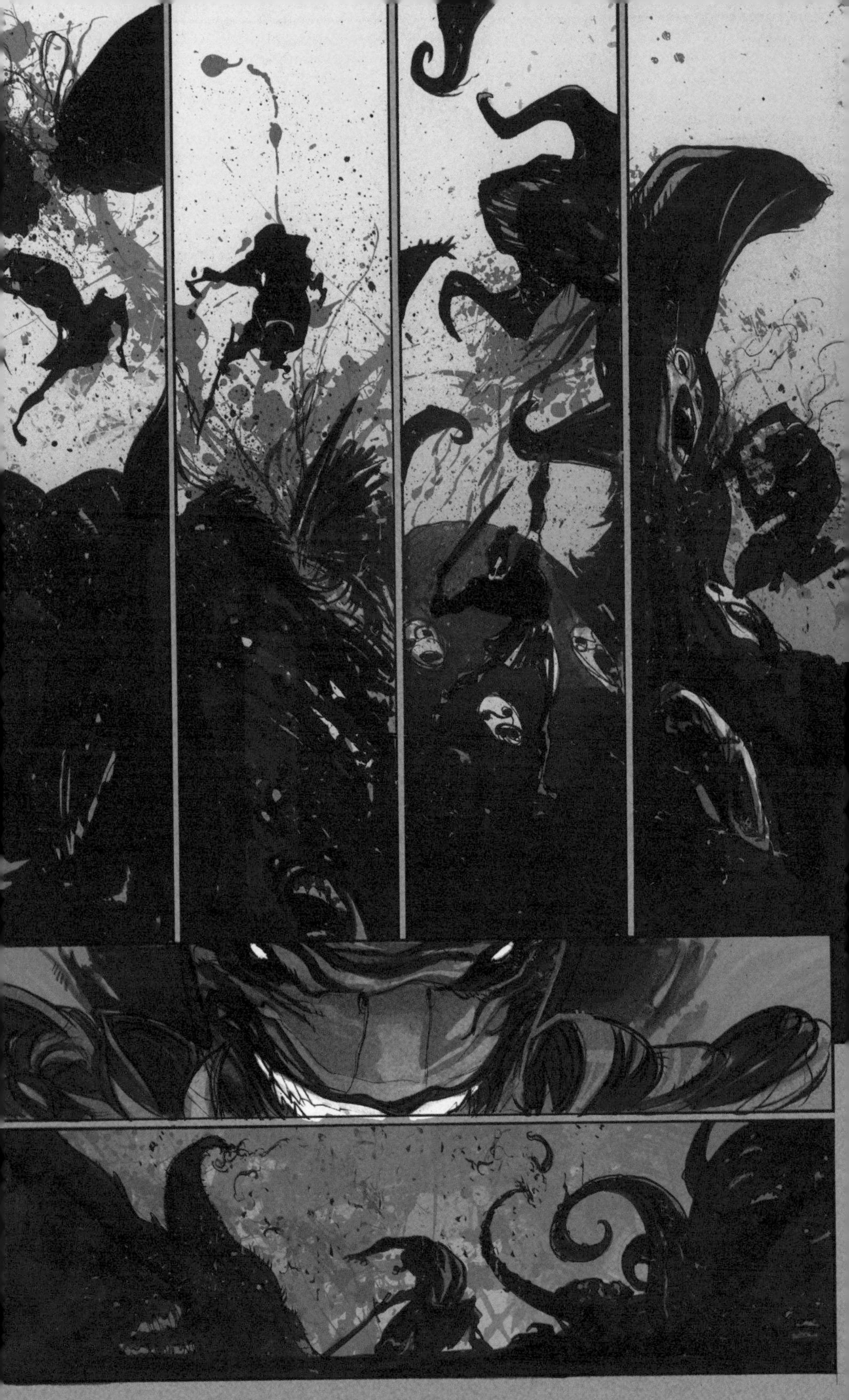

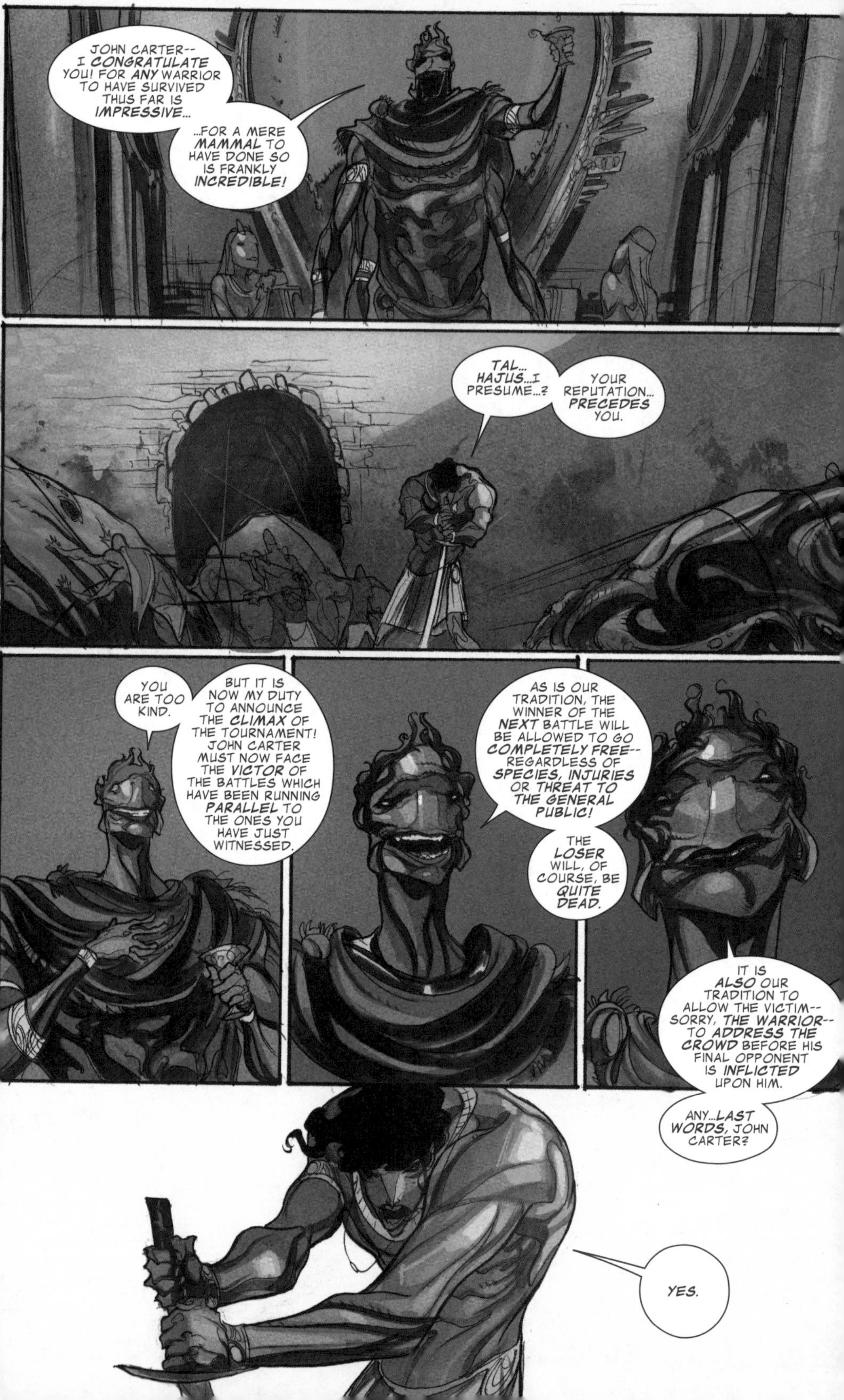

JOHN CARTER-- I CONGRATULATE YOU! FOR ANY WARRIOR TO HAVE SURVIVED THUS FAR IS IMPRESSIVE...
...FOR A MERE MAMMAL TO HAVE DONE SO IS FRANKLY INCREDIBLE!
TAL... HAJUS...I PRESUME...?
YOUR REPUTATION... PRECEDES YOU.
YOU ARE TOO KIND.
BUT IT IS NOW MY DUTY TO ANNOUNCE THE CLIMAX OF THE TOURNAMENT! JOHN CARTER MUST NOW FACE THE VICTOR OF THE BATTLES WHICH HAVE BEEN RUNNING PARALLEL TO THE ONES YOU HAVE JUST WITNESSED.
AS IS OUR TRADITION, THE WINNER OF THE NEXT BATTLE WILL BE ALLOWED TO GO COMPLETELY FREE-- REGARDLESS OF SPECIES, INJURIES OR THREAT TO THE GENERAL PUBLIC!
THE LOSER WILL, OF COURSE, BE QUITE DEAD.
IT IS ALSO OUR TRADITION TO ALLOW THE VICTIM-- SORRY, THE WARRIOR-- TO ADDRESS THE CROWD BEFORE HIS FINAL OPPONENT IS INFLICTED UPON HIM.
ANY...LAST WORDS, JOHN CARTER?
YES.

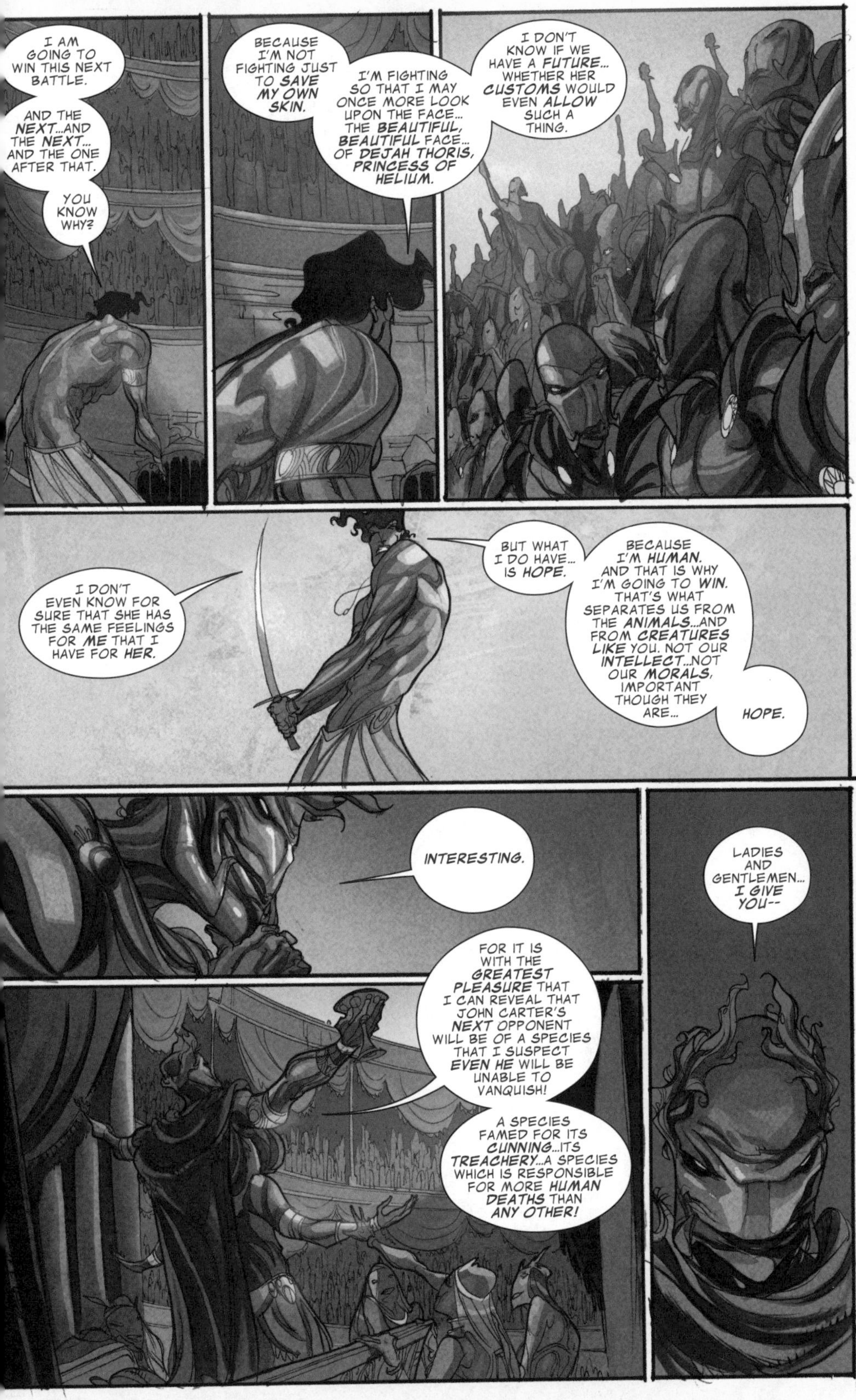
I AM GOING TO WIN THIS NEXT BATTLE.
AND THE NEXT...AND THE NEXT... AND THE ONE AFTER THAT.
YOU KNOW WHY?
BECAUSE I'M NOT FIGHTING JUST TO SAVE MY OWN SKIN.
I'M FIGHTING SO THAT I MAY ONCE MORE LOOK UPON THE FACE... THE BEAUTIFUL, BEAUTIFUL FACE... OF DEJAH THORIS, PRINCESS OF HELIUM.
I DON'T KNOW IF WE HAVE A FUTURE... WHETHER HER CUSTOMS WOULD EVEN ALLOW SUCH A THING.
I DON'T EVEN KNOW FOR SURE THAT SHE HAS THE SAME FEELINGS FOR ME THAT I HAVE FOR HER.
BUT WHAT I DO HAVE... IS HOPE.
BECAUSE I'M HUMAN. AND THAT IS WHY I'M GOING TO WIN. THAT'S WHAT SEPARATES US FROM THE ANIMALS...AND FROM CREATURES LIKE YOU. NOT OUR INTELLECT...NOT OUR MORALS, IMPORTANT THOUGH THEY ARE...
HOPE.
INTERESTING.
LADIES AND GENTLEMEN... I GIVE YOU--
FOR IT IS WITH THE GREATEST PLEASURE THAT I CAN REVEAL THAT JOHN CARTER'S NEXT OPPONENT WILL BE OF A SPECIES THAT I SUSPECT EVEN HE WILL BE UNABLE TO VANQUISH!
A SPECIES FAMED FOR ITS CUNNING...ITS TREACHERY...A SPECIES WHICH IS RESPONSIBLE FOR MORE HUMAN DEATHS THAN ANY OTHER!

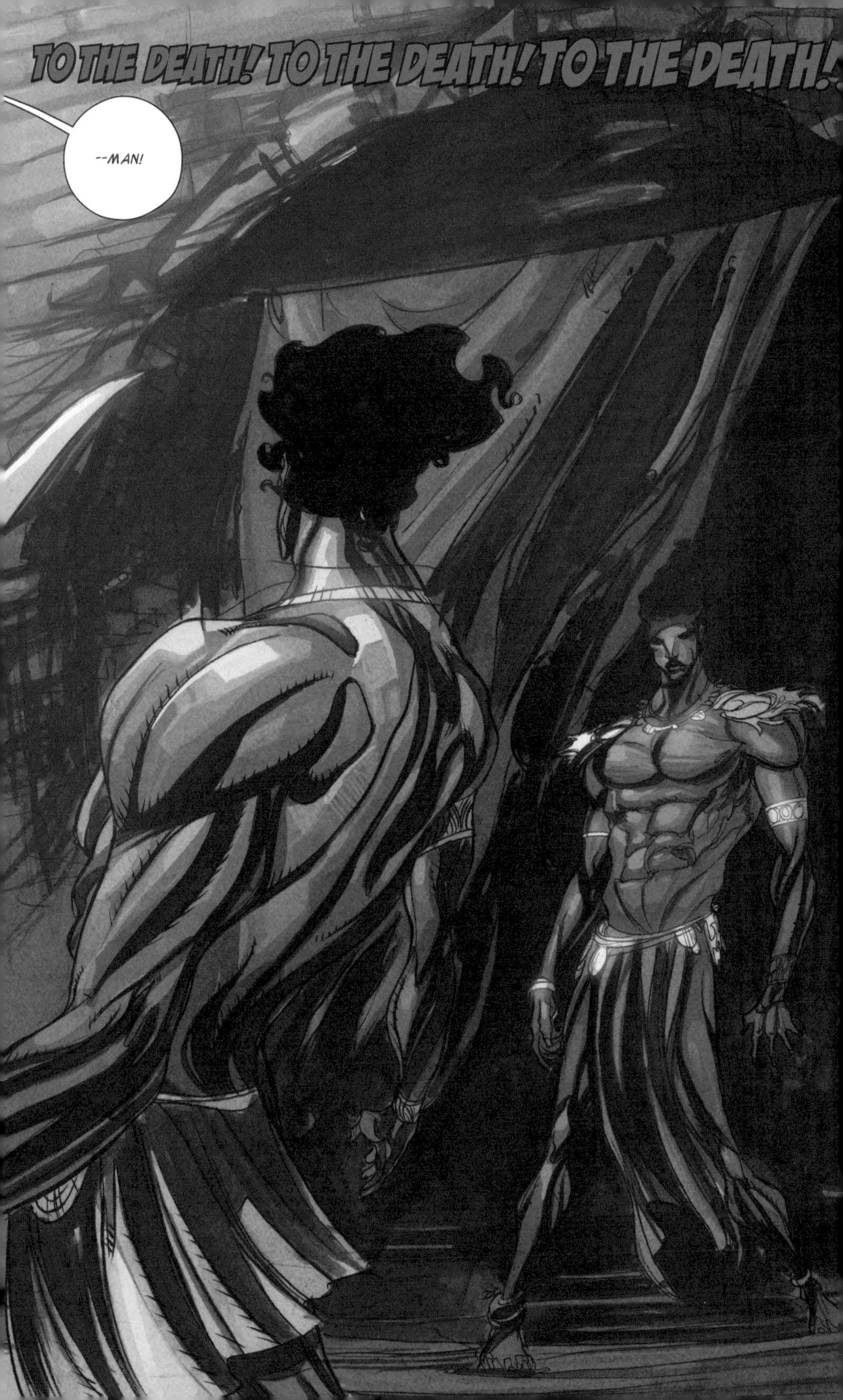
TO THE DEATH! TO THE DEATH! TO THE DEATH!
--MAN!

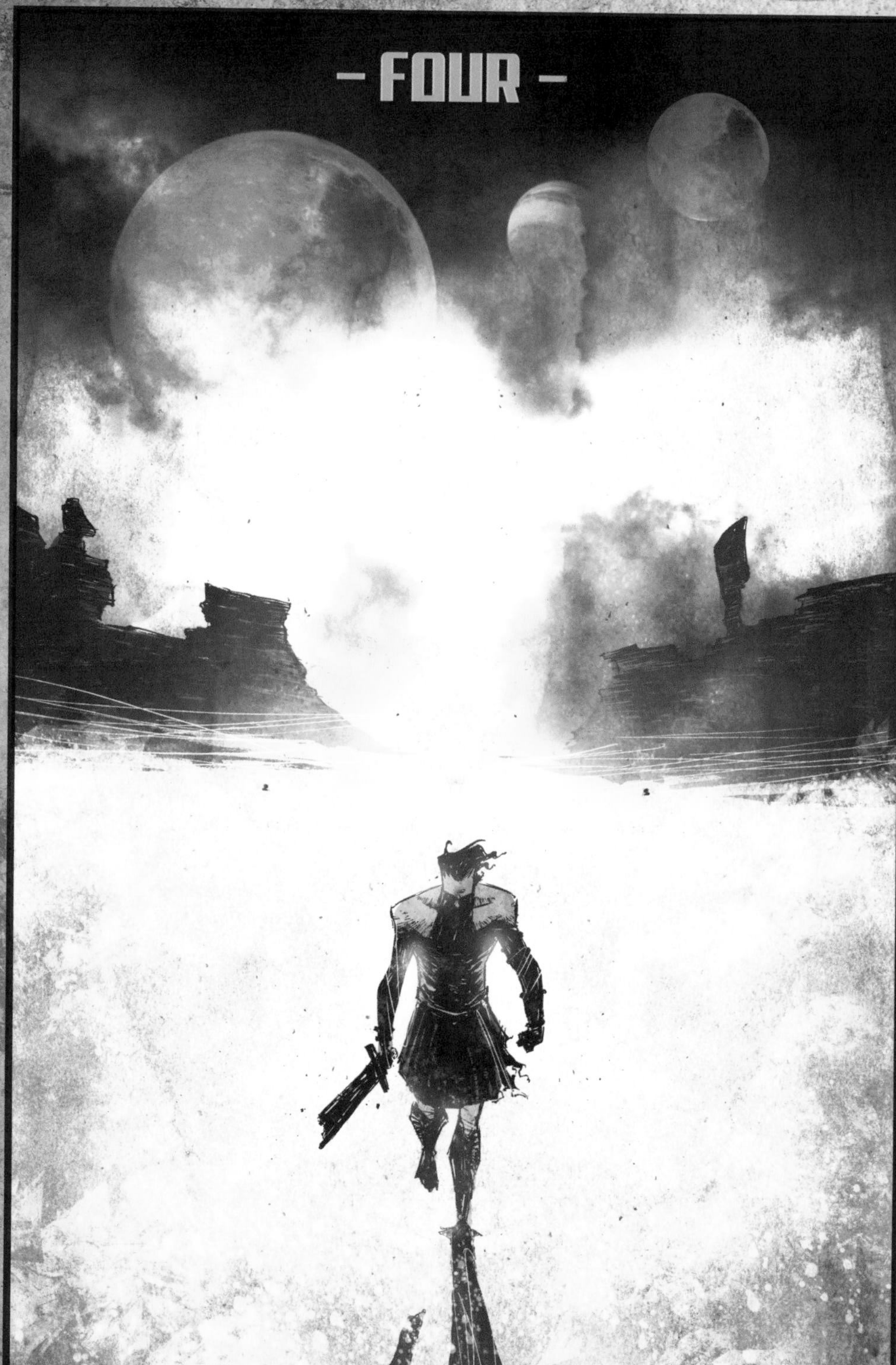
- FOUR -

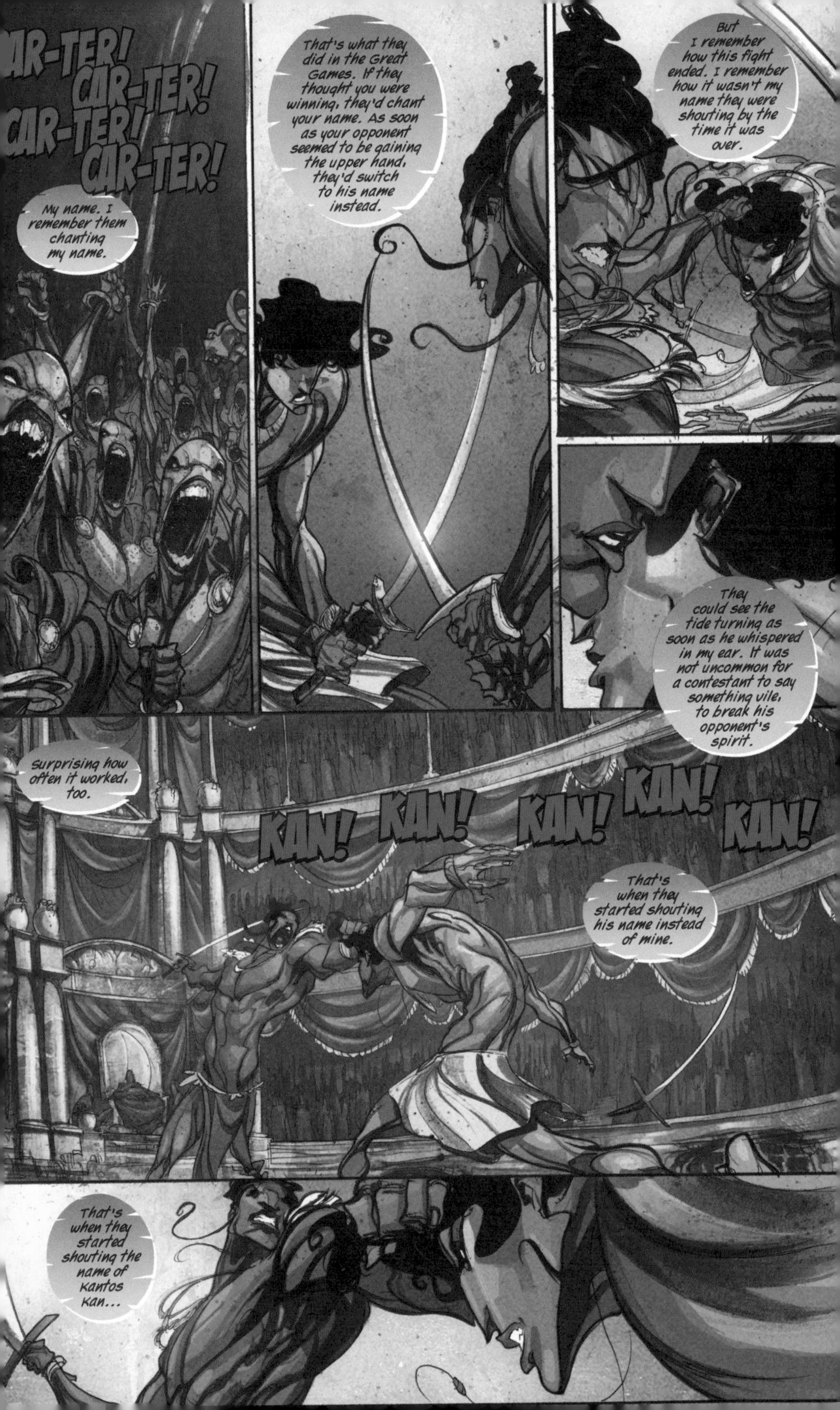
CAR-TER! CAR-TER! CAR-TER! CAR-TER!
My name. I remember them chanting my name.
That's what they did in the Great Games. If they thought you were winning, they'd chant your name. As soon as your opponent seemed to be gaining the upper hand, they'd switch to his name instead.
But I remember how this fight ended. I remember how it wasn't my name they were shouting by the time it was over.
They could see the tide turning as soon as he whispered in my ear. It was not uncommon for a contestant to say something vile, to break his opponent's spirit.
Surprising how often it worked, too.
KAN! KAN! KAN! KAN! KAN!
That's when they started shouting his name instead of mine.
That's when they started shouting the name of Kantos Kan...

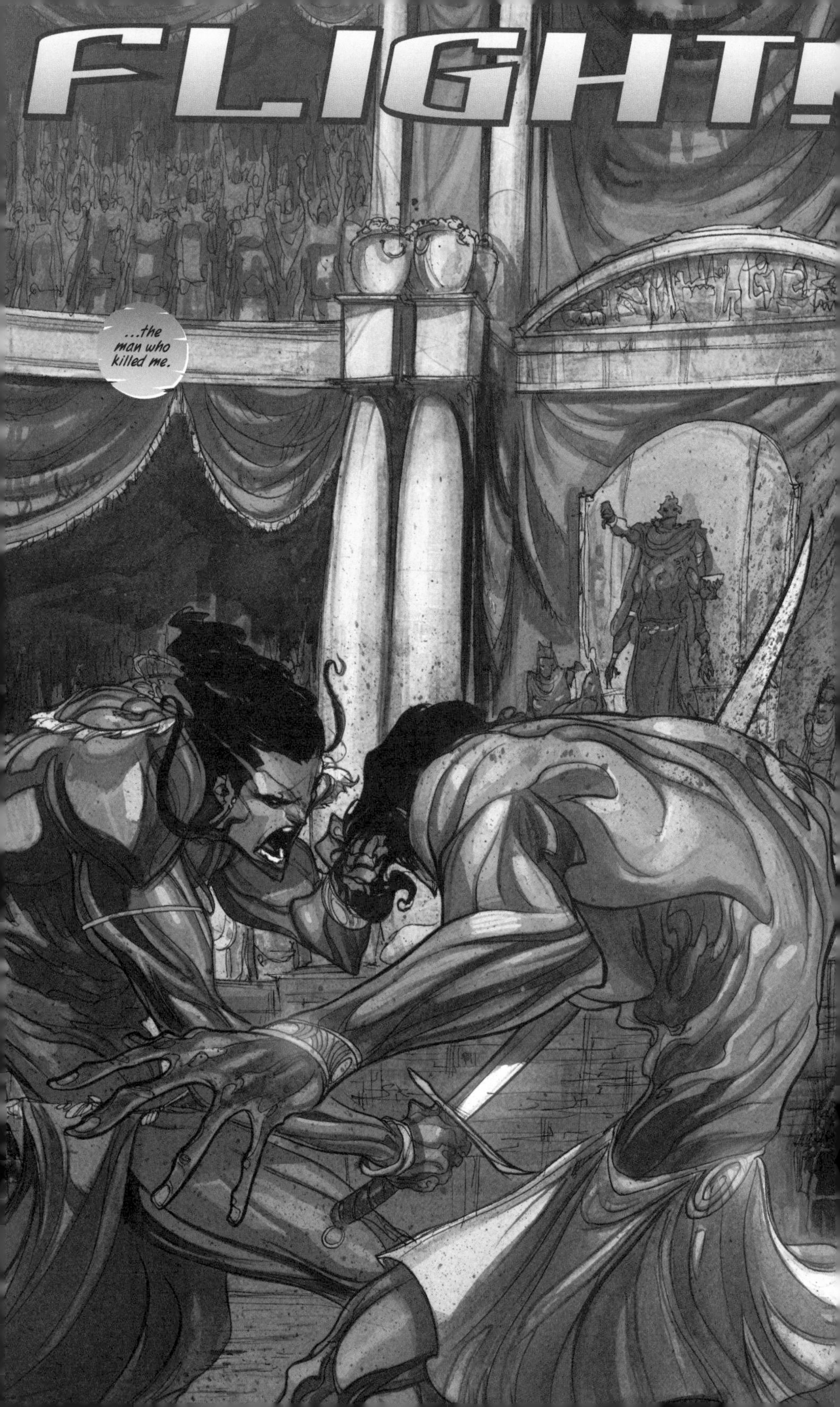
FLIGHT!
...the man who killed me.

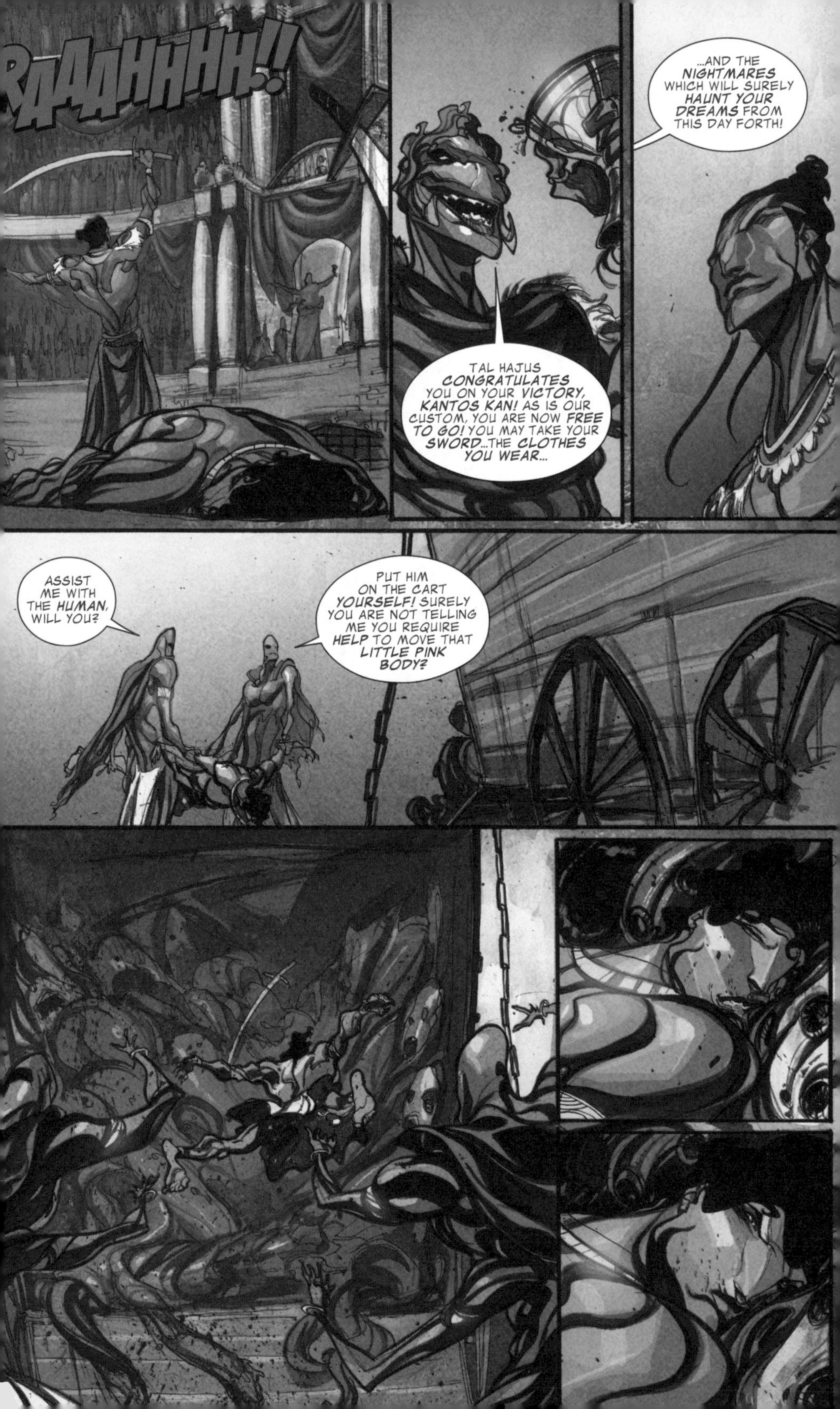
RAAAHHHH!!
TAL HAJUS CONGRATULATES YOU ON YOUR VICTORY, KANTOS KAN! AS IS OUR CUSTOM, YOU ARE NOW FREE TO GO! YOU MAY TAKE YOUR SWORD...THE CLOTHES YOU WEAR...
...AND THE NIGHTMARES WHICH WILL SURELY HAUNT YOUR DREAMS FROM THIS DAY FORTH!
ASSIST ME WITH THE HUMAN, WILL YOU?
PUT HIM ON THE CART YOURSELF! SURELY YOU ARE NOT TELLING ME YOU REQUIRE HELP TO MOVE THAT LITTLE PINK BODY?

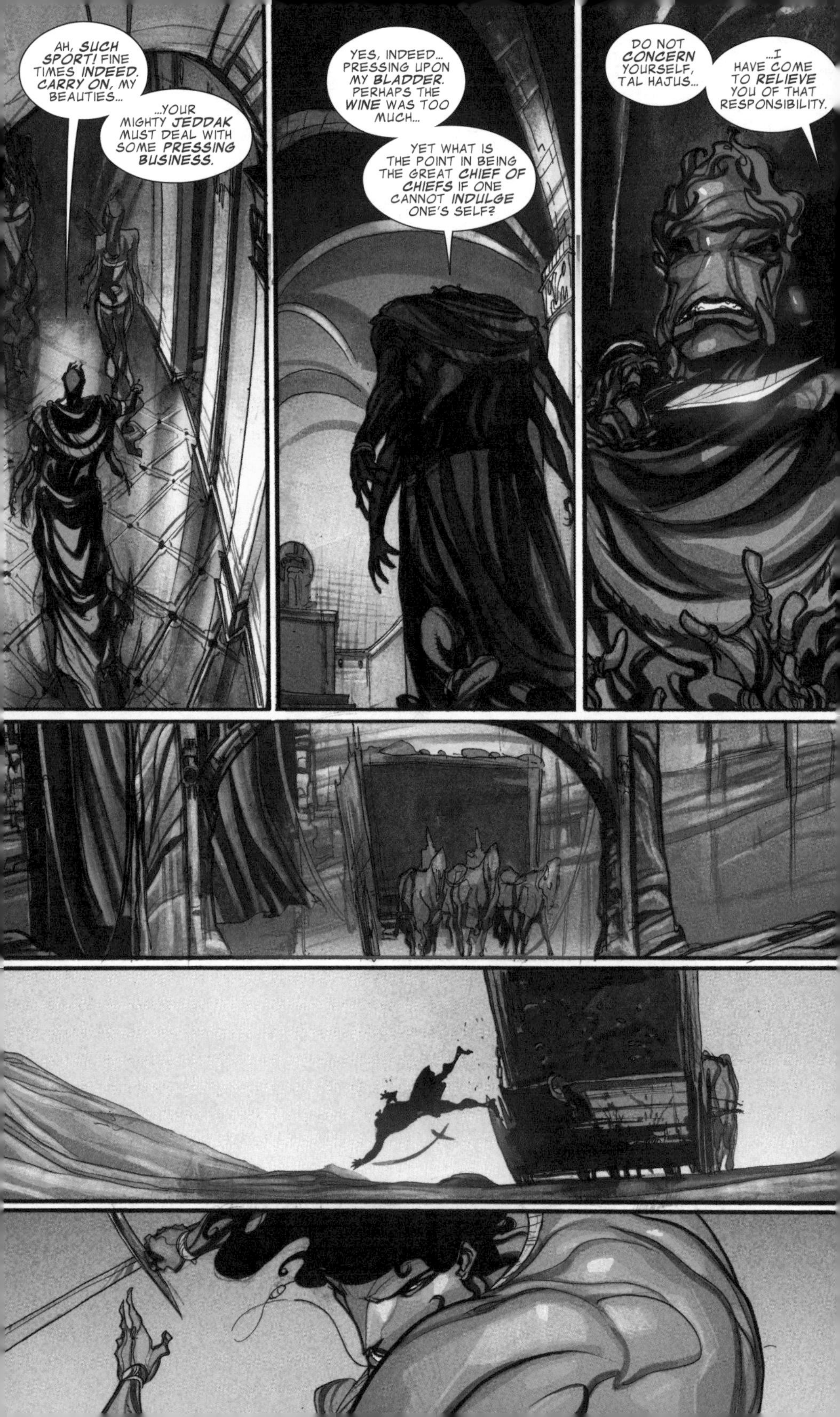
AH, SUCH SPORT! FINE TIMES INDEED. CARRY ON, MY BEAUTIES...
...YOUR MIGHTY JEDDAK MUST DEAL WITH SOME PRESSING BUSINESS.
YES, INDEED... PRESSING UPON MY BLADDER. PERHAPS THE WINE WAS TOO MUCH...
YET WHAT IS THE POINT IN BEING THE GREAT CHIEF OF CHIEFS IF ONE CANNOT INDULGE ONE'S SELF?
DO NOT CONCERN YOURSELF, TAL HAJUS...
...I HAVE COME TO RELIEVE YOU OF THAT RESPONSIBILITY.

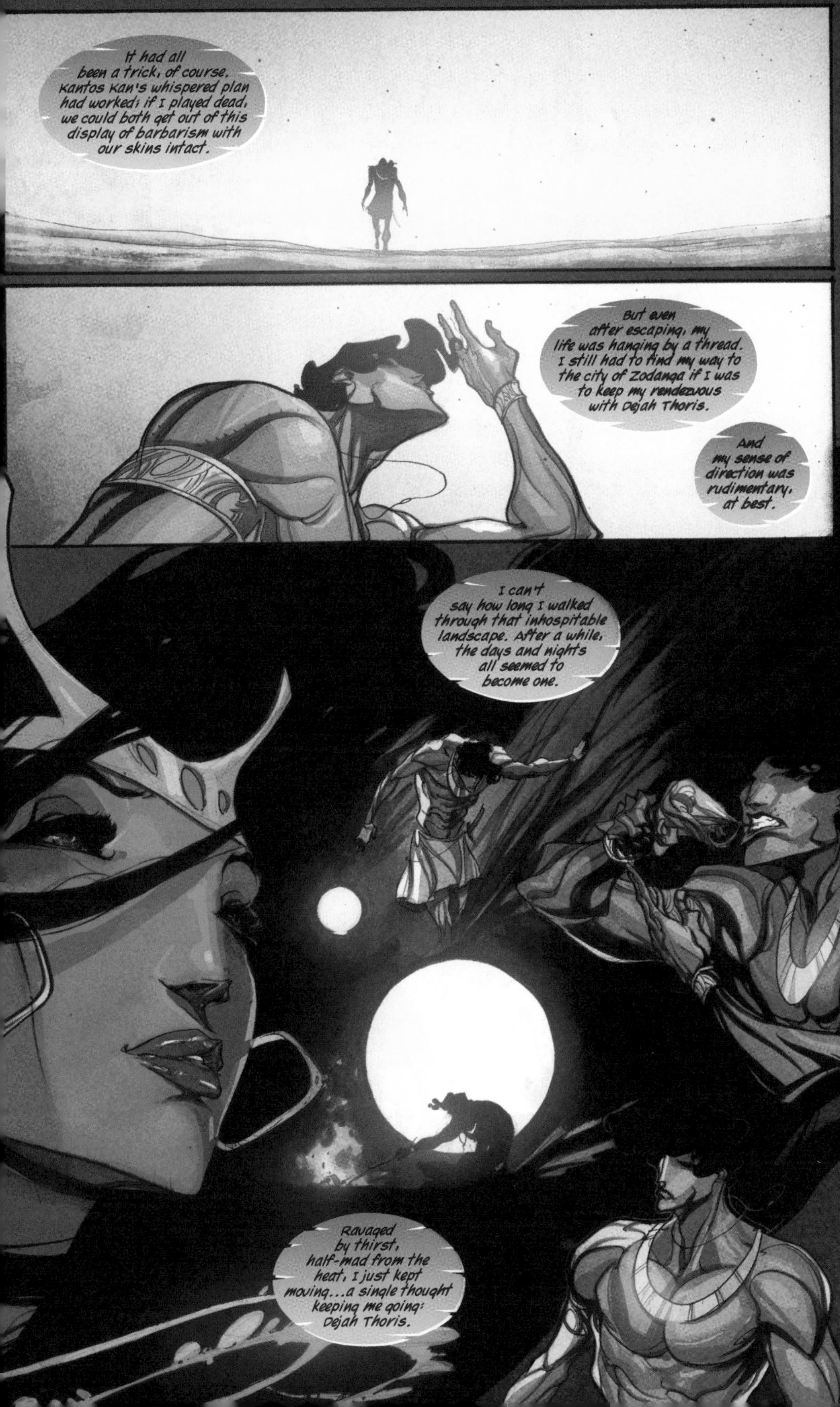
It had all been a trick, of course. Kantos Kan's whispered plan had worked: if I played dead, we could both get out of this display of barbarism with our skins intact.
But even after escaping, my life was hanging by a thread. I still had to find my way to the city of Zodanga if I was to keep my rendezvous with Dejah Thoris.
And my sense of direction was rudimentary, at best.
I can't say how long I walked through that inhospitable landscape. After a while, the days and nights all seemed to become one.
Ravaged by thirst, half-mad from the heat, I just kept moving...a single thought keeping me going: Dejah Thoris.

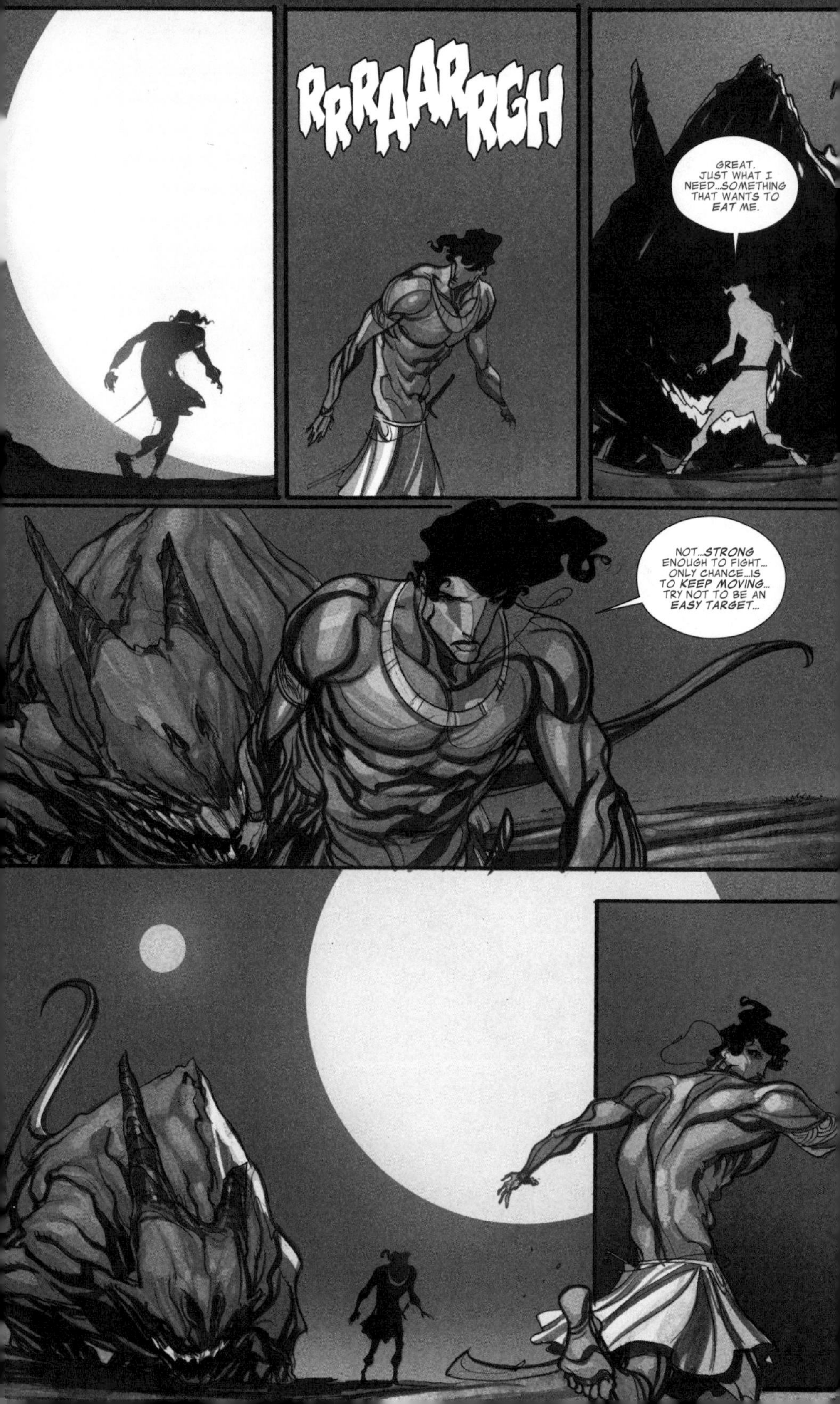
RRRAARRGH
GREAT. JUST WHAT I NEED...SOMETHING THAT WANTS TO EAT ME.
NOT...STRONG ENOUGH TO FIGHT... ONLY CHANCE...IS TO KEEP MOVING... TRY NOT TO BE AN EASY TARGET...

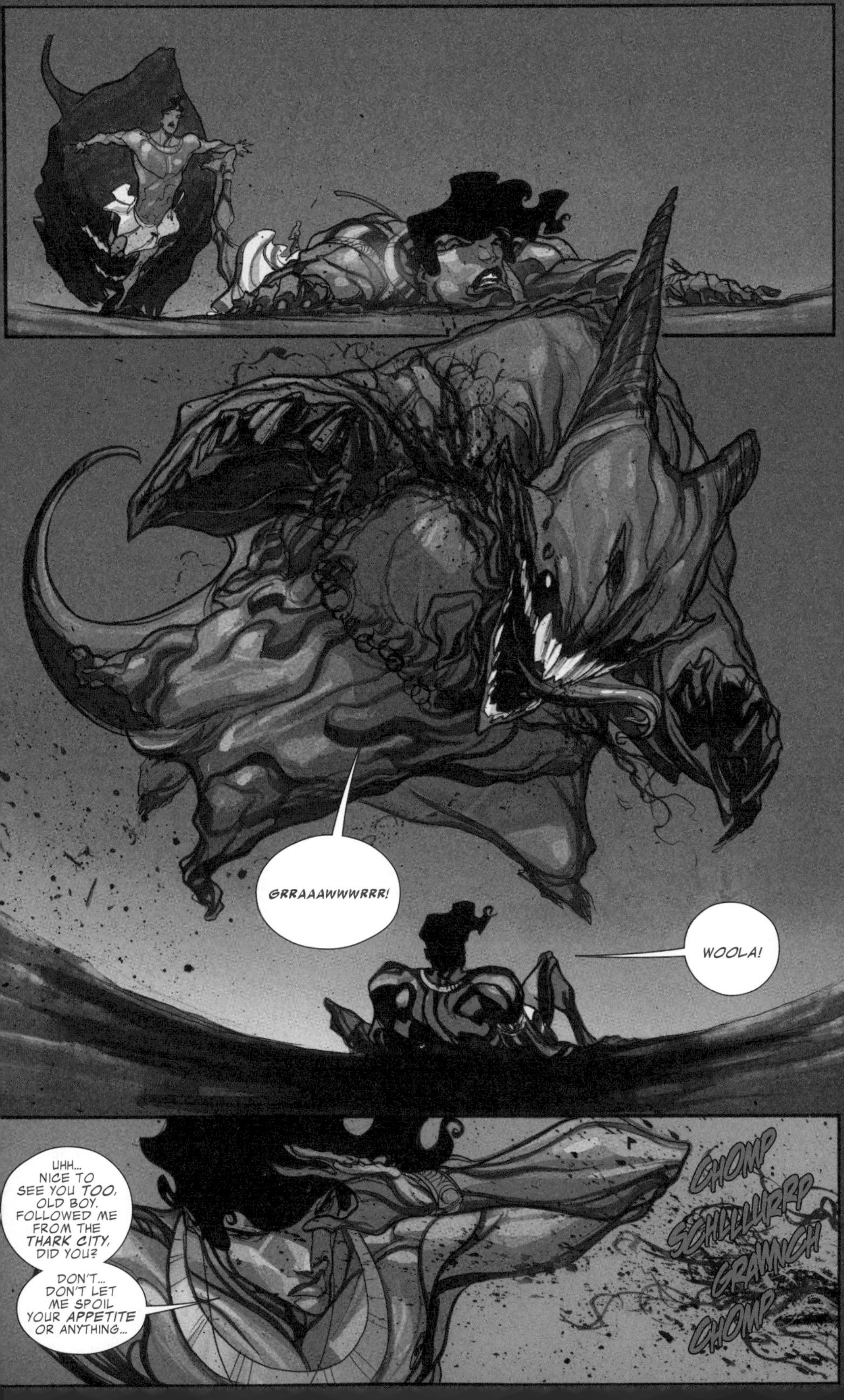
GRRAAAWWWRRR!
WOOLA!
UHH... NICE TO SEE YOU TOO, OLD BOY. FOLLOWED ME FROM THE THARK CITY, DID YOU?
DON'T... DON'T LET ME SPOIL YOUR APPETITE OR ANYTHING...
CHOMP
SCHLLLURRP
GRAWNCH
CHOMP

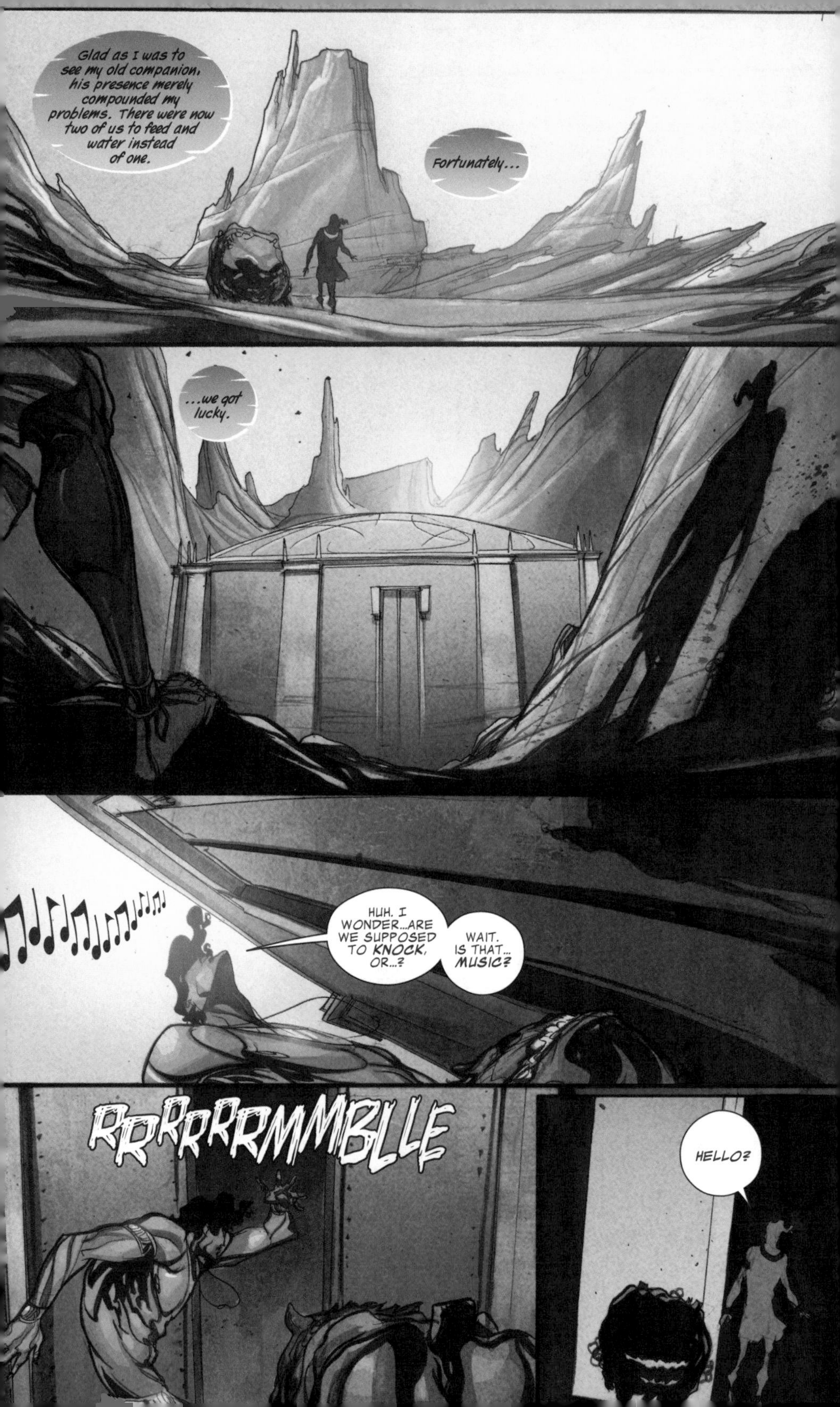
Glad as I was to see my old companion, his presence merely compounded my problems. There were now two of us to feed and water instead of one.
Fortunately...
...we got lucky.
HUH. I WONDER...ARE WE SUPPOSED TO KNOCK, OR...?
WAIT. IS THAT... MUSIC?
RRRRRRMMMBLLE
HELLO?

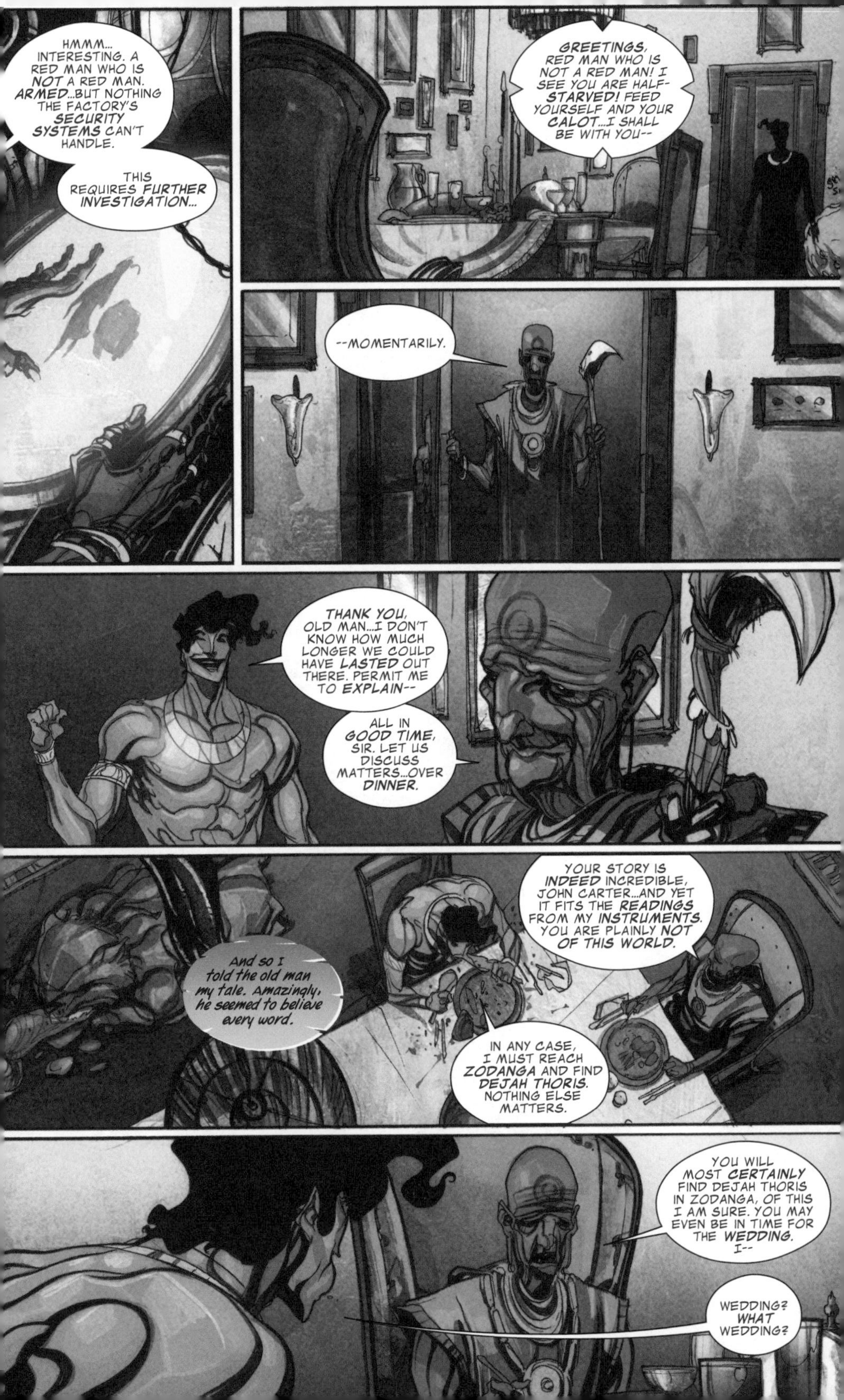
HMMM... INTERESTING. A RED MAN WHO IS NOT A RED MAN. ARMED...BUT NOTHING THE FACTORY'S SECURITY SYSTEMS CAN'T HANDLE.
THIS REQUIRES FURTHER INVESTIGATION...
GREETINGS, RED MAN WHO IS NOT A RED MAN! I SEE YOU ARE HALF-STARVED! FEED YOURSELF AND YOUR CALOT...I SHALL BE WITH YOU--
--MOMENTARILY.
THANK YOU, OLD MAN...I DON'T KNOW HOW MUCH LONGER WE COULD HAVE LASTED OUT THERE. PERMIT ME TO EXPLAIN--
ALL IN GOOD TIME, SIR. LET US DISCUSS MATTERS...OVER DINNER.
And so I told the old man my tale. Amazingly, he seemed to believe every word.
YOUR STORY IS INDEED INCREDIBLE, JOHN CARTER...AND YET IT FITS THE READINGS FROM MY INSTRUMENTS. YOU ARE PLAINLY NOT OF THIS WORLD.
IN ANY CASE, I MUST REACH ZODANGA AND FIND DEJAH THORIS. NOTHING ELSE MATTERS.
YOU WILL MOST CERTAINLY FIND DEJAH THORIS IN ZODANGA, OF THIS I AM SURE. YOU MAY EVEN BE IN TIME FOR THE WEDDING. I--
WEDDING? WHAT WEDDING?

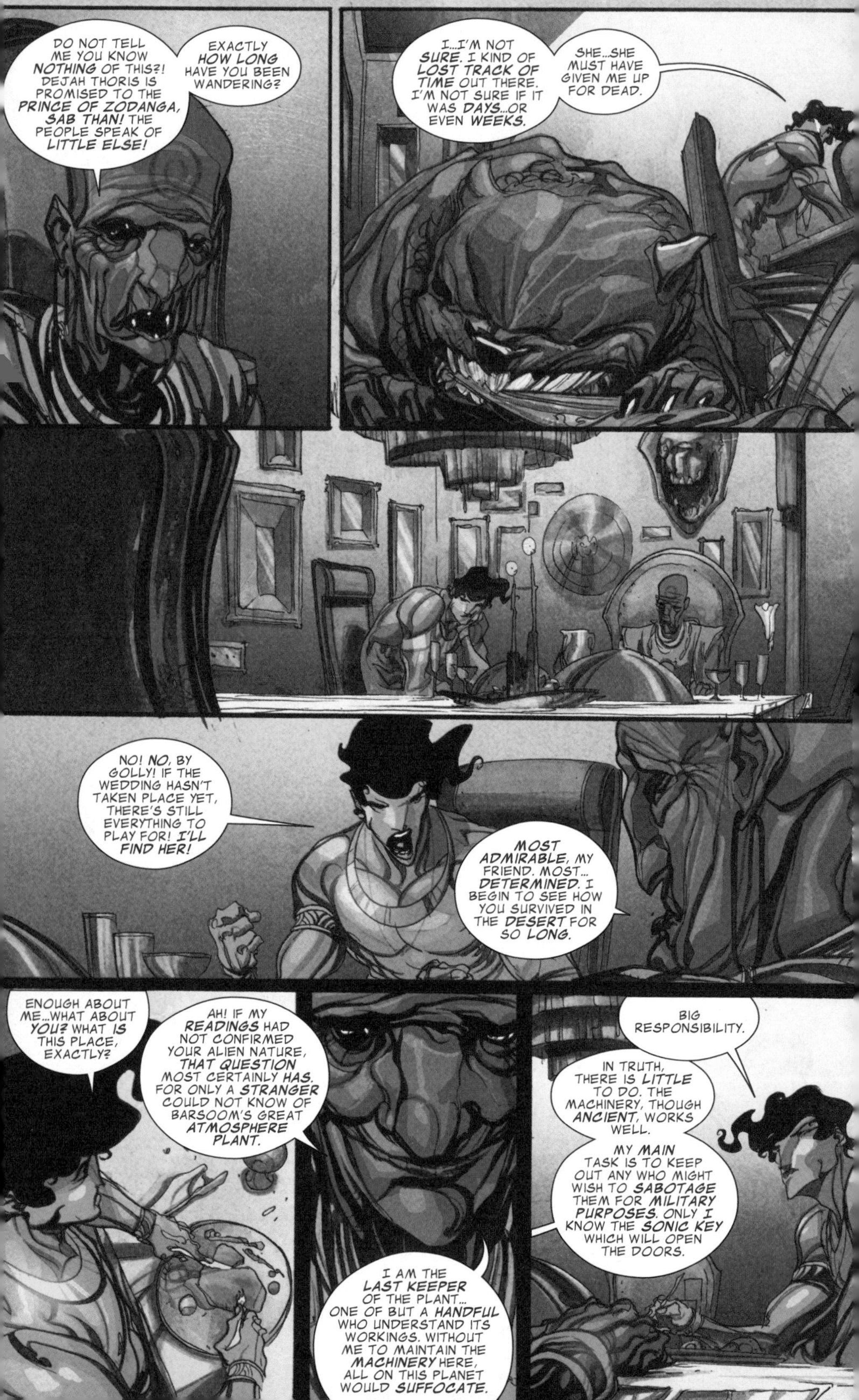
DO NOT TELL ME YOU KNOW NOTHING OF THIS?! DEJAH THORIS IS PROMISED TO THE PRINCE OF ZODANGA, SAB THAN! THE PEOPLE SPEAK OF LITTLE ELSE!
EXACTLY HOW LONG HAVE YOU BEEN WANDERING?
I...I'M NOT SURE. I KIND OF LOST TRACK OF TIME OUT THERE. I'M NOT SURE IF IT WAS DAYS...OR EVEN WEEKS.
SHE...SHE MUST HAVE GIVEN ME UP FOR DEAD.
NO! NO, BY GOLLY! IF THE WEDDING HASN'T TAKEN PLACE YET, THERE'S STILL EVERYTHING TO PLAY FOR! I'LL FIND HER!
MOST ADMIRABLE, MY FRIEND. MOST... DETERMINED. I BEGIN TO SEE HOW YOU SURVIVED IN THE DESERT FOR SO LONG.
ENOUGH ABOUT ME...WHAT ABOUT YOU? WHAT IS THIS PLACE, EXACTLY?
AH! IF MY READINGS HAD NOT CONFIRMED YOUR ALIEN NATURE, THAT QUESTION MOST CERTAINLY HAS. FOR ONLY A STRANGER COULD NOT KNOW OF BARSOOM'S GREAT ATMOSPHERE PLANT.
I AM THE LAST KEEPER OF THE PLANT... ONE OF BUT A HANDFUL WHO UNDERSTAND ITS WORKINGS. WITHOUT ME TO MAINTAIN THE MACHINERY HERE, ALL ON THIS PLANET WOULD SUFFOCATE.
BIG RESPONSIBILITY.
IN TRUTH, THERE IS LITTLE TO DO. THE MACHINERY, THOUGH ANCIENT, WORKS WELL.
MY MAIN TASK IS TO KEEP OUT ANY WHO MIGHT WISH TO SABOTAGE THEM FOR MILITARY PURPOSES. ONLY I KNOW THE SONIC KEY WHICH WILL OPEN THE DOORS.

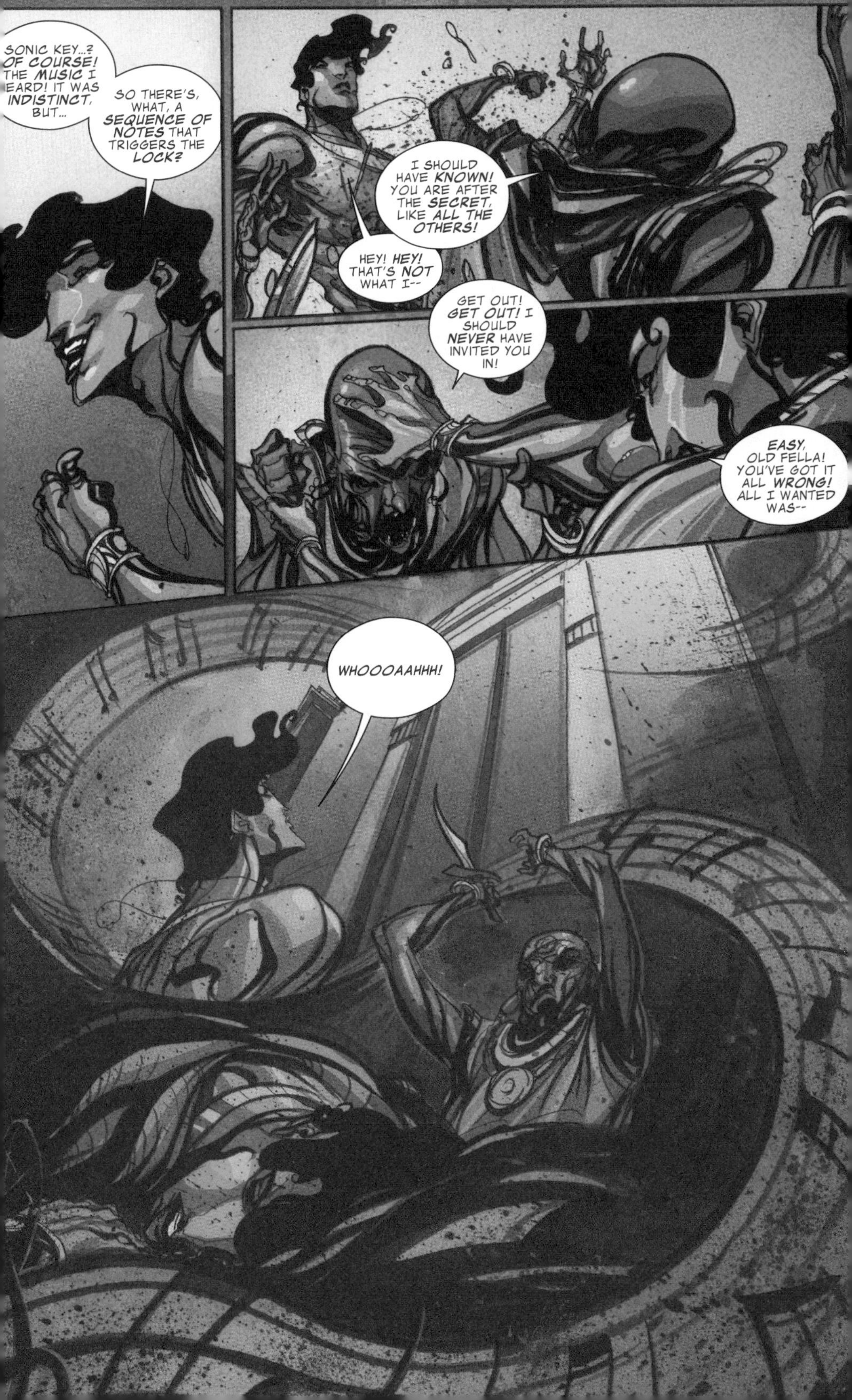
SONIC KEY...? OF COURSE! THE MUSIC I EARD! IT WAS INDISTINCT, BUT...
SO THERE'S, WHAT, A SEQUENCE OF NOTES THAT TRIGGERS THE LOCK?
I SHOULD HAVE KNOWN! YOU ARE AFTER THE SECRET, LIKE ALL THE OTHERS!
HEY! HEY! THAT'S NOT WHAT I--
GET OUT! GET OUT! I SHOULD NEVER HAVE INVITED YOU IN!
EASY, OLD FELLA! YOU'VE GOT IT ALL WRONG! ALL I WANTED WAS--
WHOOOAAHHH!

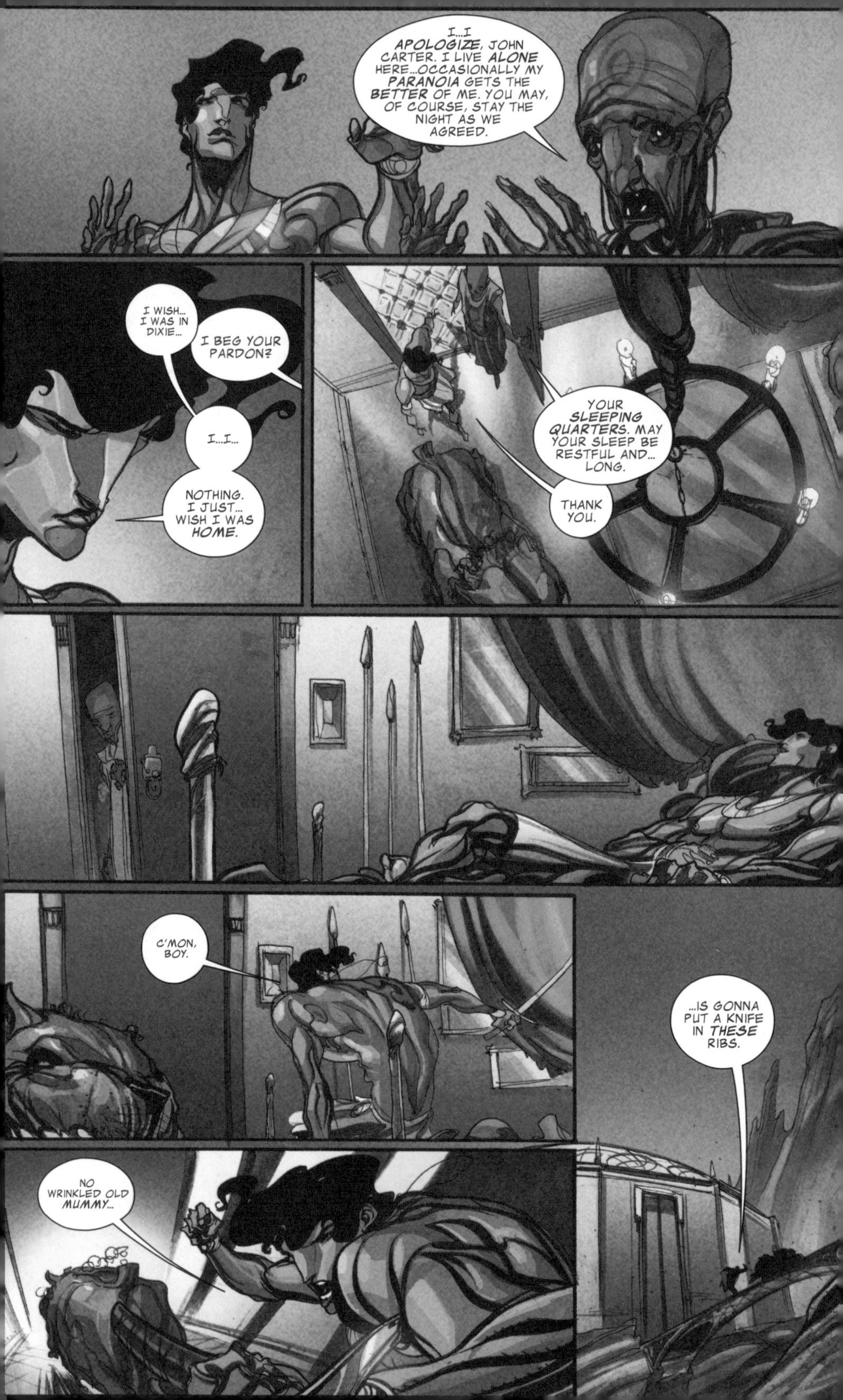

I...I APOLOGIZE, JOHN CARTER. I LIVE ALONE HERE...OCCASIONALLY MY PARANOIA GETS THE BETTER OF ME. YOU MAY, OF COURSE, STAY THE NIGHT AS WE AGREED.
I WISH... I WAS IN DIXIE...
I BEG YOUR PARDON?
I...I...
NOTHING. I JUST... WISH I WAS HOME.
YOUR SLEEPING QUARTERS. MAY YOUR SLEEP BE RESTFUL AND... LONG.
THANK YOU.
C'MON, BOY.
NO WRINKLED OLD MUMMY...
...IS GONNA PUT A KNIFE IN THESE RIBS.

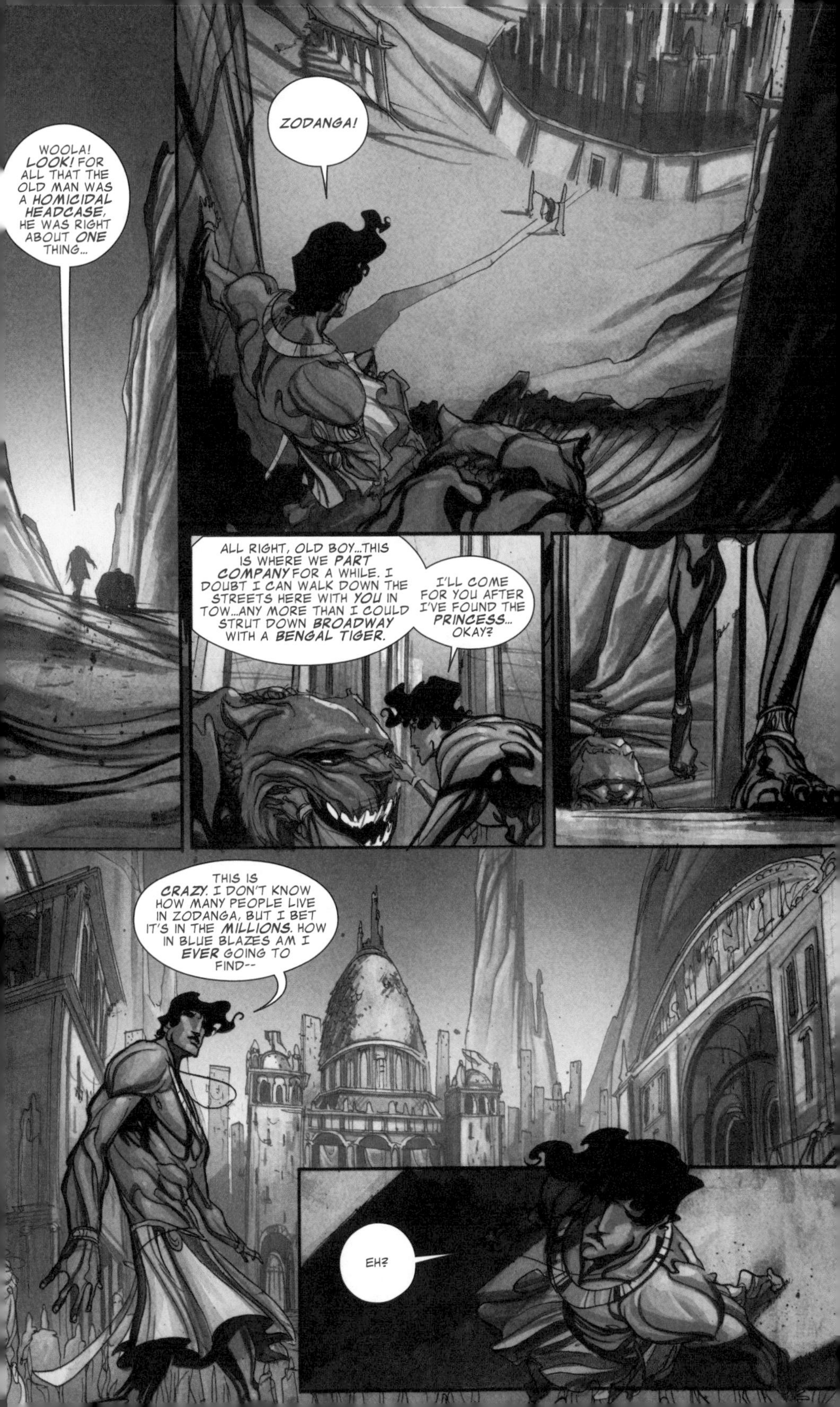
WOOLA! LOOK! FOR ALL THAT THE OLD MAN WAS A HOMICIDAL HEADCASE, HE WAS RIGHT ABOUT ONE THING...
ZODANGA!
ALL RIGHT, OLD BOY...THIS IS WHERE WE PART COMPANY FOR A WHILE. I DOUBT I CAN WALK DOWN THE STREETS HERE WITH YOU IN TOW...ANY MORE THAN I COULD STRUT DOWN BROADWAY WITH A BENGAL TIGER.
I'LL COME FOR YOU AFTER I'VE FOUND THE PRINCESS... OKAY?
THIS IS CRAZY. I DON'T KNOW HOW MANY PEOPLE LIVE IN ZODANGA, BUT I BET IT'S IN THE MILLIONS. HOW IN BLUE BLAZES AM I EVER GOING TO FIND--
EH?

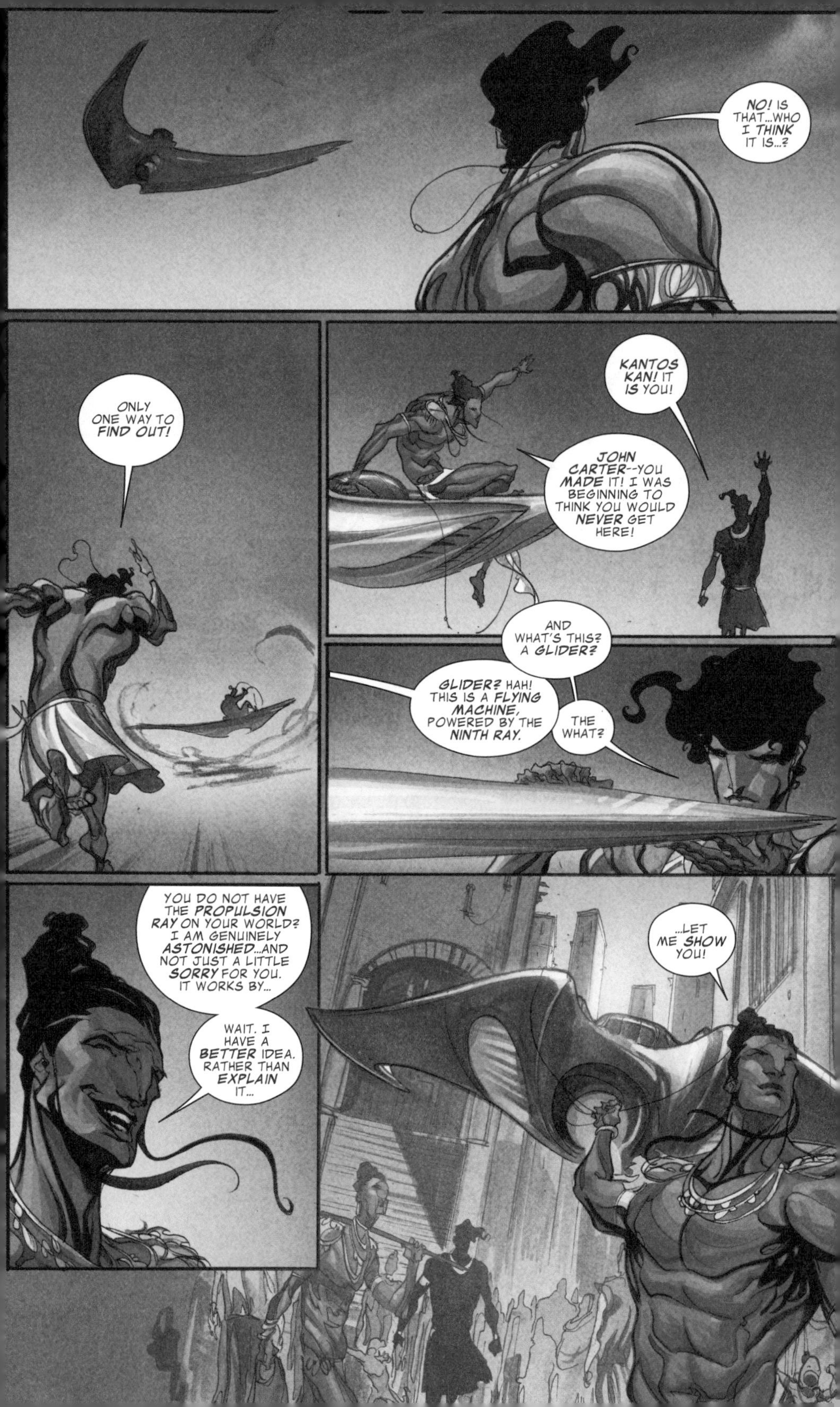
NO! IS THAT...WHO I THINK IT IS...?
ONLY ONE WAY TO FIND OUT!
KANTOS KAN! IT IS YOU!
JOHN CARTER--YOU MADE IT! I WAS BEGINNING TO THINK YOU WOULD NEVER GET HERE!
AND WHAT'S THIS? A GLIDER?
GLIDER? HAH! THIS IS A FLYING MACHINE, POWERED BY THE NINTH RAY.
THE WHAT?
YOU DO NOT HAVE THE PROPULSION RAY ON YOUR WORLD? I AM GENUINELY ASTONISHED...AND NOT JUST A LITTLE SORRY FOR YOU. IT WORKS BY...
WAIT. I HAVE A BETTER IDEA. RATHER THAN EXPLAIN IT...
...LET ME SHOW YOU!

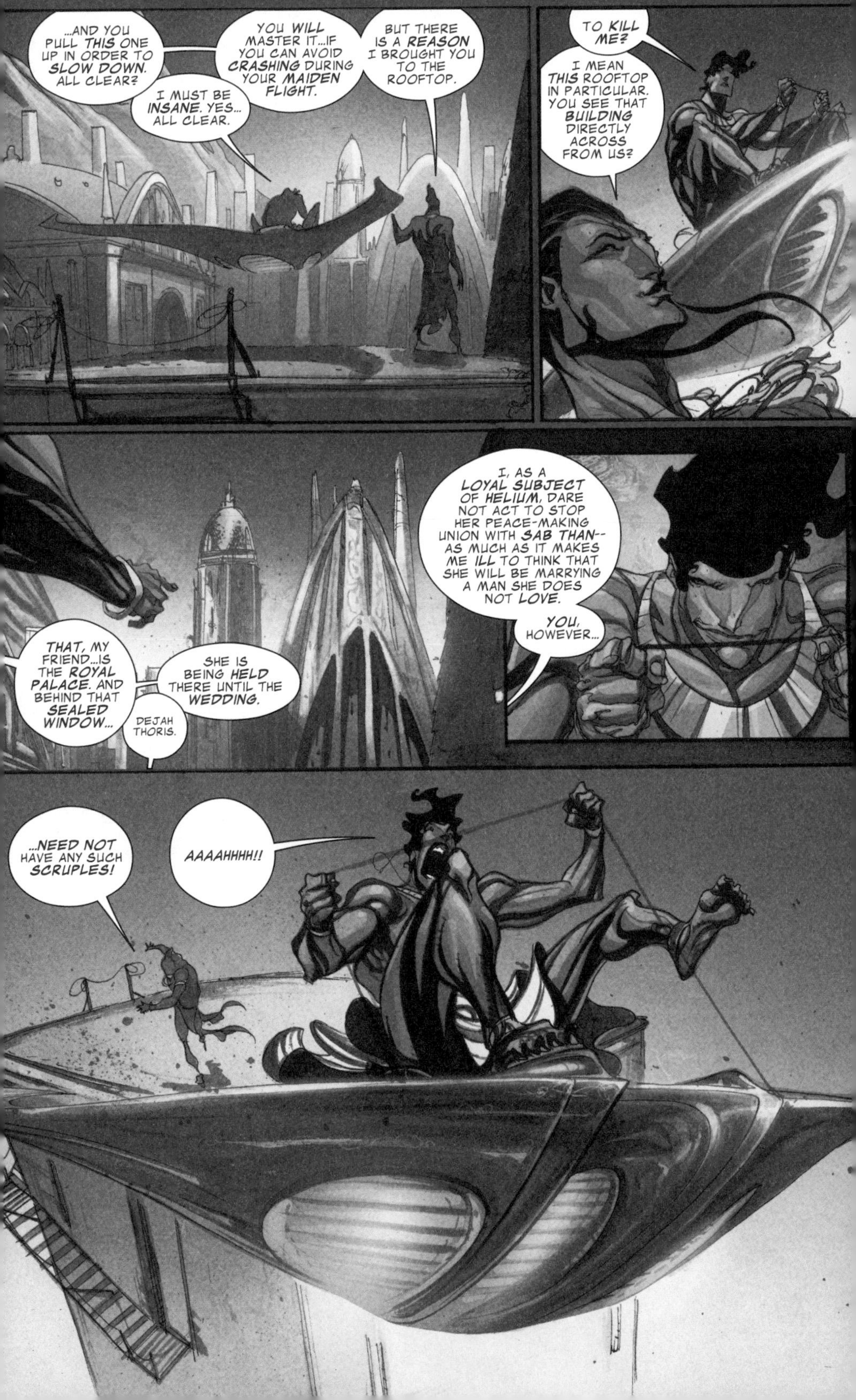
...AND YOU PULL THIS ONE UP IN ORDER TO SLOW DOWN. ALL CLEAR?
I MUST BE INSANE. YES... ALL CLEAR.
YOU WILL MASTER IT...IF YOU CAN AVOID CRASHING DURING YOUR MAIDEN FLIGHT.
BUT THERE IS A REASON I BROUGHT YOU TO THE ROOFTOP.
TO KILL ME?
I MEAN THIS ROOFTOP IN PARTICULAR. YOU SEE THAT BUILDING DIRECTLY ACROSS FROM US?
THAT, MY FRIEND...IS THE ROYAL PALACE. AND BEHIND THAT SEALED WINDOW...
SHE IS BEING HELD THERE UNTIL THE WEDDING.
DEJAH THORIS.
I, AS A LOYAL SUBJECT OF HELIUM, DARE NOT ACT TO STOP HER PEACE-MAKING UNION WITH SAB THAN--AS MUCH AS IT MAKES ME ILL TO THINK THAT SHE WILL BE MARRYING A MAN SHE DOES NOT LOVE.
YOU, HOWEVER...
...NEED NOT HAVE ANY SUCH SCRUPLES!
AAAAHHHH!!

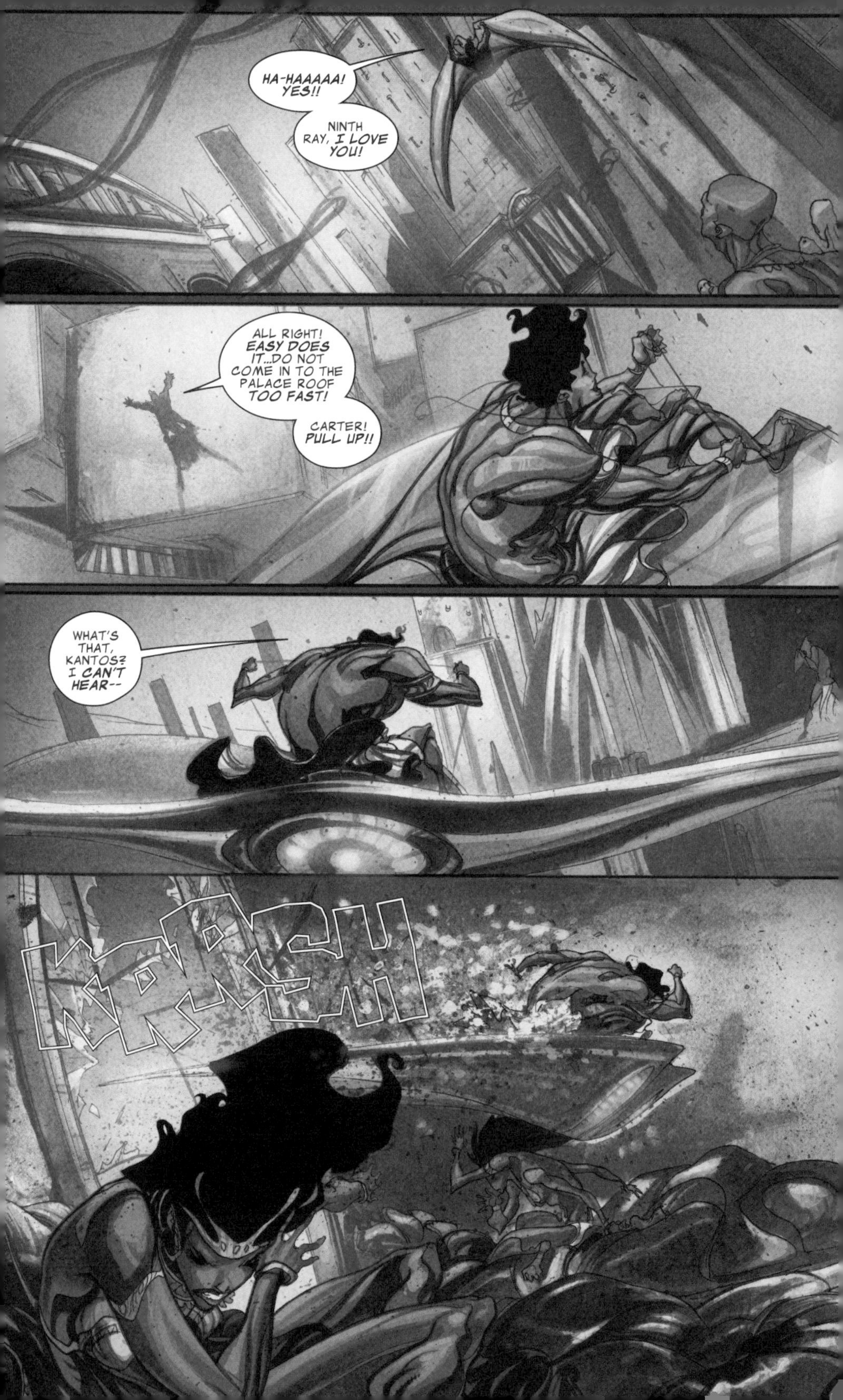
HA-HAAAAA! YES!!
NINTH RAY, I LOVE YOU!
ALL RIGHT! EASY DOES IT...DO NOT COME IN TO THE PALACE ROOF TOO FAST!
CARTER! PULL UP!!
WHAT'S THAT, KANTOS? I CAN'T HEAR--
KRASH

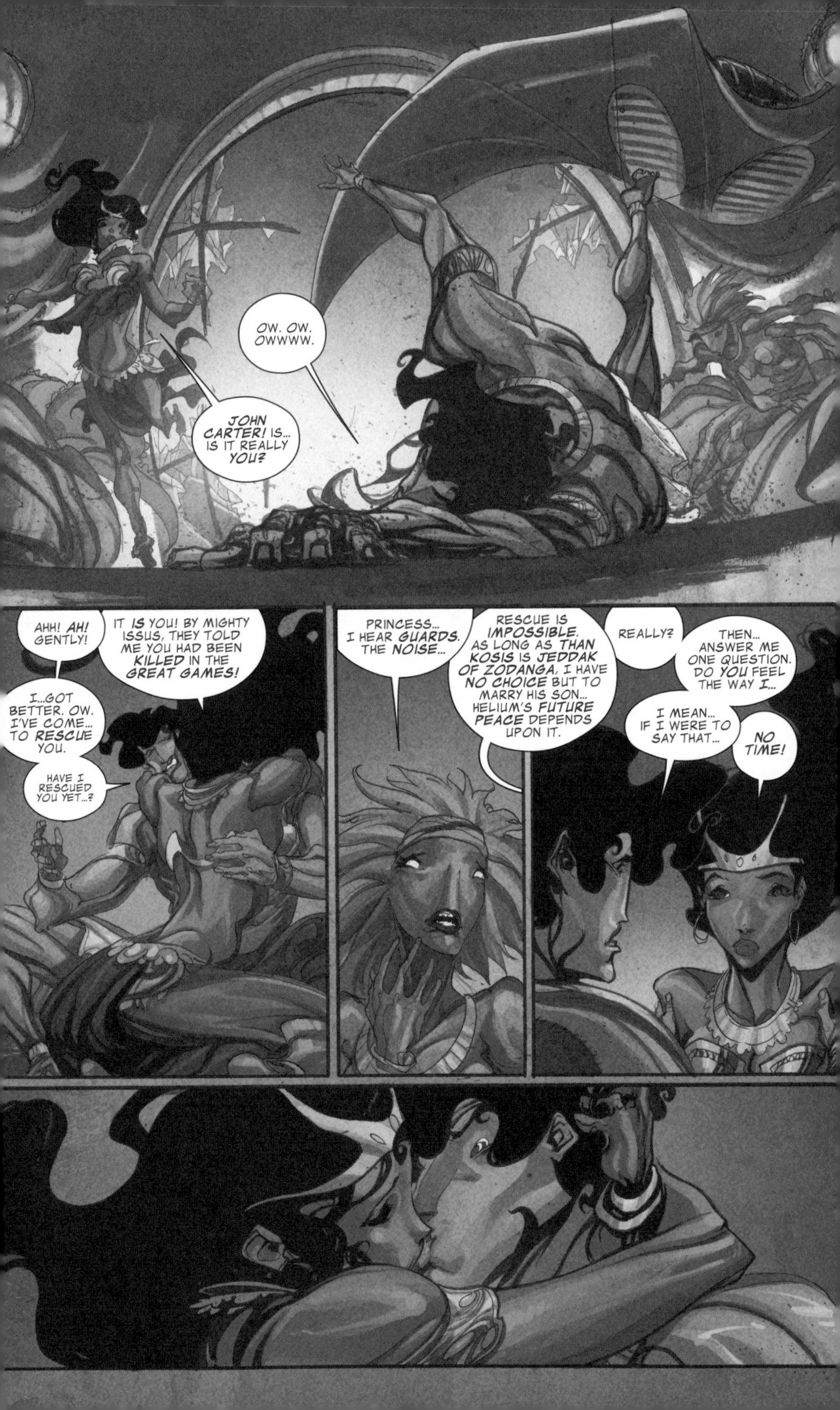

OW. OW. OWWWW.
JOHN CARTER! IS... IS IT REALLY YOU?
AHH! AH! GENTLY!
IT IS YOU! BY MIGHTY ISSUS, THEY TOLD ME YOU HAD BEEN KILLED IN THE GREAT GAMES!
I...GOT BETTER. OW. I'VE COME... TO RESCUE YOU.
HAVE I RESCUED YOU YET...?
PRINCESS... I HEAR GUARDS. THE NOISE...
RESCUE IS IMPOSSIBLE. AS LONG AS THAN KOSIS IS JEDDAK OF ZODANGA, I HAVE NO CHOICE BUT TO MARRY HIS SON... HELIUM'S FUTURE PEACE DEPENDS UPON IT.
REALLY?
THEN... ANSWER ME ONE QUESTION. DO YOU FEEL THE WAY I...
I MEAN... IF I WERE TO SAY THAT...
NO TIME!

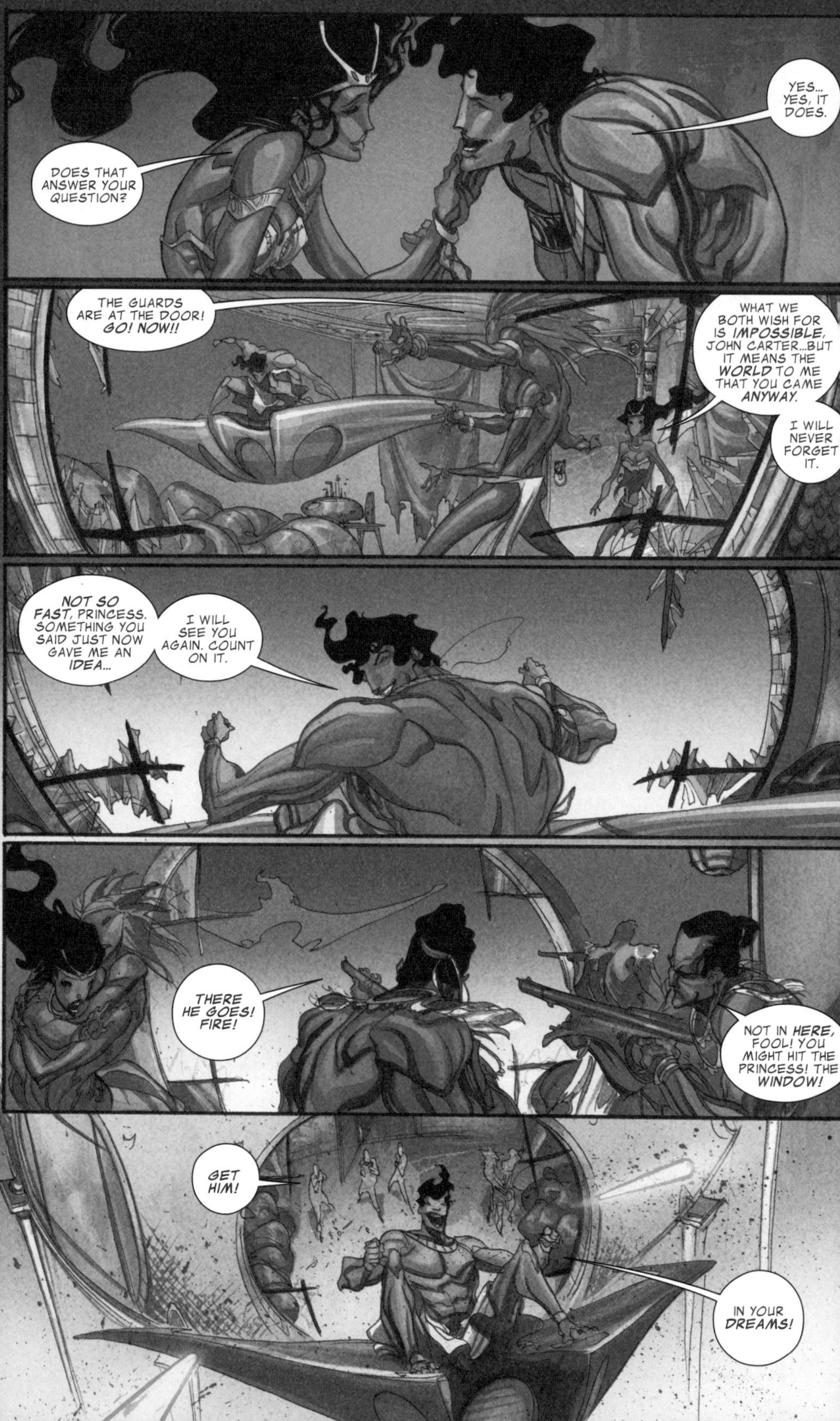
DOES THAT ANSWER YOUR QUESTION?
YES... YES, IT DOES.
THE GUARDS ARE AT THE DOOR! GO! NOW!!
WHAT WE BOTH WISH FOR IS IMPOSSIBLE, JOHN CARTER...BUT IT MEANS THE WORLD TO ME THAT YOU CAME ANYWAY.
I WILL NEVER FORGET IT.
NOT SO FAST, PRINCESS. SOMETHING YOU SAID JUST NOW GAVE ME AN IDEA...
I WILL SEE YOU AGAIN. COUNT ON IT.
THERE HE GOES! FIRE!
NOT IN HERE, FOOL! YOU MIGHT HIT THE PRINCESS! THE WINDOW!
GET HIM!
IN YOUR DREAMS!

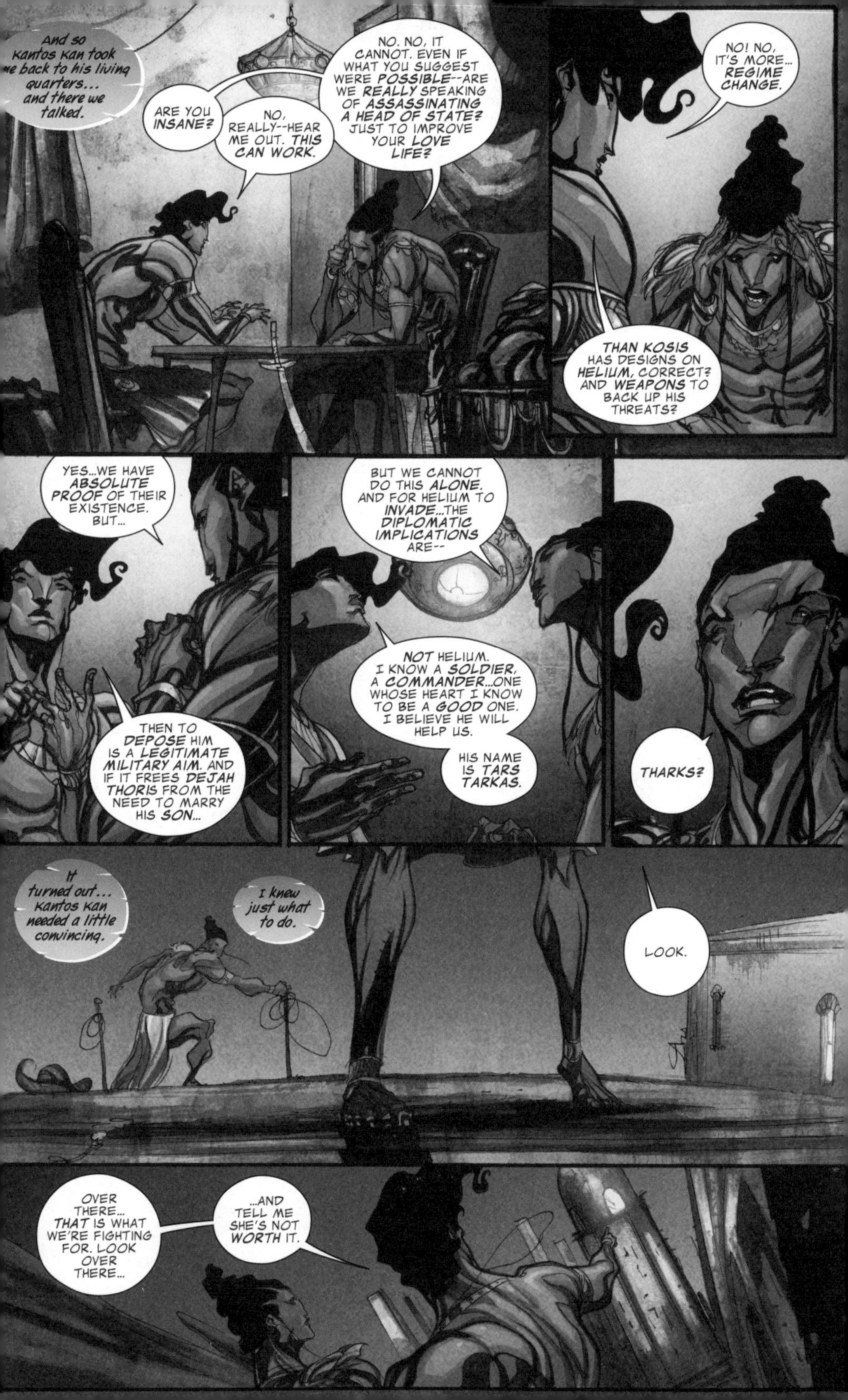
And so Kantos Kan took me back to his living quarters... and there we talked.
ARE YOU INSANE?
NO, REALLY--HEAR ME OUT. THIS CAN WORK.
NO. NO, IT CANNOT. EVEN IF WHAT YOU SUGGEST WERE POSSIBLE--ARE WE REALLY SPEAKING OF ASSASSINATING A HEAD OF STATE? JUST TO IMPROVE YOUR LOVE LIFE?
NO! NO, IT'S MORE... REGIME CHANGE.
THAN KOSIS HAS DESIGNS ON HELIUM, CORRECT? AND WEAPONS TO BACK UP HIS THREATS?
YES...WE HAVE ABSOLUTE PROOF OF THEIR EXISTENCE. BUT...
THEN TO DEPOSE HIM IS A LEGITIMATE MILITARY AIM. AND IF IT FREES DEJAH THORIS FROM THE NEED TO MARRY HIS SON...
BUT WE CANNOT DO THIS ALONE. AND FOR HELIUM TO INVADE...THE DIPLOMATIC IMPLICATIONS ARE--
NOT HELIUM. I KNOW A SOLDIER, A COMMANDER...ONE WHOSE HEART I KNOW TO BE A GOOD ONE. I BELIEVE HE WILL HELP US.
HIS NAME IS TARS TARKAS.
THARKS?
It turned out... Kantos Kan needed a little convincing.
I knew just what to do.
LOOK.
OVER THERE... THAT IS WHAT WE'RE FIGHTING FOR. LOOK OVER THERE...
...AND TELL ME SHE'S NOT WORTH IT.

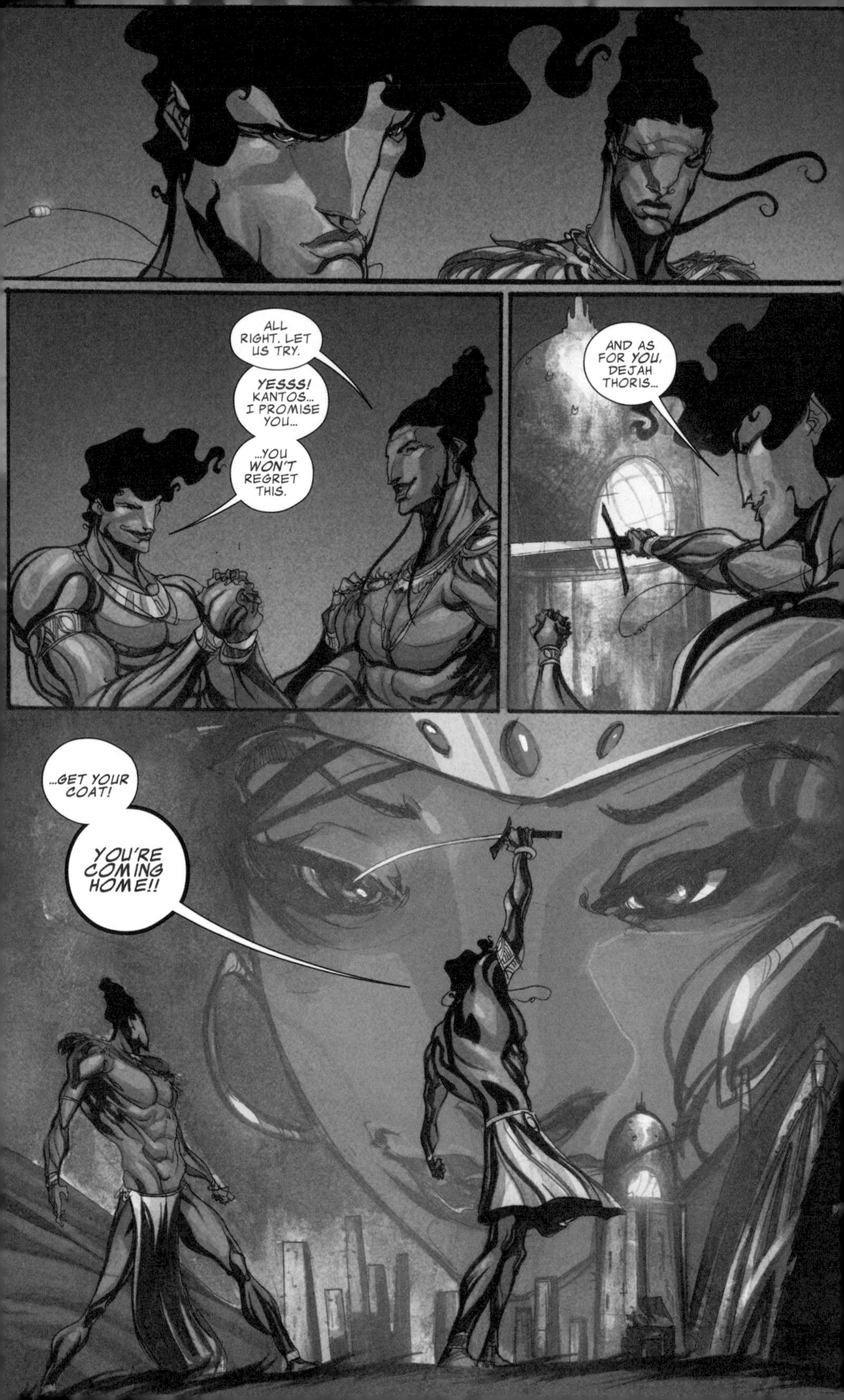
ALL RIGHT. LET US TRY.
YESSS! KANTOS... I PROMISE YOU...
...YOU WON'T REGRET THIS.
AND AS FOR YOU, DEJAH THORIS...
...GET YOUR COAT!
YOU'RE COMING HOME!!

– FIVE –

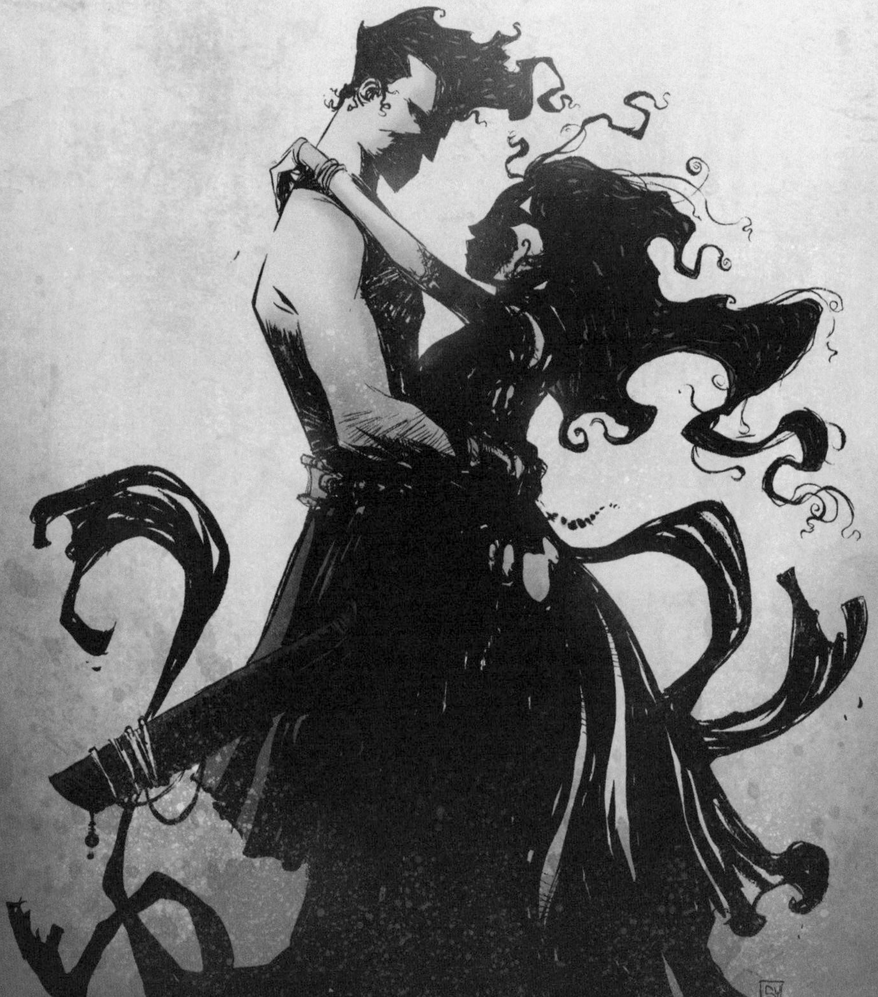

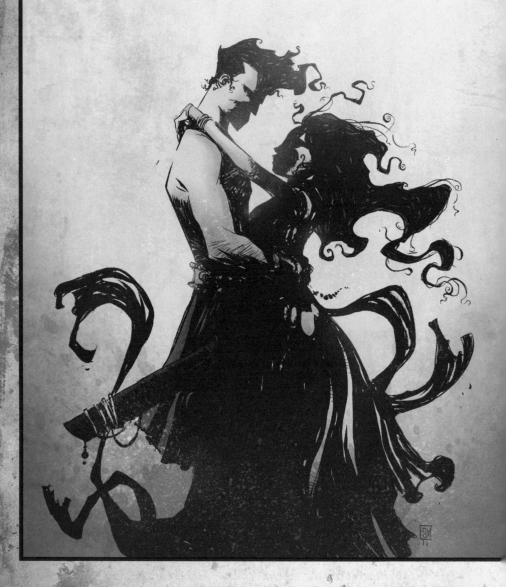

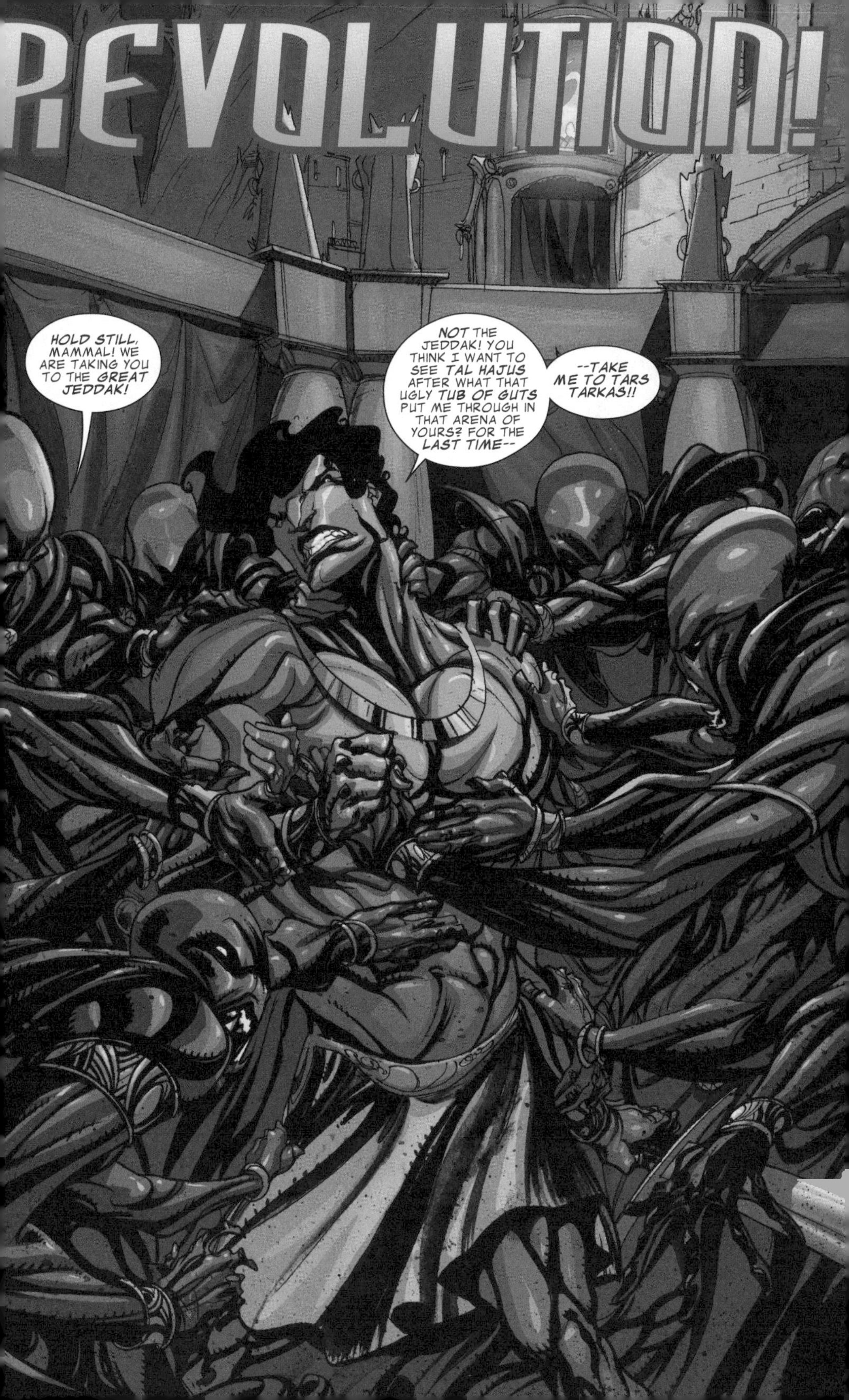
REVOLUTION!
HOLD STILL, MAMMAL! WE ARE TAKING YOU TO THE GREAT JEDDAK!
NOT THE JEDDAK! YOU THINK I WANT TO SEE TAL HAJUS AFTER WHAT THAT UGLY TUB OF GUTS PUT ME THROUGH IN THAT ARENA OF YOURS? FOR THE LAST TIME--
--TAKE ME TO TARS TARKAS!!

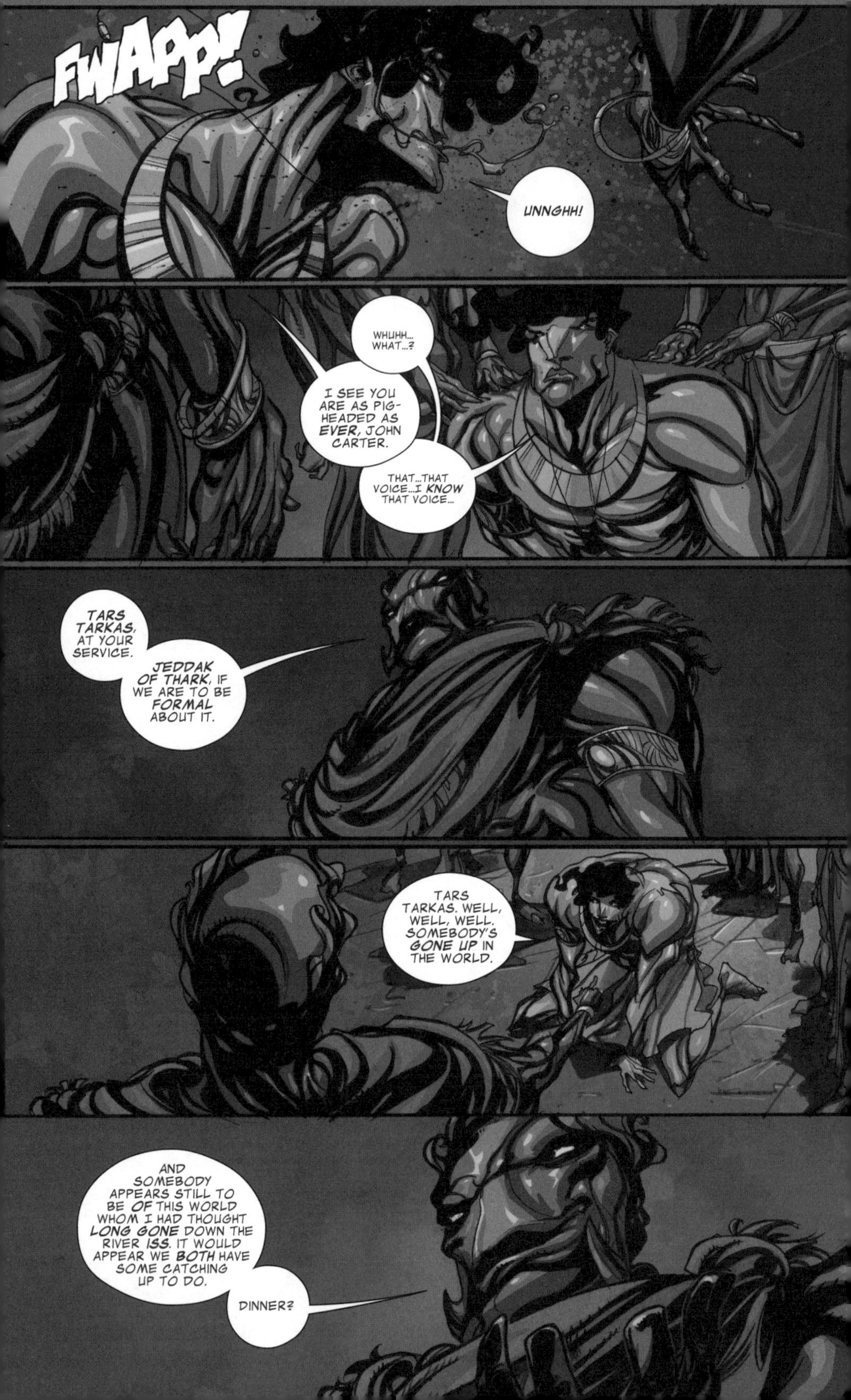
FWAPP!
UNNGHH!
WHUHH... WHAT...?
I SEE YOU ARE AS PIG-HEADED AS EVER, JOHN CARTER.
THAT...THAT VOICE...I KNOW THAT VOICE...
TARS TARKAS, AT YOUR SERVICE.
JEDDAK OF THARK, IF WE ARE TO BE FORMAL ABOUT IT.
TARS TARKAS. WELL, WELL, WELL. SOMEBODY'S GONE UP IN THE WORLD.
AND SOMEBODY APPEARS STILL TO BE OF THIS WORLD WHOM I HAD THOUGHT LONG GONE DOWN THE RIVER ISS. IT WOULD APPEAR WE BOTH HAVE SOME CATCHING UP TO DO.
DINNER?

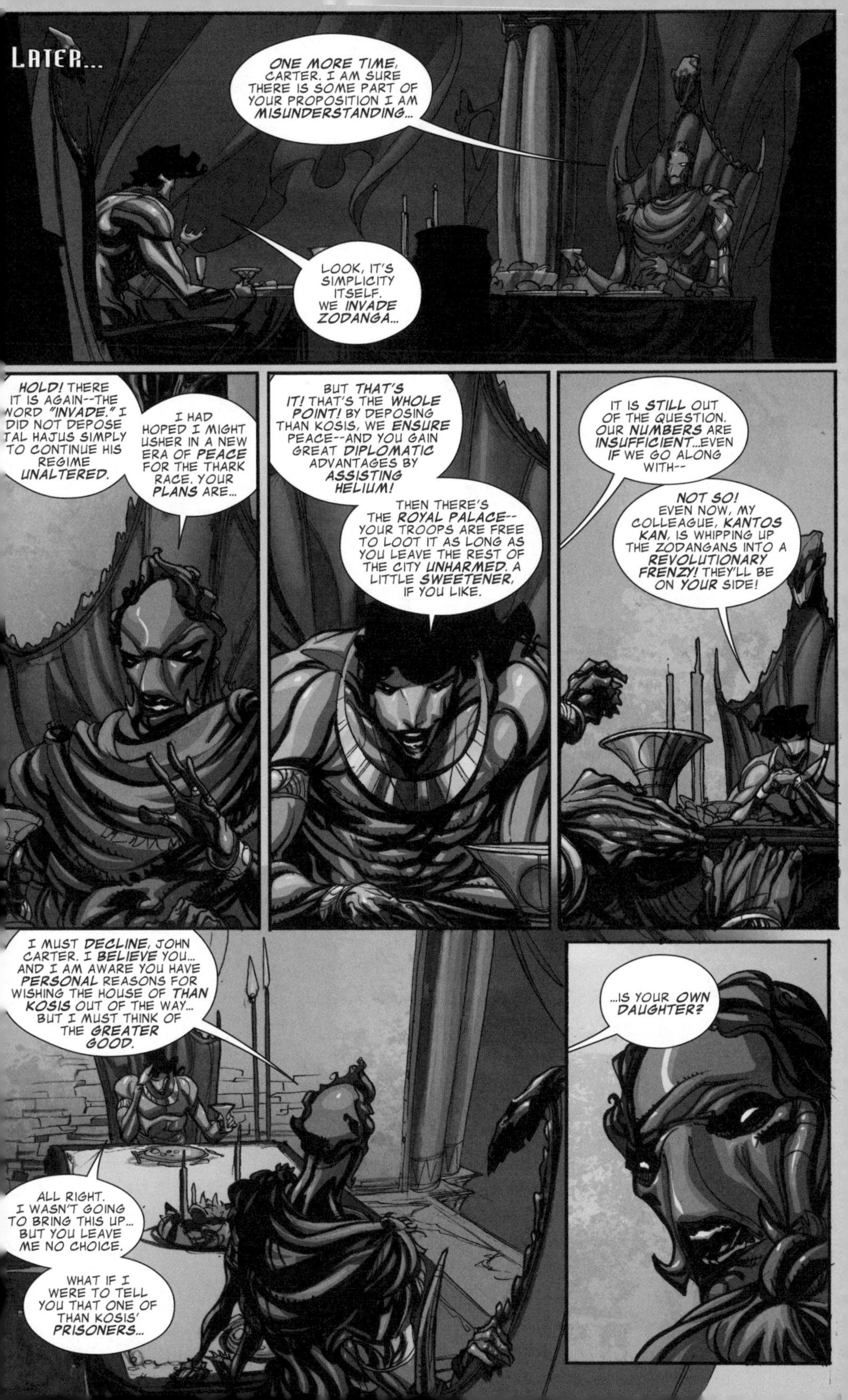
LATER...
ONE MORE TIME, CARTER. I AM SURE THERE IS SOME PART OF YOUR PROPOSITION I AM MISUNDERSTANDING...
LOOK, IT'S SIMPLICITY ITSELF. WE INVADE ZODANGA...
HOLD! THERE IT IS AGAIN--THE WORD "INVADE." I DID NOT DEPOSE TAL HAJUS SIMPLY TO CONTINUE HIS REGIME UNALTERED.
I HAD HOPED I MIGHT USHER IN A NEW ERA OF PEACE FOR THE THARK RACE. YOUR PLANS ARE...
BUT THAT'S IT! THAT'S THE WHOLE POINT! BY DEPOSING THAN KOSIS, WE ENSURE PEACE--AND YOU GAIN GREAT DIPLOMATIC ADVANTAGES BY ASSISTING HELIUM!
THEN THERE'S THE ROYAL PALACE--YOUR TROOPS ARE FREE TO LOOT IT AS LONG AS YOU LEAVE THE REST OF THE CITY UNHARMED. A LITTLE SWEETENER, IF YOU LIKE.
IT IS STILL OUT OF THE QUESTION. OUR NUMBERS ARE INSUFFICIENT...EVEN IF WE GO ALONG WITH--
NOT SO! EVEN NOW, MY COLLEAGUE, KANTOS KAN, IS WHIPPING UP THE ZODANGANS INTO A REVOLUTIONARY FRENZY! THEY'LL BE ON YOUR SIDE!
I MUST DECLINE, JOHN CARTER. I BELIEVE YOU... AND I AM AWARE YOU HAVE PERSONAL REASONS FOR WISHING THE HOUSE OF THAN KOSIS OUT OF THE WAY... BUT I MUST THINK OF THE GREATER GOOD.
ALL RIGHT. I WASN'T GOING TO BRING THIS UP... BUT YOU LEAVE ME NO CHOICE.
WHAT IF I WERE TO TELL YOU THAT ONE OF THAN KOSIS' PRISONERS...
...IS YOUR OWN DAUGHTER?

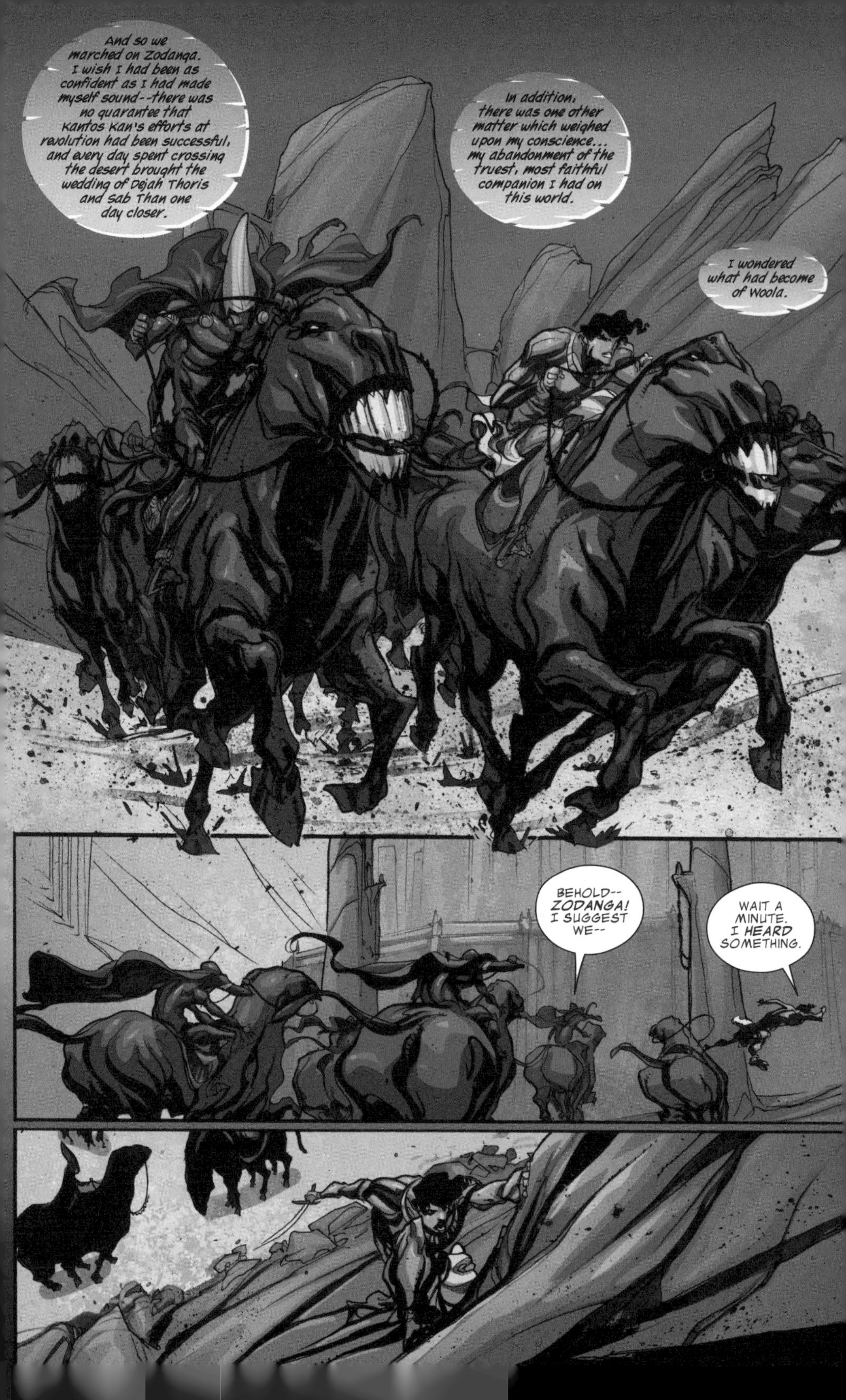

And so we marched on Zodanga. I wish I had been as confident as I had made myself sound--there was no guarantee that Kantos Kan's efforts at revolution had been successful, and every day spent crossing the desert brought the wedding of Dejah Thoris and Sab Than one day closer.
In addition, there was one other matter which weighed upon my conscience... my abandonment of the truest, most faithful companion I had on this world.
I wondered what had become of Woola.
BEHOLD-- ZODANGA! I SUGGEST WE--
WAIT A MINUTE. I HEARD SOMETHING.

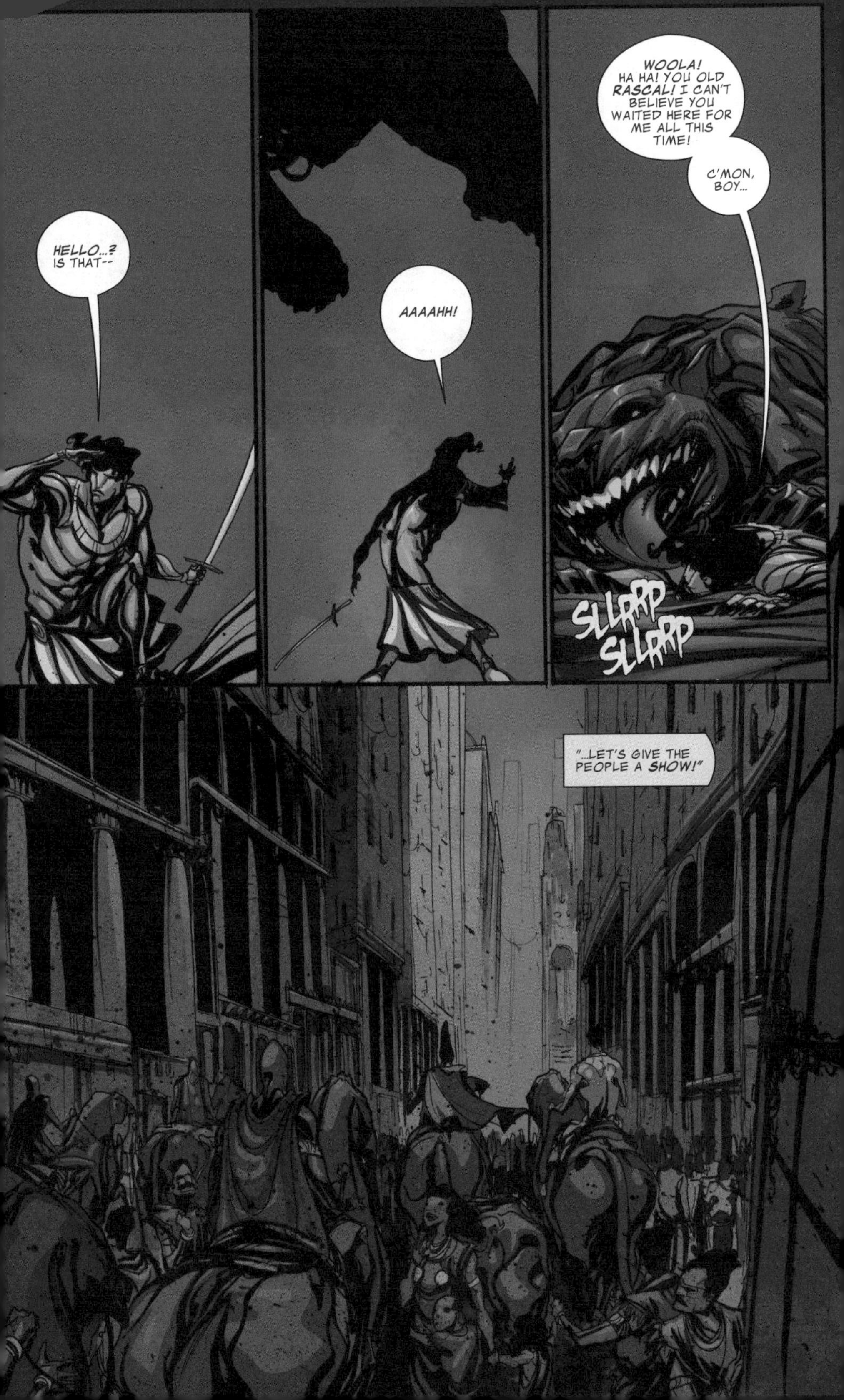
HELLO...? IS THAT--
AAAAHH!
WOOLA! HA HA! YOU OLD RASCAL! I CAN'T BELIEVE YOU WAITED HERE FOR ME ALL THIS TIME!
C'MON, BOY...
SLLRRP SLLRRP
"...LET'S GIVE THE PEOPLE A SHOW!"

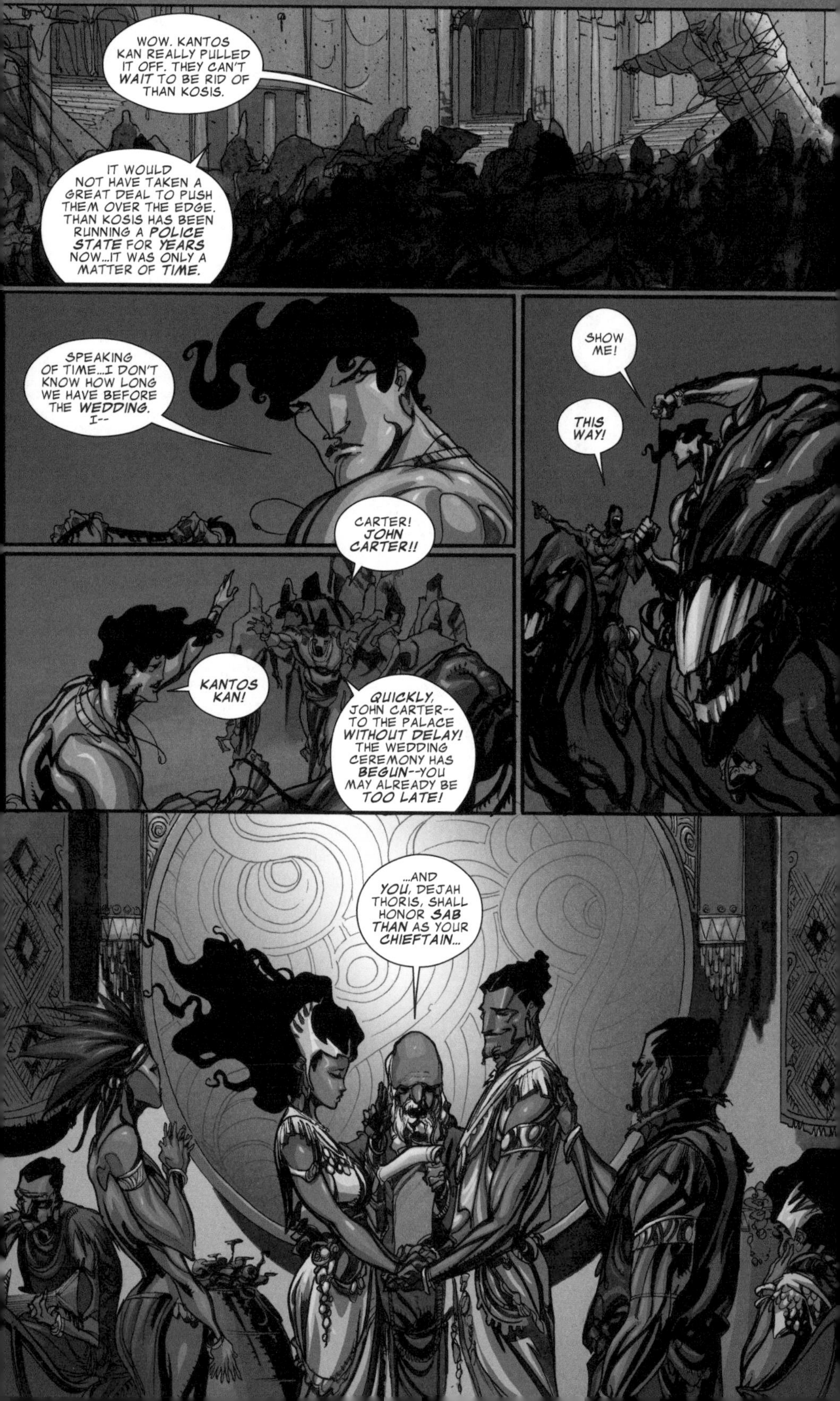
WOW. KANTOS KAN REALLY PULLED IT OFF. THEY CAN'T WAIT TO BE RID OF THAN KOSIS.
IT WOULD NOT HAVE TAKEN A GREAT DEAL TO PUSH THEM OVER THE EDGE. THAN KOSIS HAS BEEN RUNNING A POLICE STATE FOR YEARS NOW...IT WAS ONLY A MATTER OF TIME.
SPEAKING OF TIME...I DON'T KNOW HOW LONG WE HAVE BEFORE THE WEDDING. I--
CARTER! JOHN CARTER!!
KANTOS KAN!
QUICKLY, JOHN CARTER--TO THE PALACE WITHOUT DELAY! THE WEDDING CEREMONY HAS BEGUN--YOU MAY ALREADY BE TOO LATE!
SHOW ME!
THIS WAY!
...AND YOU, DEJAH THORIS, SHALL HONOR SAB THAN AS YOUR CHIEFTAIN...

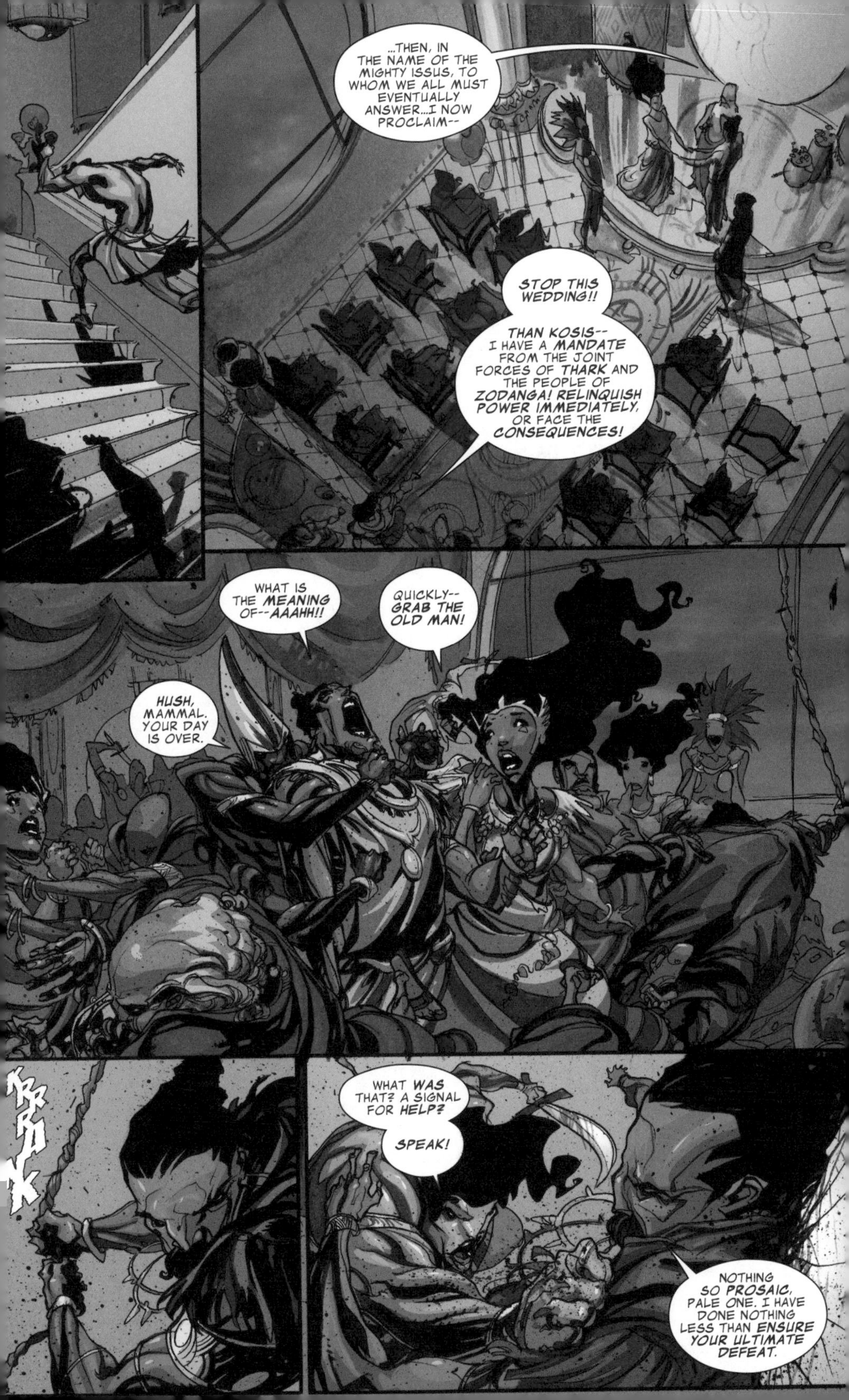
...THEN, IN THE NAME OF THE MIGHTY ISSUS, TO WHOM WE ALL MUST EVENTUALLY ANSWER...I NOW PROCLAIM--
STOP THIS WEDDING!!
THAN KOSIS-- I HAVE A MANDATE FROM THE JOINT FORCES OF THARK AND THE PEOPLE OF ZODANGA! RELINQUISH POWER IMMEDIATELY, OR FACE THE CONSEQUENCES!
WHAT IS THE MEANING OF--AAAHH!!
QUICKLY-- GRAB THE OLD MAN!
HUSH, MAMMAL. YOUR DAY IS OVER.
KRRONK
WHAT WAS THAT? A SIGNAL FOR HELP?
SPEAK!
NOTHING SO PROSAIC, PALE ONE. I HAVE DONE NOTHING LESS THAN ENSURE YOUR ULTIMATE DEFEAT.

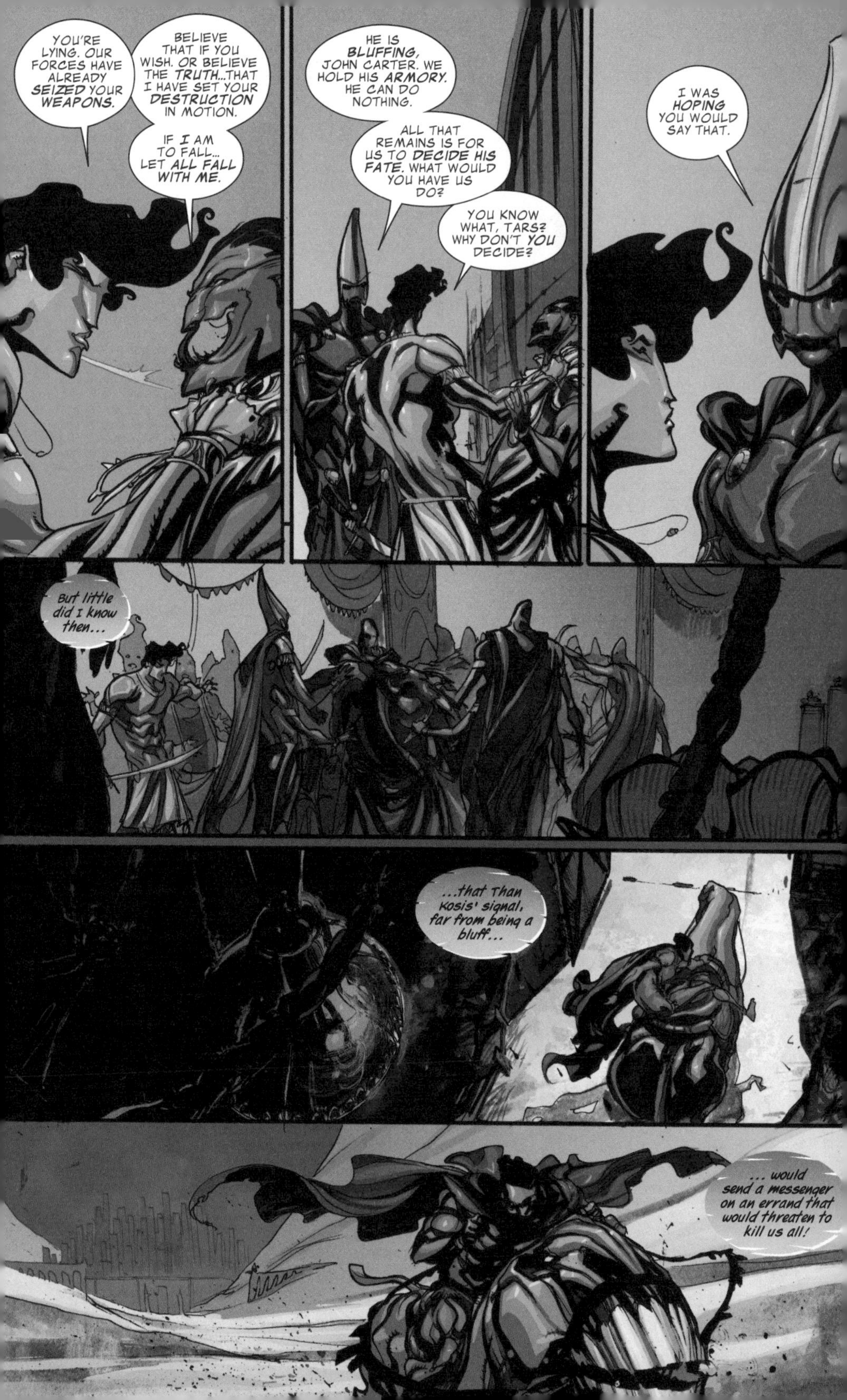
YOU'RE LYING. OUR FORCES HAVE ALREADY SEIZED YOUR WEAPONS.
BELIEVE THAT IF YOU WISH. OR BELIEVE THE TRUTH...THAT I HAVE SET YOUR DESTRUCTION IN MOTION.
IF I AM TO FALL... LET ALL FALL WITH ME.
HE IS BLUFFING, JOHN CARTER. WE HOLD HIS ARMORY. HE CAN DO NOTHING.
ALL THAT REMAINS IS FOR US TO DECIDE HIS FATE. WHAT WOULD YOU HAVE US DO?
YOU KNOW WHAT, TARS? WHY DON'T YOU DECIDE?
I WAS HOPING YOU WOULD SAY THAT.
But little did I know then...
...that Than Kosis' signal, far from being a bluff...
... would send a messenger on an errand that would threaten to kill us all!

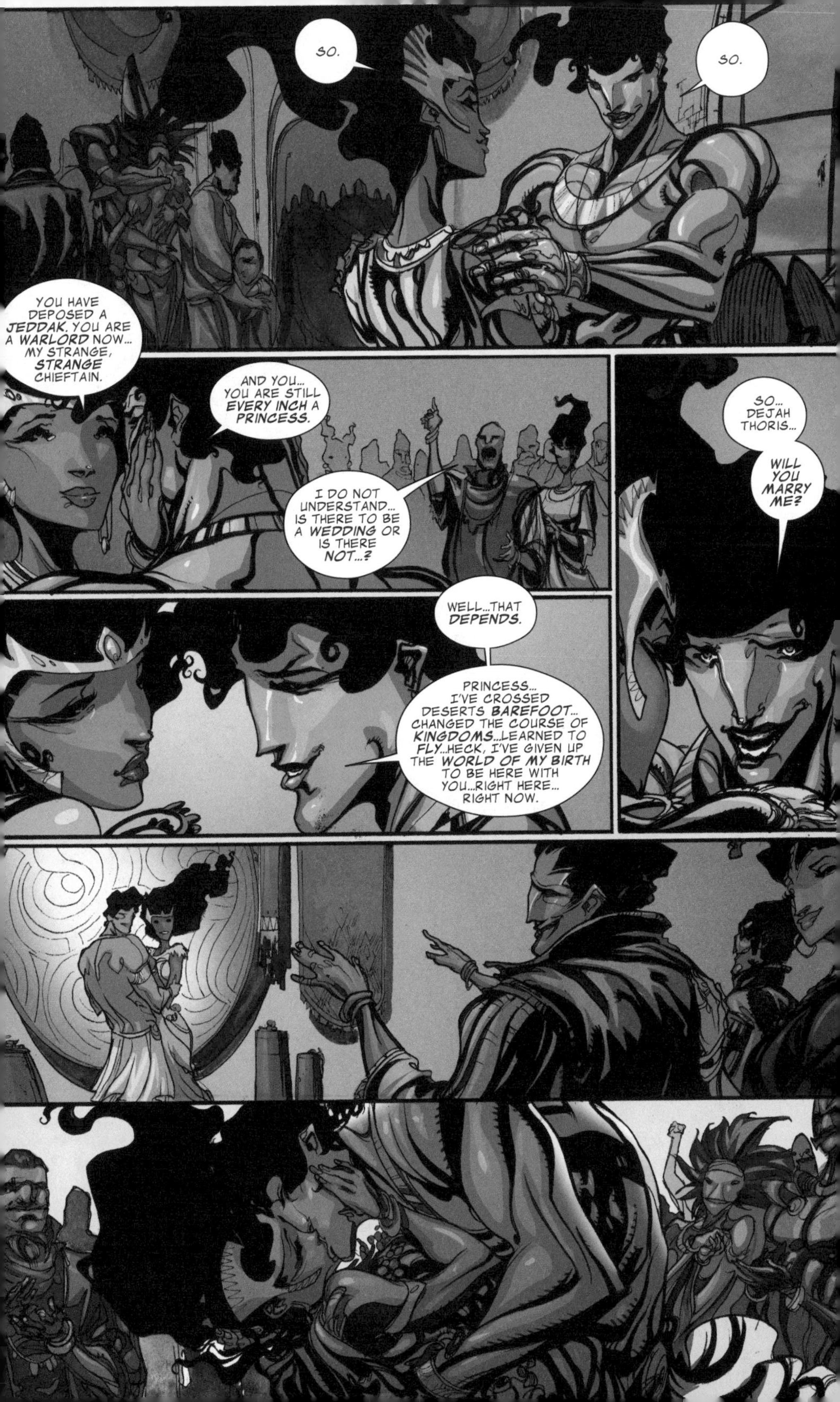
SO.
SO.
YOU HAVE DEPOSED A JEDDAK. YOU ARE A WARLORD NOW... MY STRANGE, STRANGE CHIEFTAIN.
AND YOU... YOU ARE STILL EVERY INCH A PRINCESS.
I DO NOT UNDERSTAND... IS THERE TO BE A WEDDING OR IS THERE NOT...?
WELL...THAT DEPENDS.
PRINCESS... I'VE CROSSED DESERTS BAREFOOT... CHANGED THE COURSE OF KINGDOMS...LEARNED TO FLY...HECK, I'VE GIVEN UP THE WORLD OF MY BIRTH TO BE HERE WITH YOU...RIGHT HERE... RIGHT NOW.
SO... DEJAH THORIS...
WILL YOU MARRY ME?

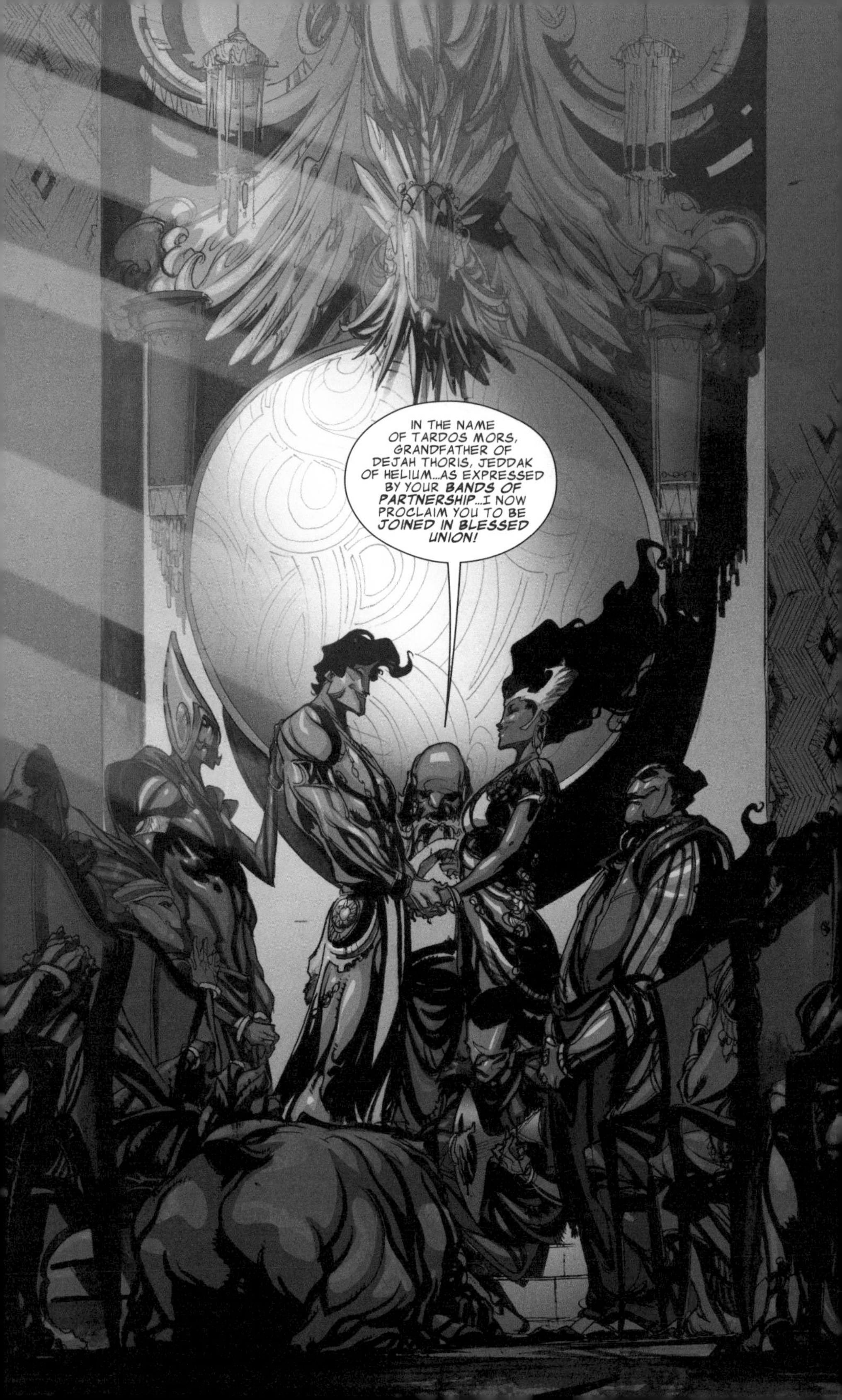
IN THE NAME OF TARDOS MORS, GRANDFATHER OF DEJAH THORIS, JEDDAK OF HELIUM...AS EXPRESSED BY YOUR **BANDS OF PARTNERSHIP**...I NOW PROCLAIM YOU TO BE ***JOINED IN BLESSED UNION!***

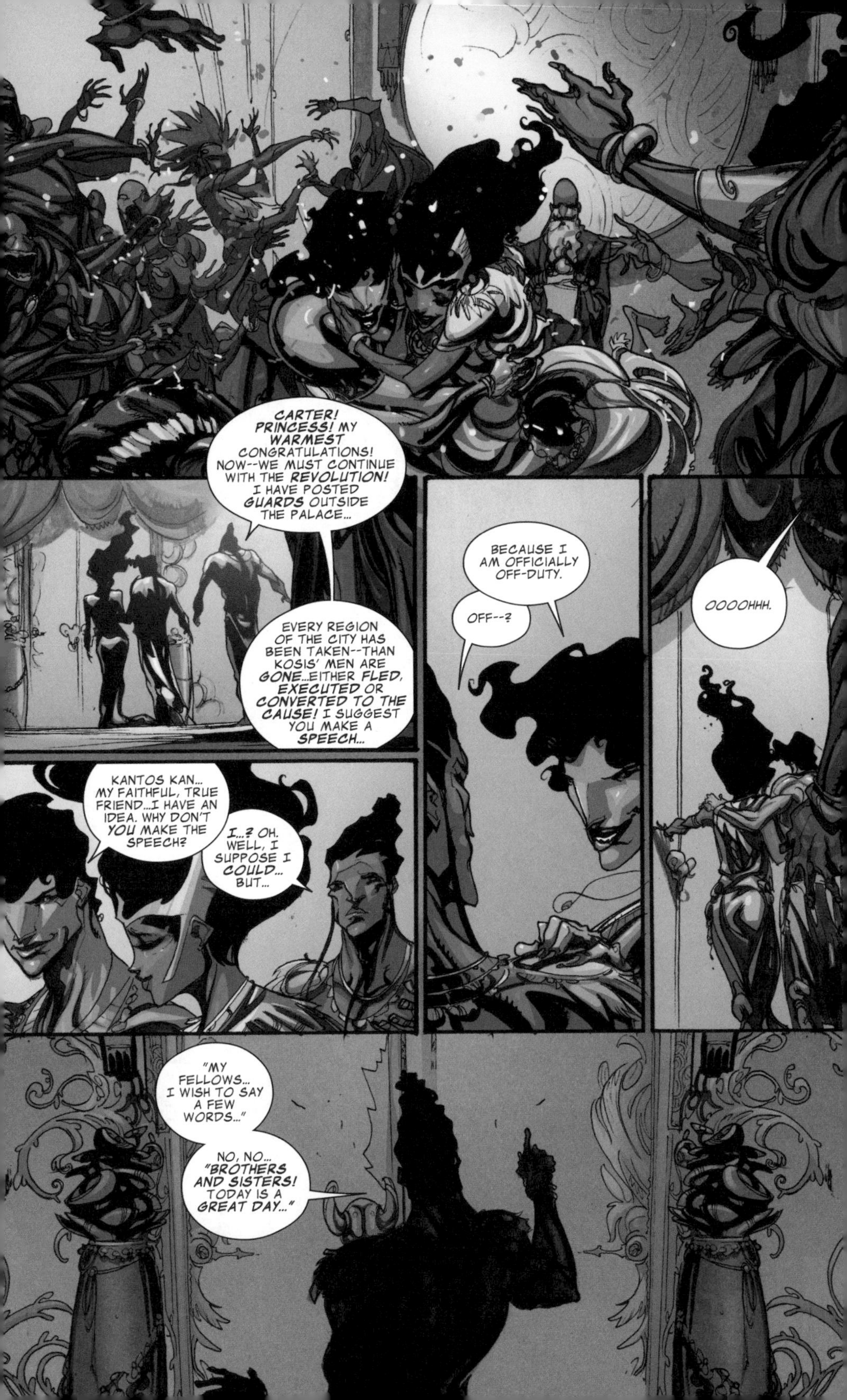
CARTER! PRINCESS! MY WARMEST CONGRATULATIONS! NOW--WE MUST CONTINUE WITH THE REVOLUTION! I HAVE POSTED GUARDS OUTSIDE THE PALACE...
EVERY REGION OF THE CITY HAS BEEN TAKEN--THAN KOSIS' MEN ARE GONE...EITHER FLED, EXECUTED OR CONVERTED TO THE CAUSE! I SUGGEST YOU MAKE A SPEECH...
KANTOS KAN... MY FAITHFUL, TRUE FRIEND...I HAVE AN IDEA. WHY DON'T YOU MAKE THE SPEECH?
I...? OH. WELL, I SUPPOSE I COULD... BUT...
BECAUSE I AM OFFICIALLY OFF-DUTY.
OFF--?
OOOOHHH.
"MY FELLOWS... I WISH TO SAY A FEW WORDS..."
NO, NO... "BROTHERS AND SISTERS! TODAY IS A GREAT DAY..."

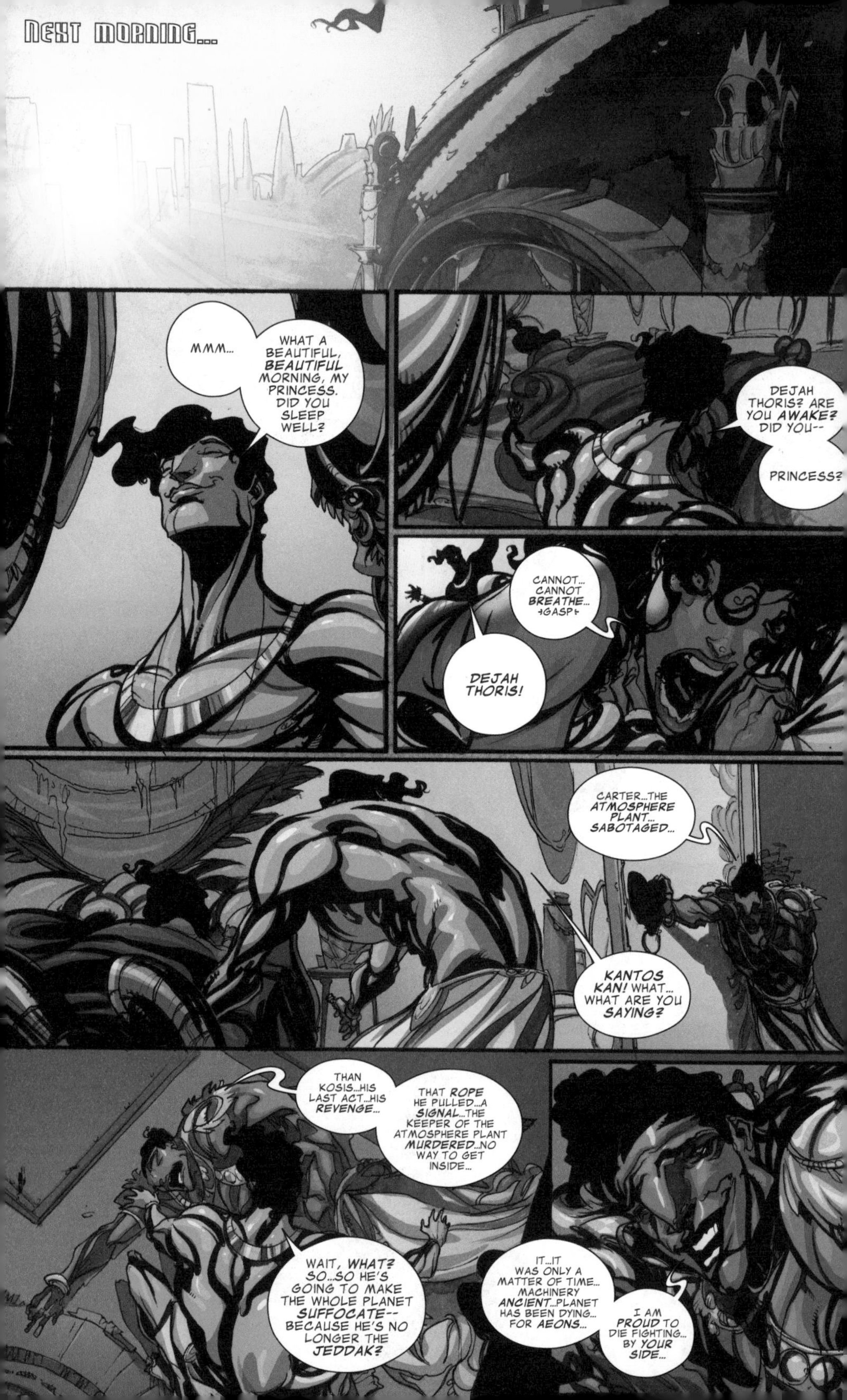
NEXT MORNING...
MMM...
WHAT A BEAUTIFUL, BEAUTIFUL MORNING, MY PRINCESS. DID YOU SLEEP WELL?
DEJAH THORIS? ARE YOU AWAKE? DID YOU--
PRINCESS?
CANNOT... CANNOT BREATHE... +GASP+
DEJAH THORIS!
CARTER...THE ATMOSPHERE PLANT... SABOTAGED...
KANTOS KAN! WHAT... WHAT ARE YOU SAYING?
THAN KOSIS...HIS LAST ACT...HIS REVENGE...
THAT ROPE HE PULLED...A SIGNAL...THE KEEPER OF THE ATMOSPHERE PLANT MURDERED...NO WAY TO GET INSIDE...
WAIT, WHAT? SO...SO HE'S GOING TO MAKE THE WHOLE PLANET SUFFOCATE-- BECAUSE HE'S NO LONGER THE JEDDAK?
IT...IT WAS ONLY A MATTER OF TIME... MACHINERY ANCIENT...PLANET HAS BEEN DYING... FOR AEONS...
I AM PROUD TO DIE FIGHTING... BY YOUR SIDE...

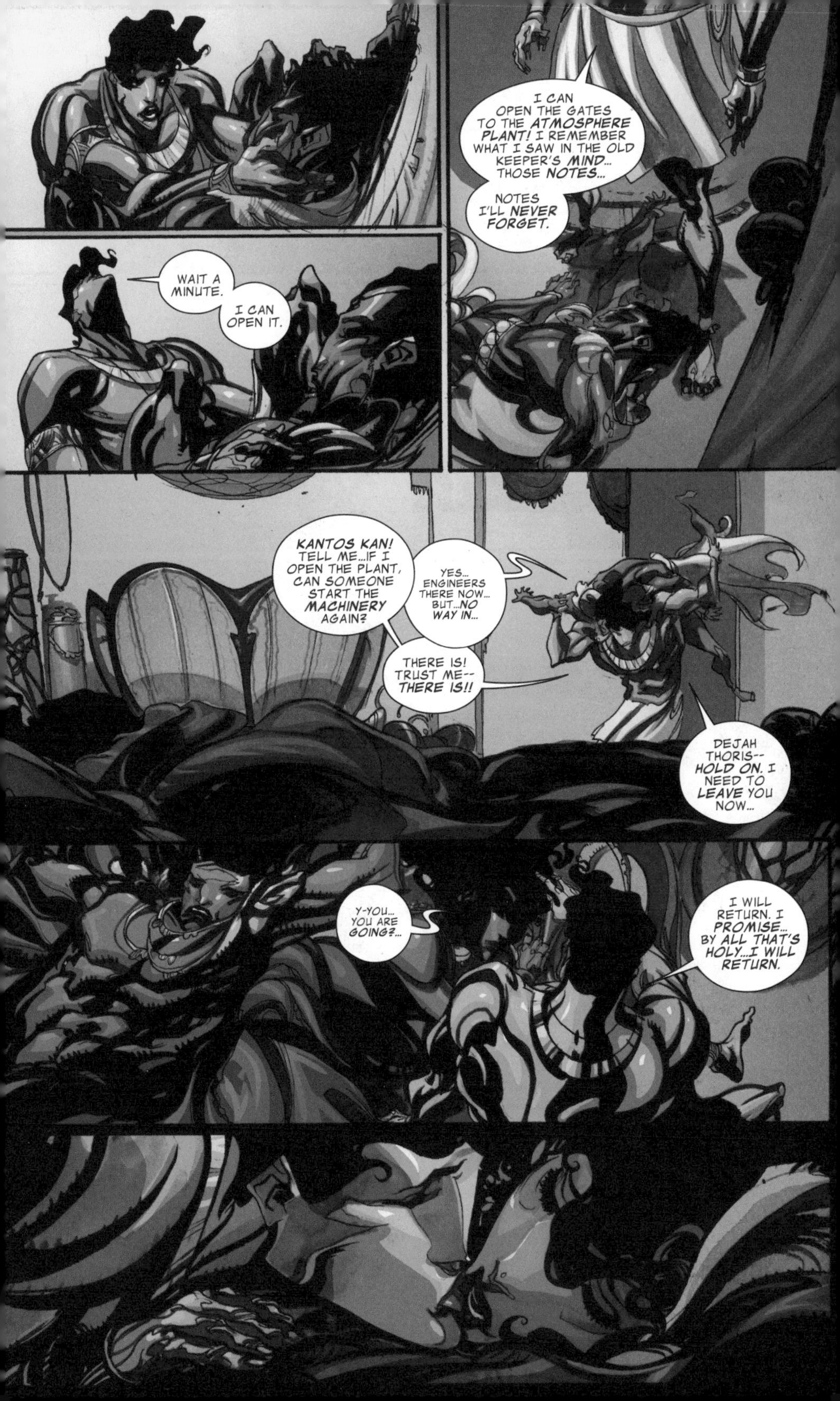
I CAN OPEN THE GATES TO THE ATMOSPHERE PLANT! I REMEMBER WHAT I SAW IN THE OLD KEEPER'S MIND... THOSE NOTES...
NOTES I'LL NEVER FORGET.
WAIT A MINUTE.
I CAN OPEN IT.
KANTOS KAN! TELL ME...IF I OPEN THE PLANT, CAN SOMEONE START THE MACHINERY AGAIN?
YES... ENGINEERS THERE NOW... BUT...NO WAY IN...
THERE IS! TRUST ME-- THERE IS!!
DEJAH THORIS-- HOLD ON. I NEED TO LEAVE YOU NOW...
Y-YOU... YOU ARE GOING?...
I WILL RETURN. I PROMISE... BY ALL THAT'S HOLY...I WILL RETURN.

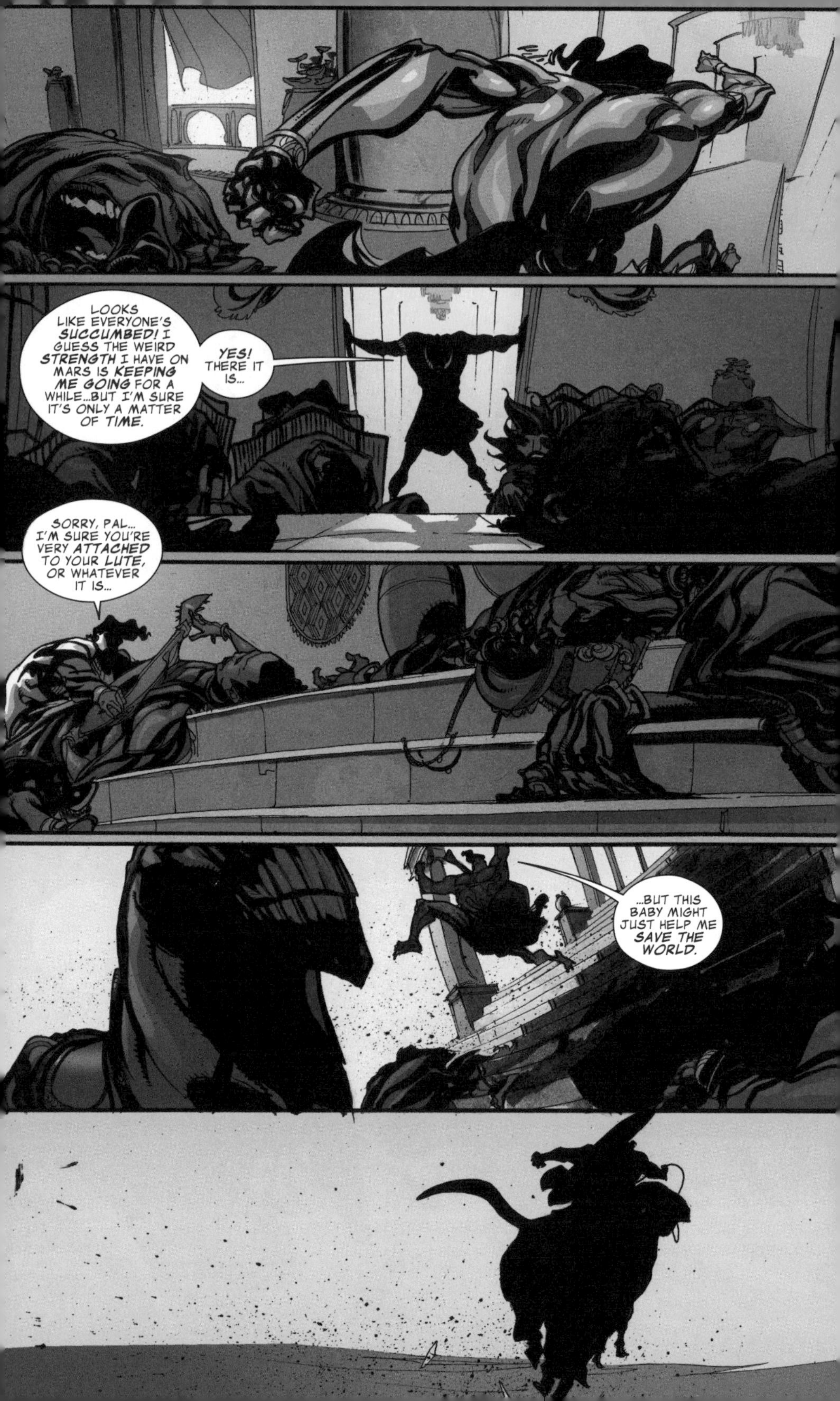

LOOKS LIKE EVERYONE'S SUCCUMBED! I GUESS THE WEIRD STRENGTH I HAVE ON MARS IS KEEPING ME GOING FOR A WHILE...BUT I'M SURE IT'S ONLY A MATTER OF TIME.
YES! THERE IT IS...
SORRY, PAL... I'M SURE YOU'RE VERY ATTACHED TO YOUR LUTE, OR WHATEVER IT IS...
...BUT THIS BABY MIGHT JUST HELP ME SAVE THE WORLD.

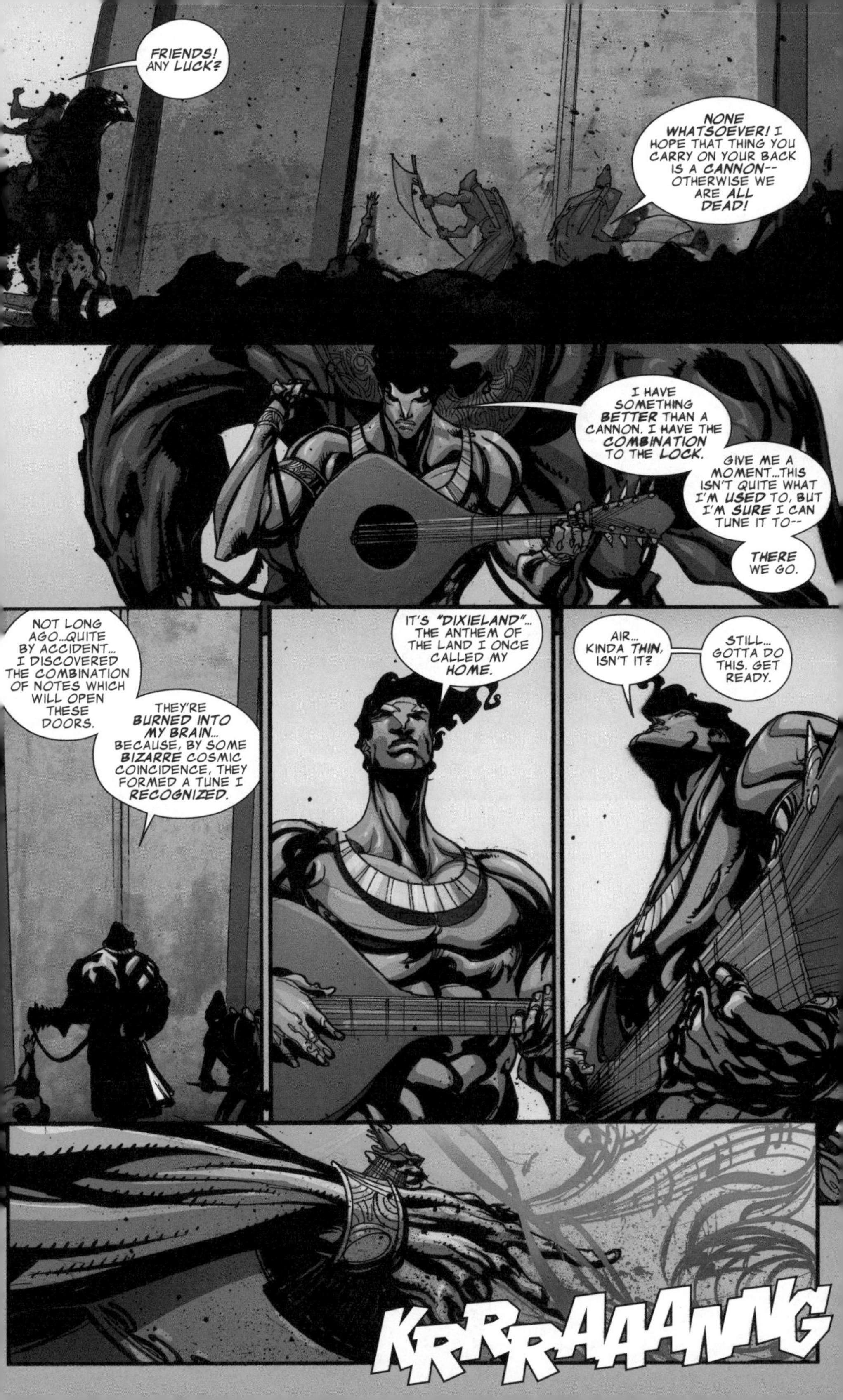
FRIENDS! ANY LUCK?
NONE WHATSOEVER! I HOPE THAT THING YOU CARRY ON YOUR BACK IS A CANNON-- OTHERWISE WE ARE ALL DEAD!
I HAVE SOMETHING BETTER THAN A CANNON. I HAVE THE COMBINATION TO THE LOCK.
GIVE ME A MOMENT...THIS ISN'T QUITE WHAT I'M USED TO, BUT I'M SURE I CAN TUNE IT TO--
THERE WE GO.
NOT LONG AGO...QUITE BY ACCIDENT... I DISCOVERED THE COMBINATION OF NOTES WHICH WILL OPEN THESE DOORS.
THEY'RE BURNED INTO MY BRAIN... BECAUSE, BY SOME BIZARRE COSMIC COINCIDENCE, THEY FORMED A TUNE I RECOGNIZED.
IT'S "DIXIELAND"... THE ANTHEM OF THE LAND I ONCE CALLED MY HOME.
AIR... KINDA THIN, ISN'T IT?
STILL... GOTTA DO THIS. GET READY.
KRRRAAAANNG

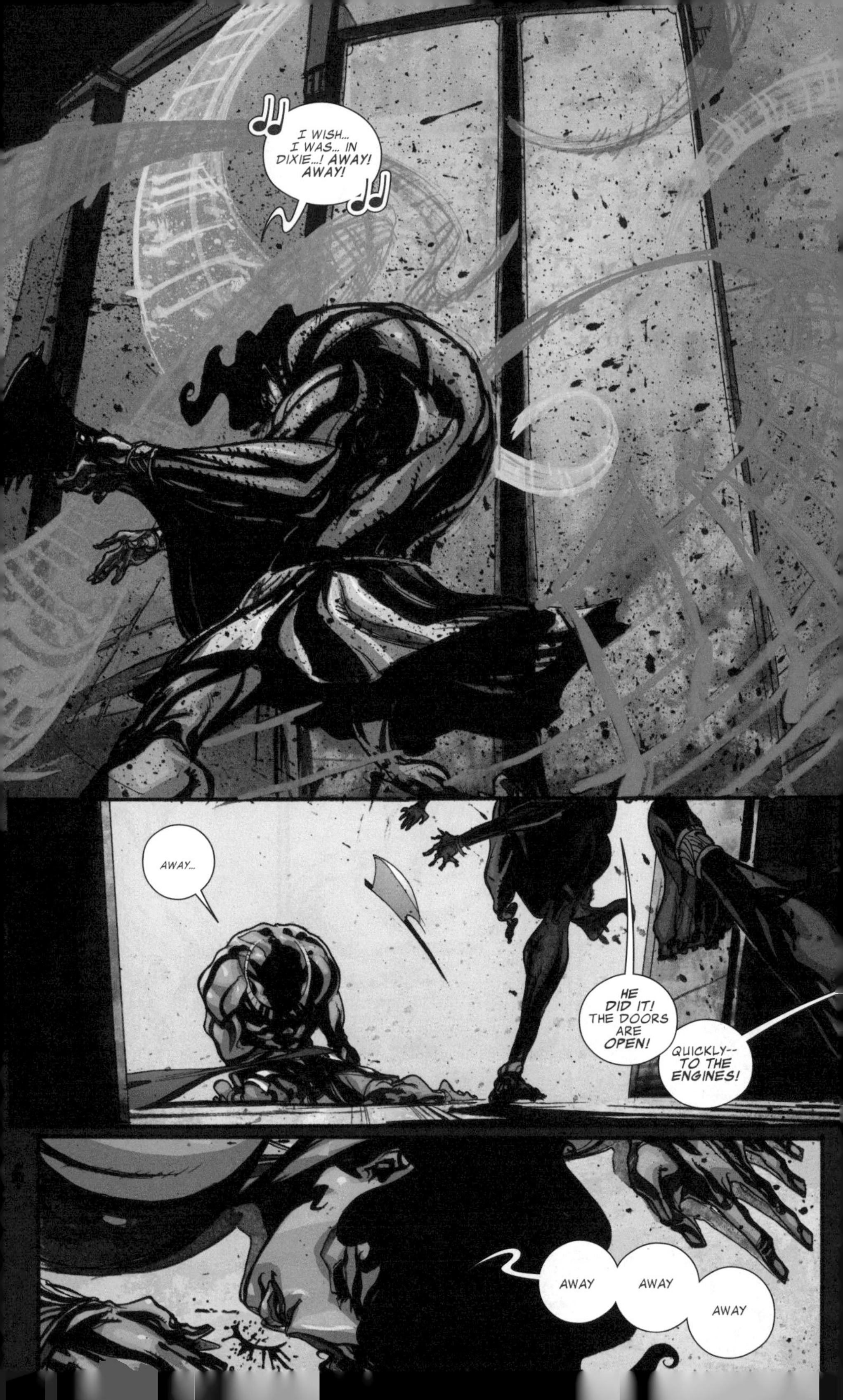
I WISH... I WAS... IN DIXIE...! AWAY! AWAY!
AWAY...
HE DID IT! THE DOORS ARE OPEN!
QUICKLY-- TO THE ENGINES!
AWAY
AWAY
AWAY

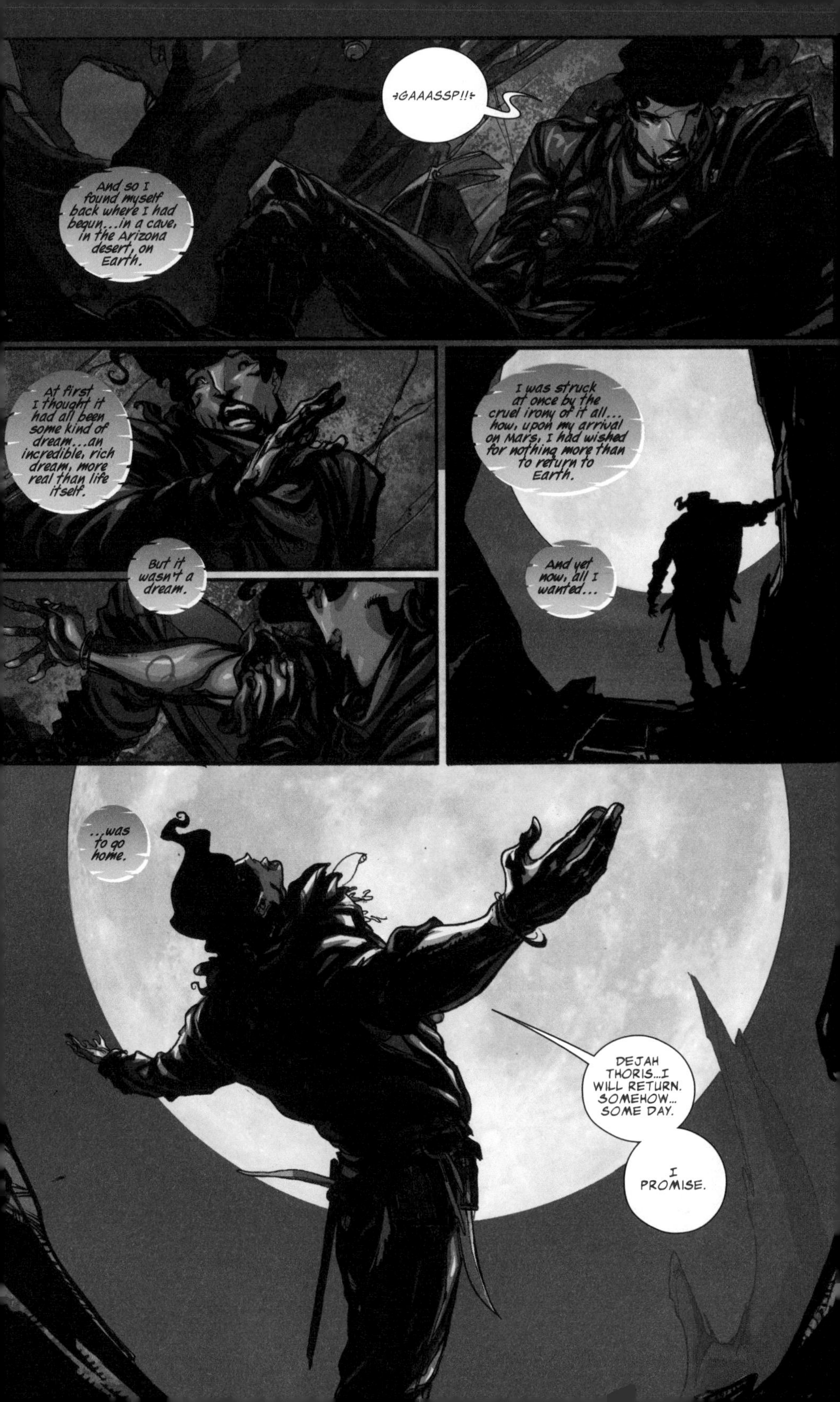

-GAAASSP!!-
And so I found myself back where I had begun...in a cave, in the Arizona desert, on Earth.
At first I thought it had all been some kind of dream...an incredible, rich dream, more real than life itself.
But it wasn't a dream.
I was struck at once by the cruel irony of it all... how, upon my arrival on Mars, I had wished for nothing more than to return to Earth.
And yet now, all I wanted...
...was to go home.
DEJAH THORIS...I WILL RETURN. SOMEHOW... SOME DAY.
I PROMISE.

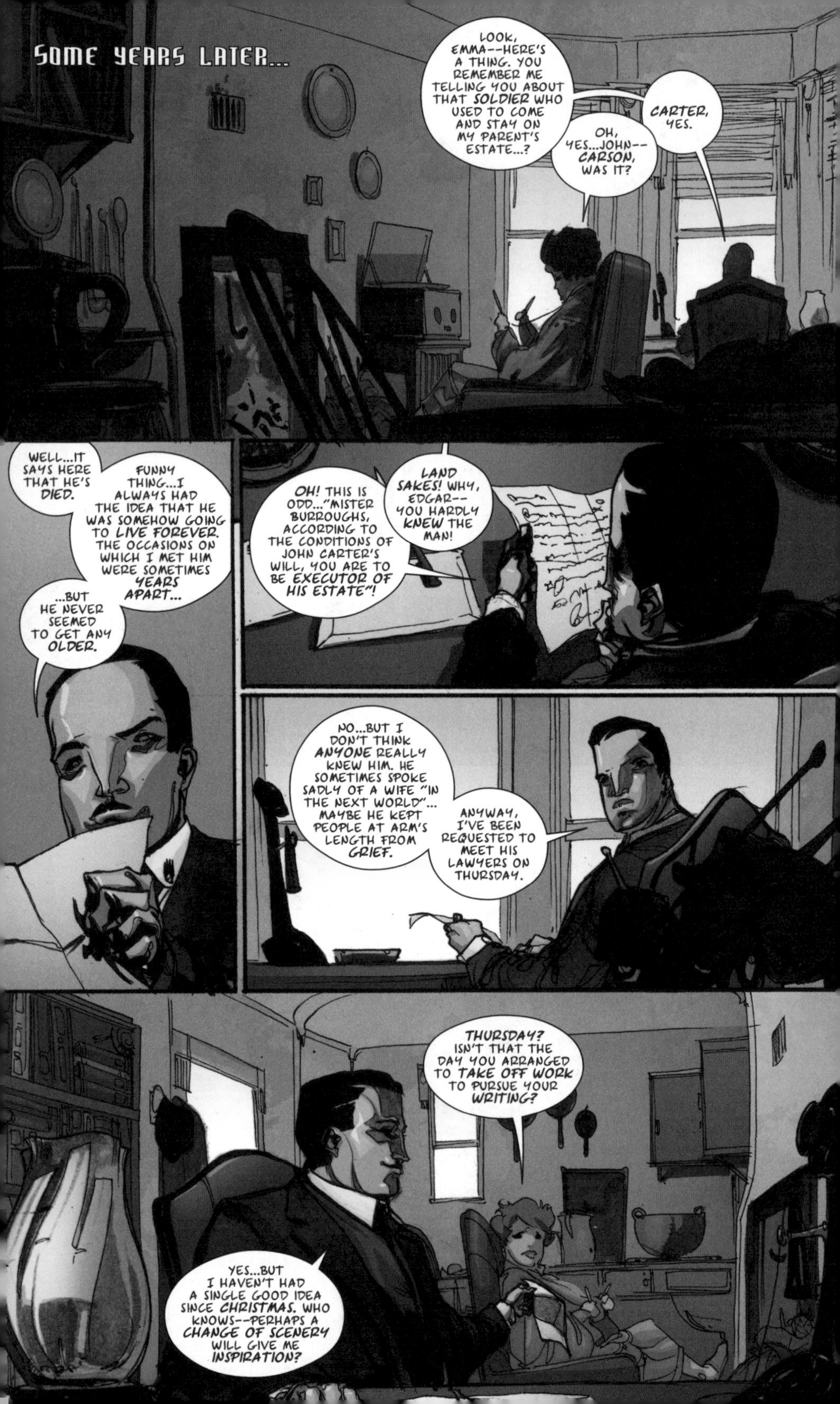
SOME YEARS LATER...
LOOK, EMMA--HERE'S A THING. YOU REMEMBER ME TELLING YOU ABOUT THAT SOLDIER WHO USED TO COME AND STAY ON MY PARENT'S ESTATE...?
OH, YES...JOHN--CARSON, WAS IT?
CARTER, YES.
WELL...IT SAYS HERE THAT HE'S DIED.
FUNNY THING...I ALWAYS HAD THE IDEA THAT HE WAS SOMEHOW GOING TO LIVE FOREVER. THE OCCASIONS ON WHICH I MET HIM WERE SOMETIMES YEARS APART...
...BUT HE NEVER SEEMED TO GET ANY OLDER.
OH! THIS IS ODD..."MISTER BURROUGHS, ACCORDING TO THE CONDITIONS OF JOHN CARTER'S WILL, YOU ARE TO BE EXECUTOR OF HIS ESTATE"!
LAND SAKES! WHY, EDGAR--YOU HARDLY KNEW THE MAN!
NO...BUT I DON'T THINK ANYONE REALLY KNEW HIM. HE SOMETIMES SPOKE SADLY OF A WIFE "IN THE NEXT WORLD"... MAYBE HE KEPT PEOPLE AT ARM'S LENGTH FROM GRIEF.
ANYWAY, I'VE BEEN REQUESTED TO MEET HIS LAWYERS ON THURSDAY.
THURSDAY? ISN'T THAT THE DAY YOU ARRANGED TO TAKE OFF WORK TO PURSUE YOUR WRITING?
YES...BUT I HAVEN'T HAD A SINGLE GOOD IDEA SINCE CHRISTMAS. WHO KNOWS--PERHAPS A CHANGE OF SCENERY WILL GIVE ME INSPIRATION?

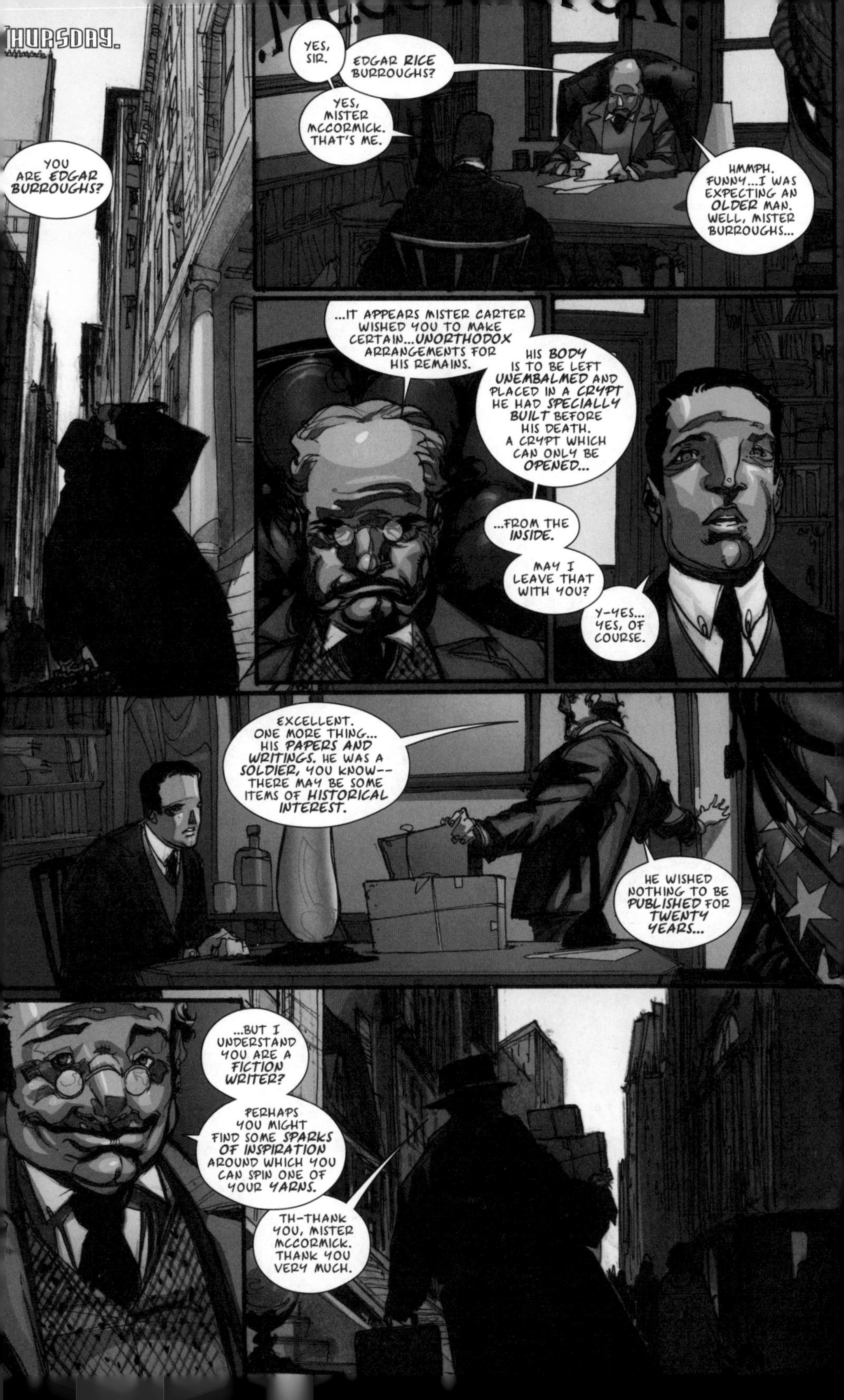
THURSDAY.
YOU ARE EDGAR BURROUGHS?
YES, SIR.
EDGAR RICE BURROUGHS?
YES, MISTER McCORMICK. THAT'S ME.
HMMPH. FUNNY...I WAS EXPECTING AN OLDER MAN. WELL, MISTER BURROUGHS...
...IT APPEARS MISTER CARTER WISHED YOU TO MAKE CERTAIN...UNORTHODOX ARRANGEMENTS FOR HIS REMAINS.
HIS BODY IS TO BE LEFT UNEMBALMED AND PLACED IN A CRYPT HE HAD SPECIALLY BUILT BEFORE HIS DEATH. A CRYPT WHICH CAN ONLY BE OPENED...
...FROM THE INSIDE.
MAY I LEAVE THAT WITH YOU?
Y-YES... YES, OF COURSE.
EXCELLENT. ONE MORE THING... HIS PAPERS AND WRITINGS. HE WAS A SOLDIER, YOU KNOW-- THERE MAY BE SOME ITEMS OF HISTORICAL INTEREST.
HE WISHED NOTHING TO BE PUBLISHED FOR TWENTY YEARS...
...BUT I UNDERSTAND YOU ARE A FICTION WRITER?
PERHAPS YOU MIGHT FIND SOME SPARKS OF INSPIRATION AROUND WHICH YOU CAN SPIN ONE OF YOUR YARNS.
TH-THANK YOU, MISTER McCORMICK. THANK YOU VERY MUCH.

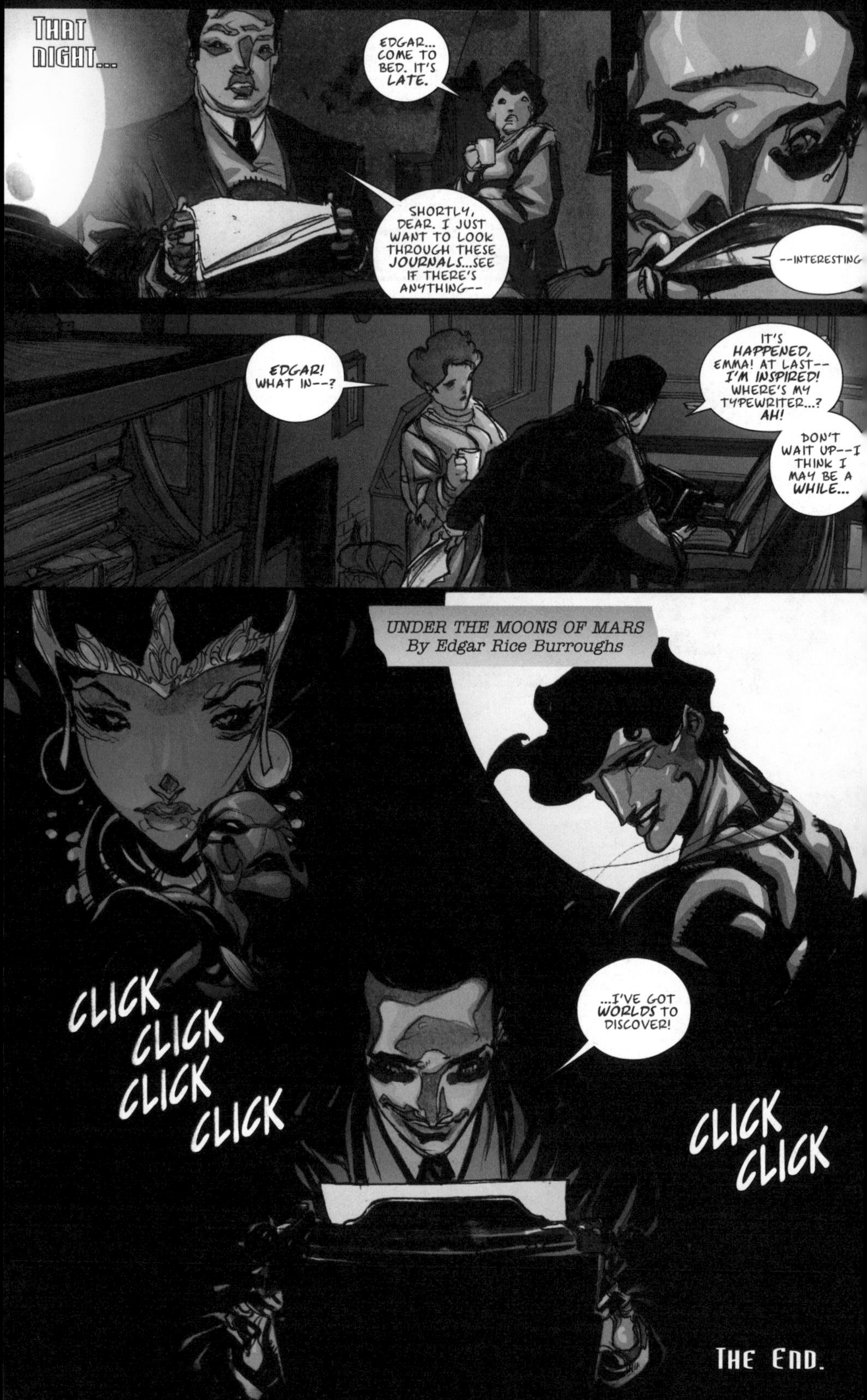
THAT NIGHT...
EDGAR... COME TO BED. IT'S LATE.
SHORTLY, DEAR. I JUST WANT TO LOOK THROUGH THESE JOURNALS...SEE IF THERE'S ANYTHING--
--INTERESTING
EDGAR! WHAT IN--?
IT'S HAPPENED, EMMA! AT LAST--I'M INSPIRED! WHERE'S MY TYPEWRITER...? AH!
DON'T WAIT UP--I THINK I MAY BE A WHILE...
UNDER THE MOONS OF MARS
By Edgar Rice Burroughs
CLICK
CLICK
CLICK
CLICK
...I'VE GOT WORLDS TO DISCOVER!
CLICK
CLICK
THE END.

THE STORY CONTINUES IN...

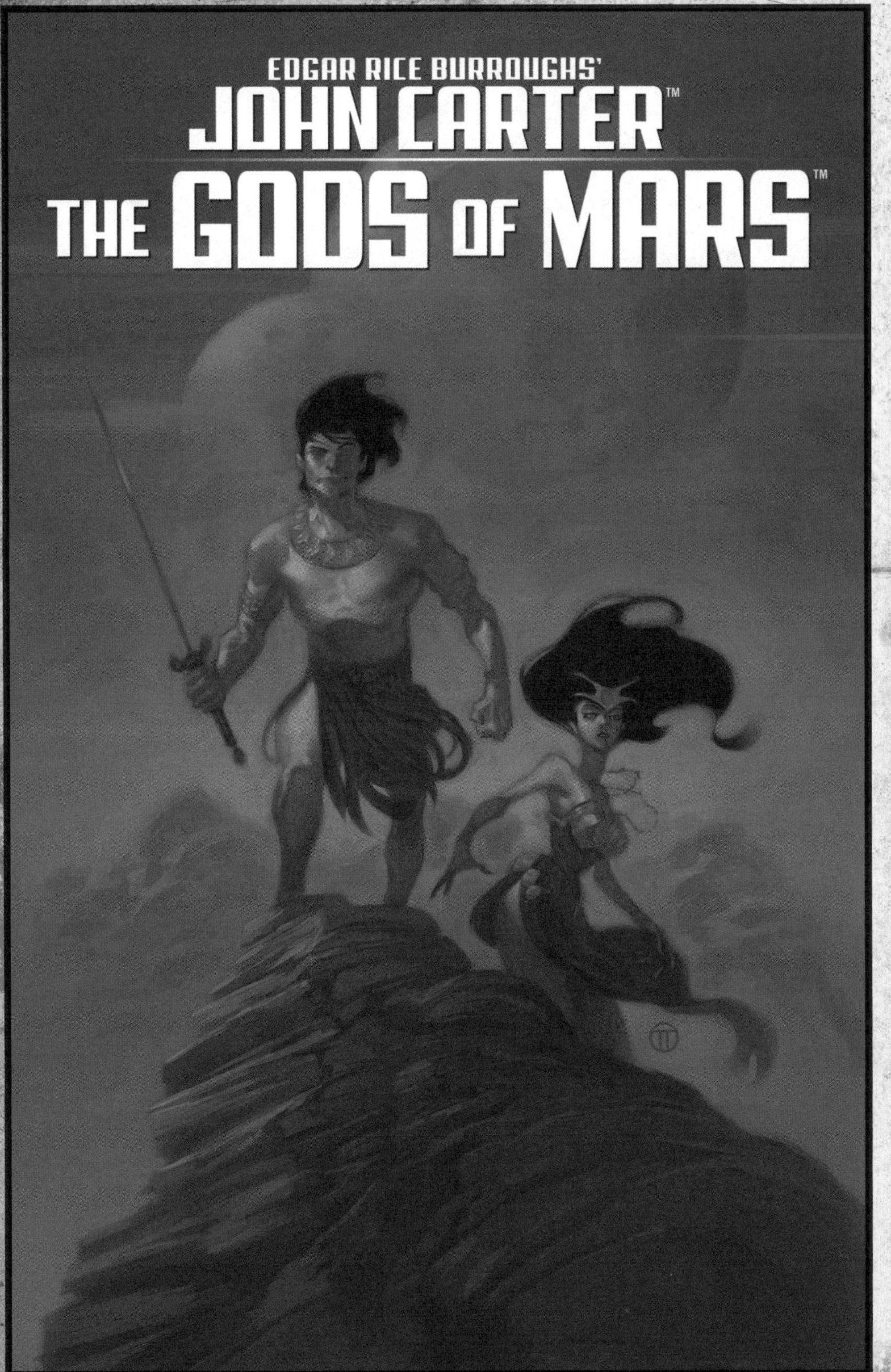
EDGAR RICE BURROUGHS'
JOHN CARTER™
THE GODS OF MARS™

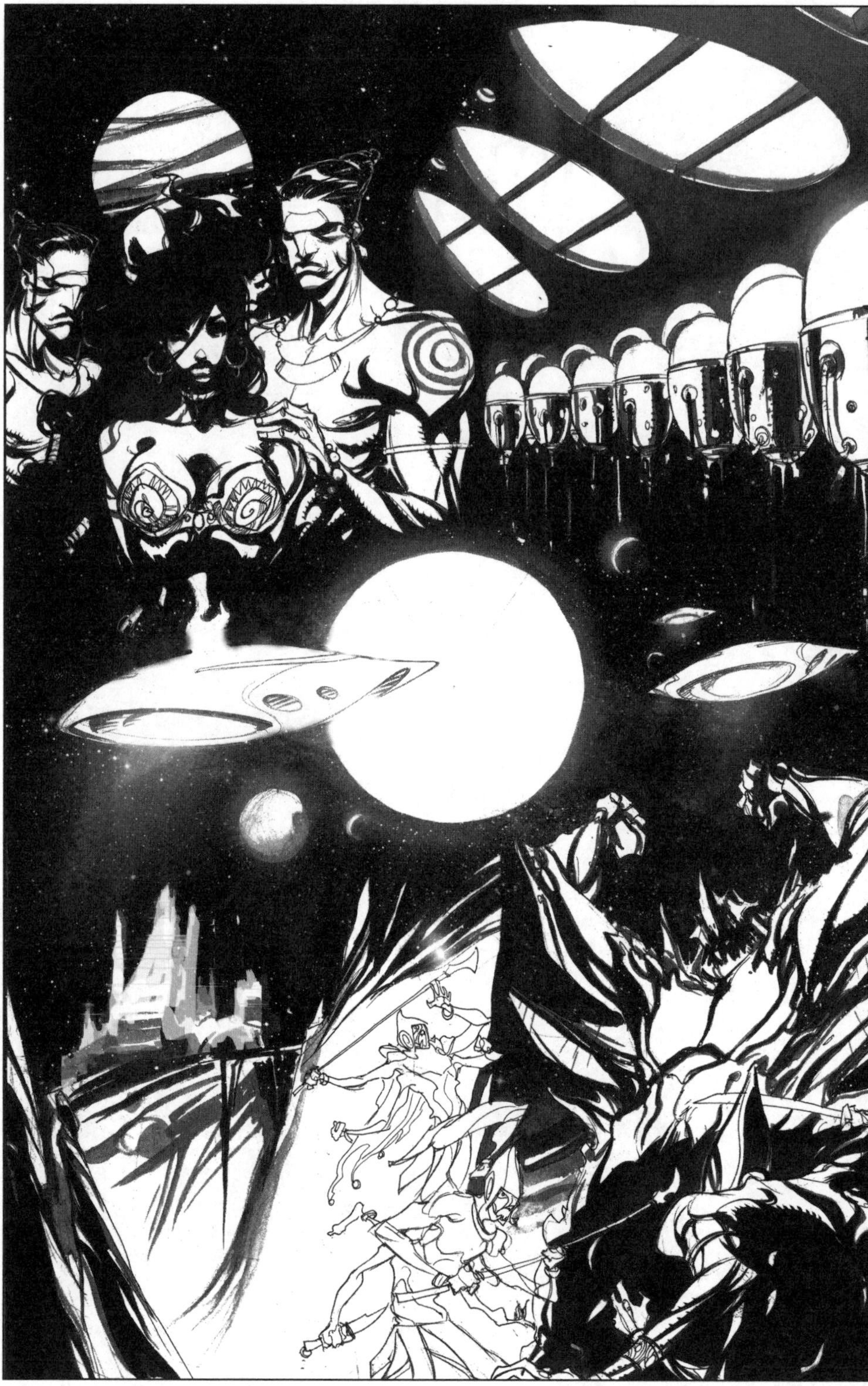

JOHN CARTER: A PRINCESS OF MARS #1, PAGE 5 ART BY FILIPE ANDRADE

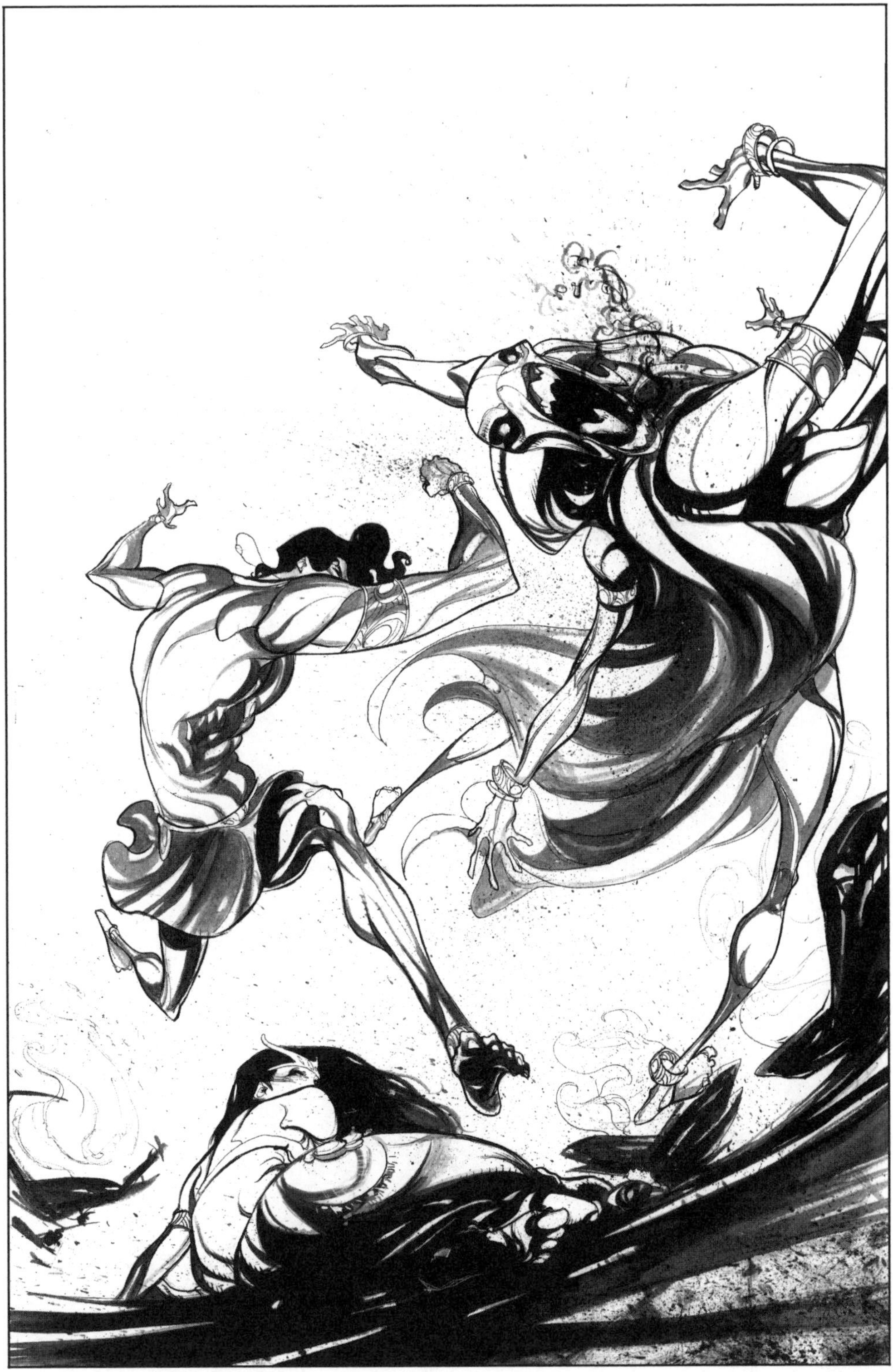

JOHN CARTER: A PRINCESS OF MARS #2, PAGE 5 ART BY FILIPE ANDRADE

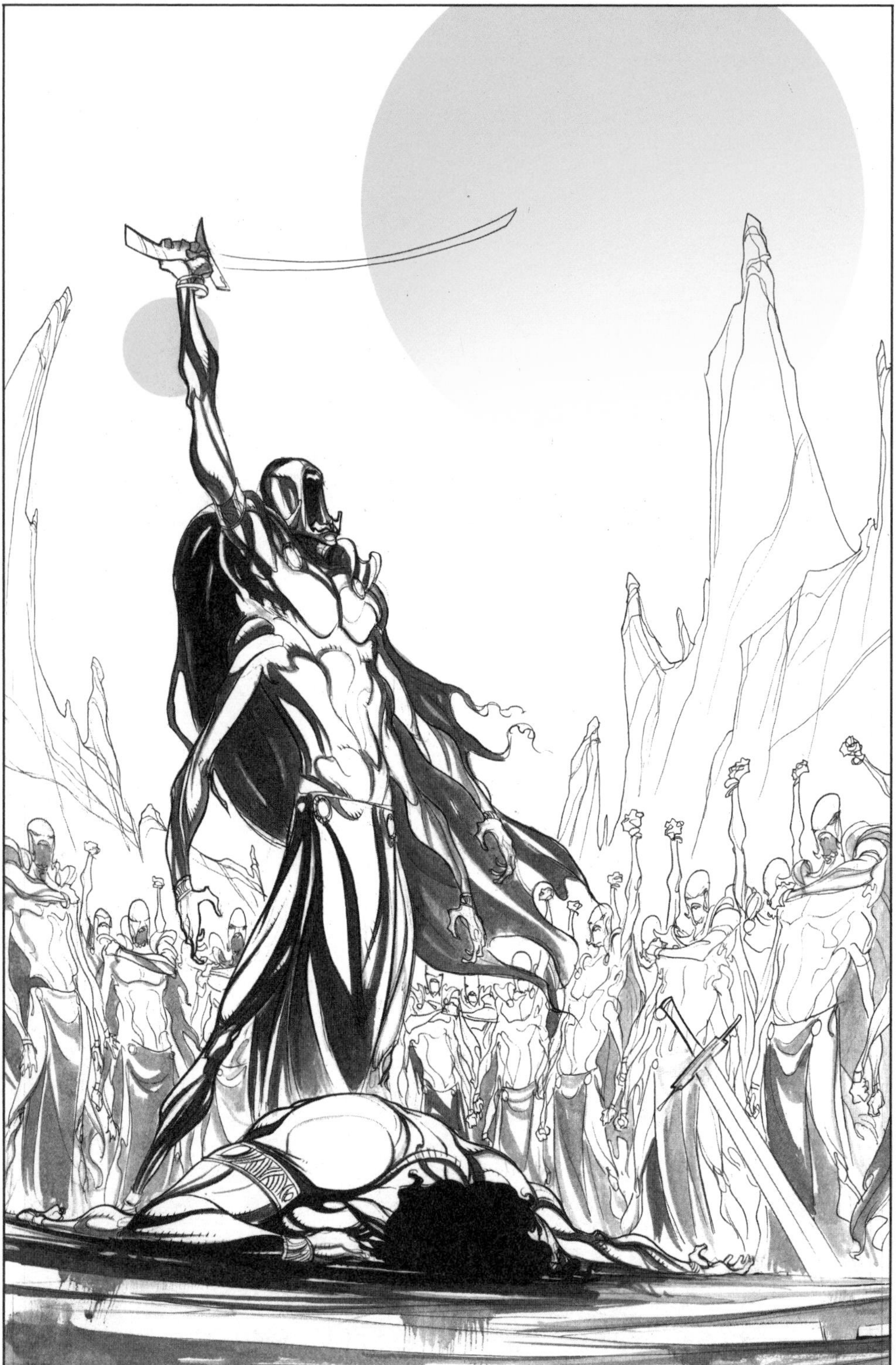

JOHN CARTER: A PRINCESS OF MARS #2, PAGE 20 ART BY FILIPE ANDRADE

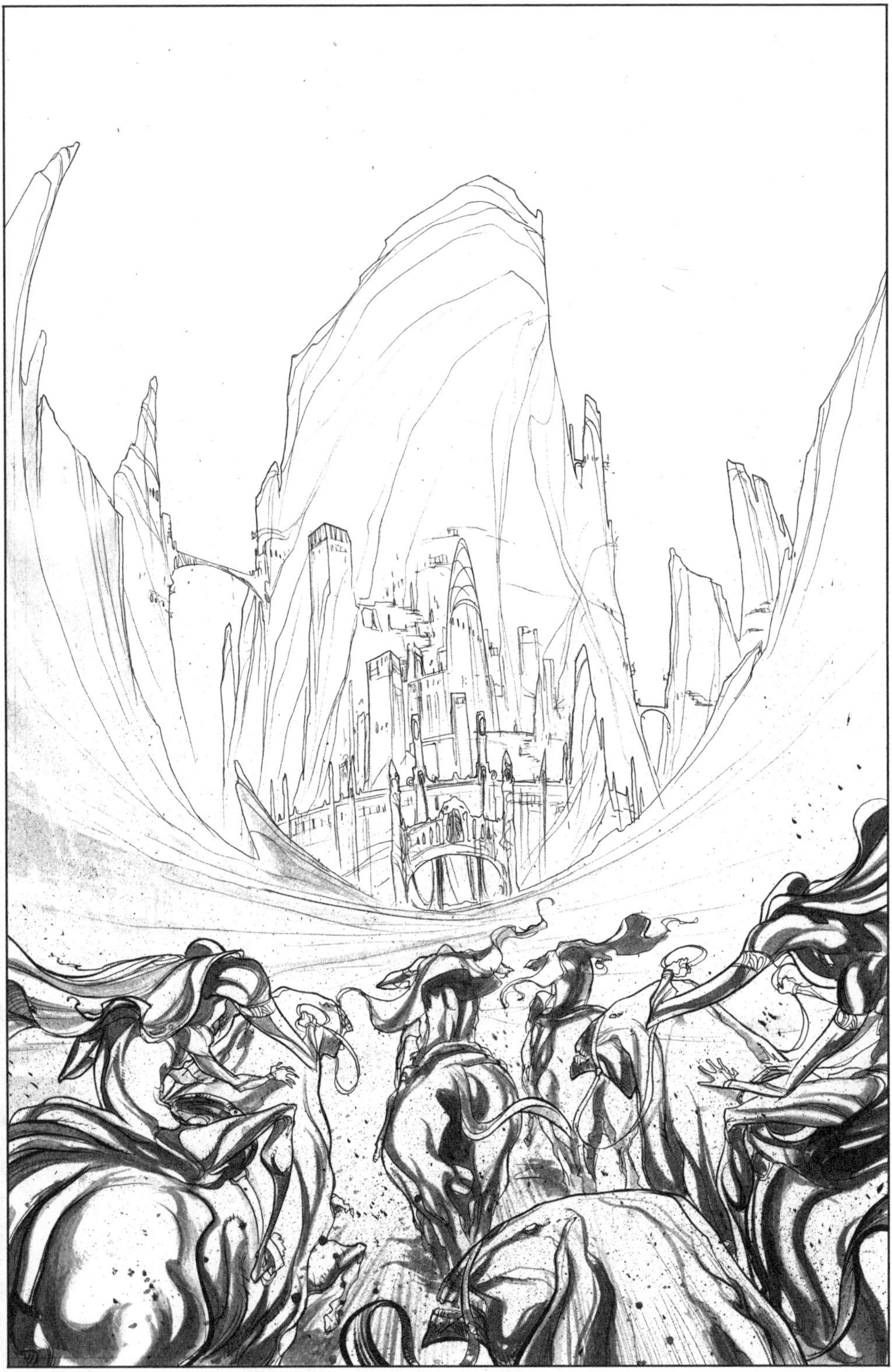

JOHN CARTER: A PRINCESS OF MARS #3, PAGE 4 ART BY FILIPE ANDRADE

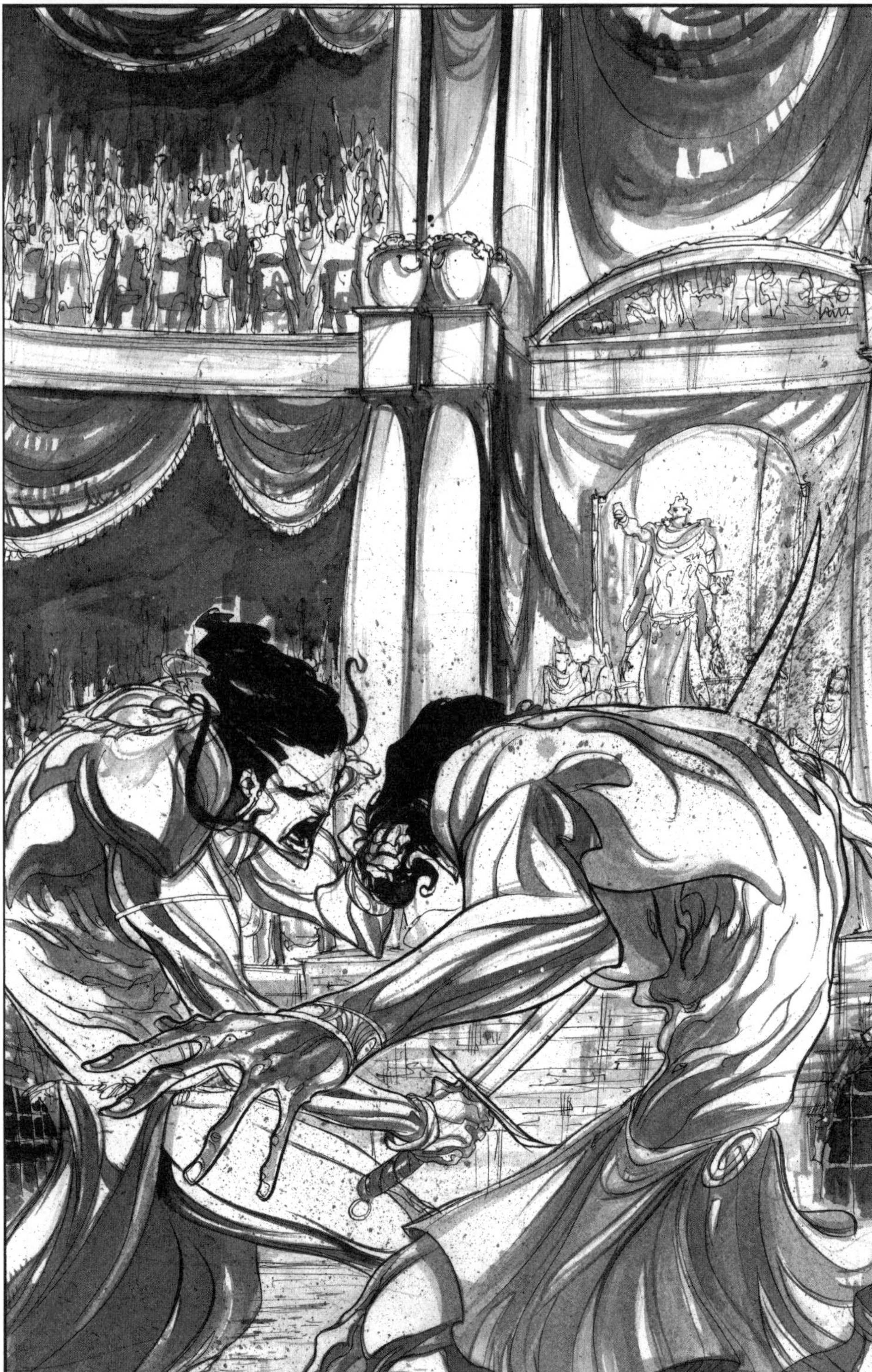

JOHN CARTER: A PRINCESS OF MARS #4, PAGE 2 ART BY FILIPE ANDRADE

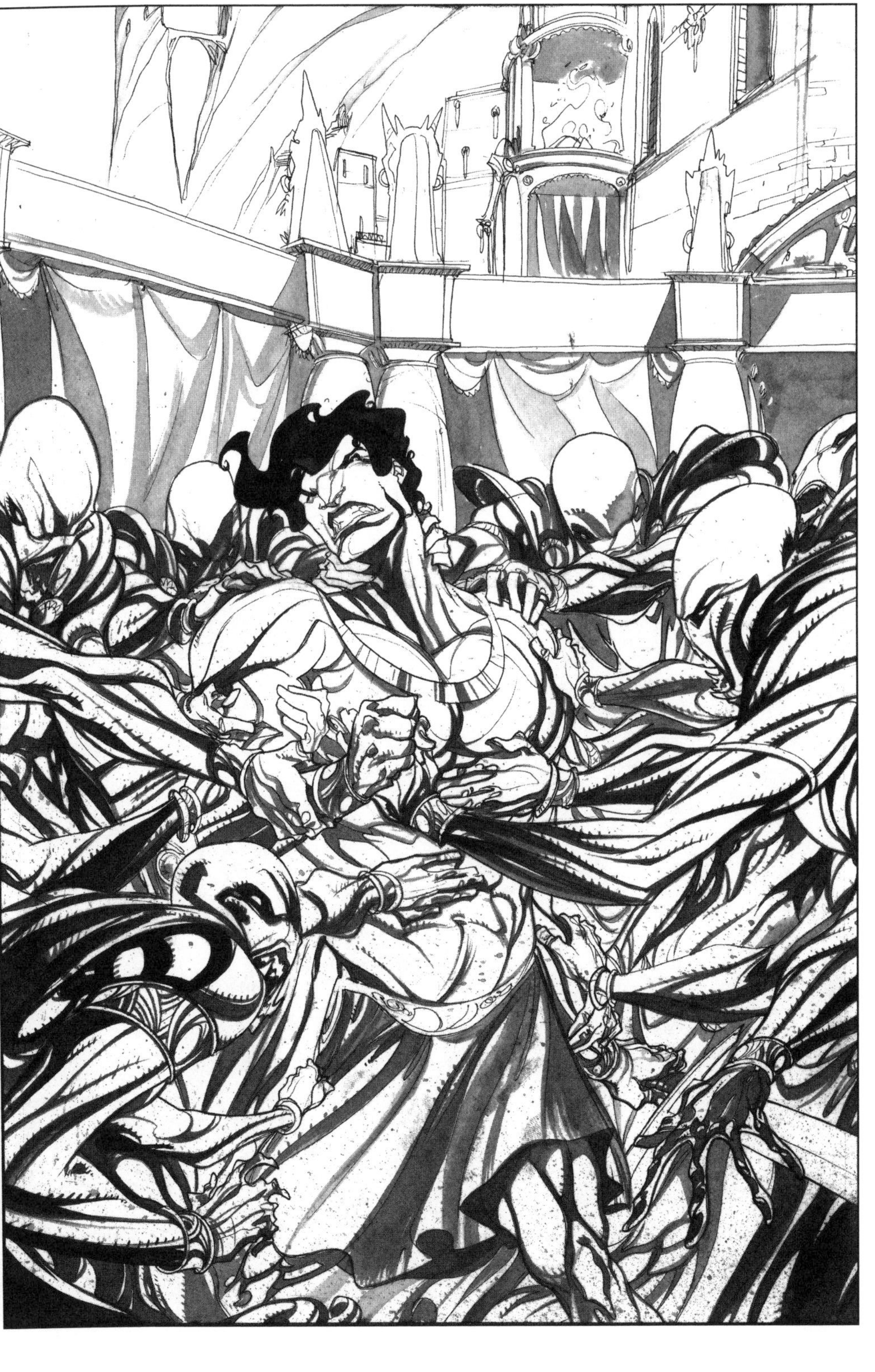

JOHN CARTER: A PRINCESS OF MARS #5, PAGE 1 ART BY FILIPE ANDRADE

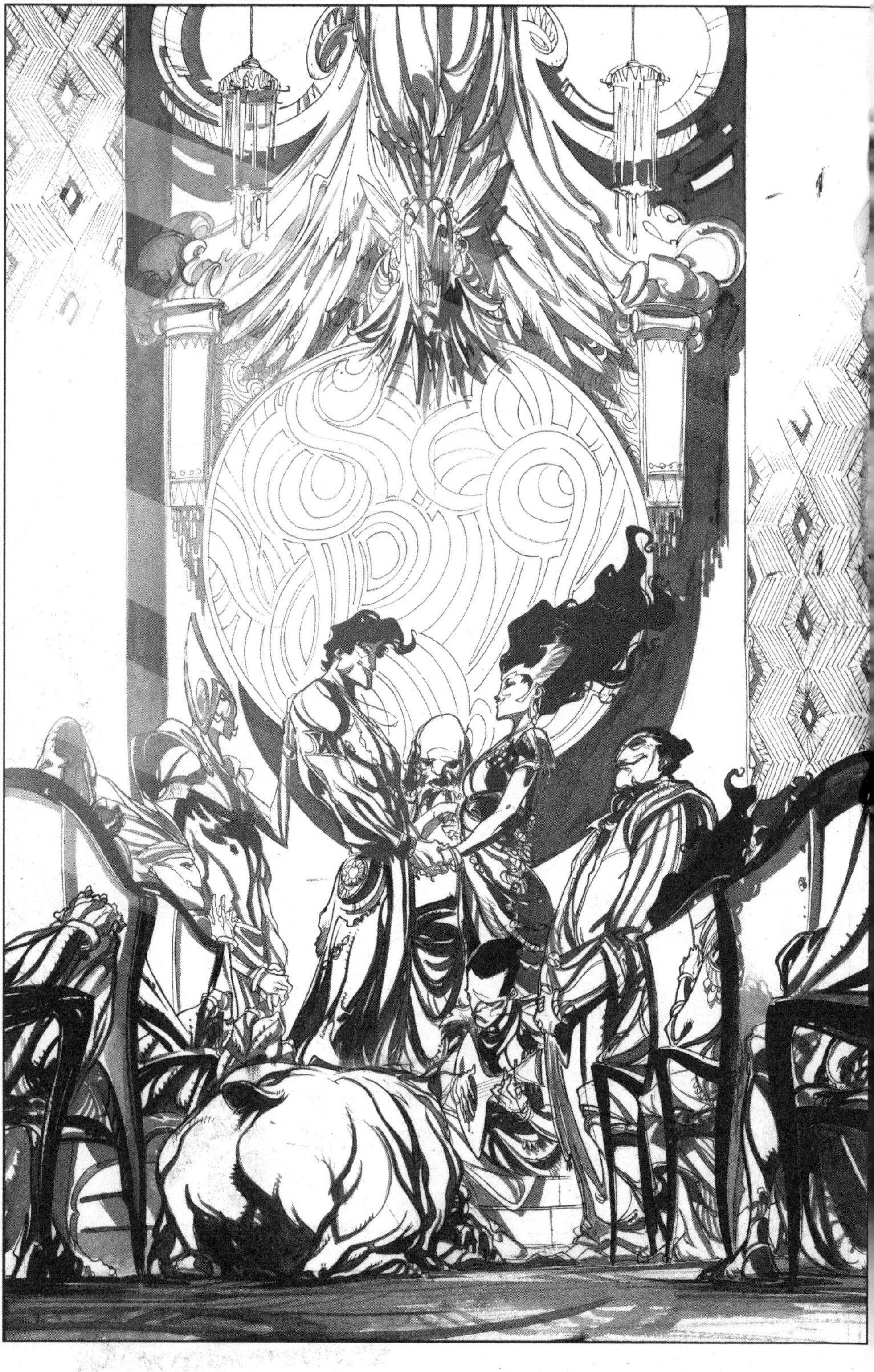

JOHN CARTER: A PRINCESS OF MARS #5, PAGE 10 ART BY FILIPE ANDRADE